The
Mathematics
of Collective
Action

METHODOLOGICAL
PERSPECTIVES

A series edited by
RICHARD J. HILL
Purdue University

The Mathematics of Collective Action

**JAMES
COLEMAN**
Johns Hopkins University

Aldine Publishing Company/Chicago

ABOUT THE AUTHOR

James S. Coleman received his B.S. from Purdue University and his
Ph.D. from Columbia University. He has done extensive research
and published his work in social research in the major sociological
journals. His other books include *Community Conflict, Introduction to
Mathematical Sociology, The Adolescent Society,* and *Adolescents
and the Schools.* Professor Coleman has taught at the University of
Chicago and is presently teaching in the Department of Social Relations
at Johns Hopkins University.

Copyright © 1973 by James Coleman

First published in Great Britain, 1973

First U.S. edition published 1973 by
Aldine Publishing Company
529 South Wabash Avenue
Chicago, Illinois 60605

ISBN 0-202-30258-X
Library of Congress Catalog Number 73-75372

Printed in Great Britain by
William Clowes & Sons Limited

Contents

Preface

Several years ago, I devised a game. It was a legislative game, in which players—that is, legislators—began with constituents' interests for or against particular bills, with their right to vote in the legislature on those bills, and with the knowledge that constituents would vote for their re-election if their interests were satisfied, against it if they were not. That was all, except for a few rules of parliamentary procedure.

What was curious about the game was the behaviour that transpired among the legislators during play. Voting itself was a minor part of the action. Nor was effort directed toward trying to convince another player that he should vote for or against a bill. Instead, most of the action involved negotiations: agreements between two players to support each other on two bills, one of which was of interest to the constituents of each. Sometimes, more than two bills were involved in the discussion, and sometimes, though infrequently, more than two persons were involved.[1]

As I examined available information on real legislatures, I found it didn't work just that way: both more and less transpired. Legislators had more than their vote that other legislators were interested in: influence in a committee, their time or attention, their influence over other legislators. And many other groups besides other legislators were involved in the activities that finally culminated in a vote, each with resources of its own: government agencies, trade associations, business firms, trade unions, professional associations.[2] But less took

---

[1] The game is described in Coleman (1967), and is published as an academic game for schools, by Western Publishing Company.

[2] See Bauer, Pool, and Dexter (1963, Chapters 1–5), for detailed observation on the functioning of a legislative committee, and Peabody and Polsby (1963) for other case studies.

place as well: there was seldom explicit log-rolling, seldom explicit trades, a less fully developed market in votes than I found in the game. There appears to be an implicit system of political credit among legislators, but on many issues there were no explicit trades or political deals.

I began to notice also that in other far more loosely organized collectivities similar processes appeared to be operating, and in formally organized bureaucracies as well, there was much that observers referred to as 'political,' by which they meant negotiations, implicit debts and obligations, and explicit trades.[3]

It began to be clear that all this could be conceptualized with a relatively simple set of concepts: actors, events, control of actors over events, interest of actors in events. The development of this set of concepts led me into a theoretical direction I had previously avoided: purposive action. I had previously, both in mathematical and non-mathematical work, limited any consideration of theory to causal processes, in which cause precedes effect, and only proximate causes are examined.

This book constitutes the first fruits of that direction of work. It is only the first fruits, and gives a very partial view of what will be necessary in a theory of action. I expect to correct this before long, but this book contains a partial mathematical basis for such a theory of action. It will, I expect, satisfy no one. It is not empirical enough for sociologists, not theoretical enough for economists, too psychologically barren for psychologists, and too devoid of concrete referents for political scientists. I hope, however, that this dissatisfaction will lead in productive directions.

I have incurred many debts along the way. Robert Peabody and a host of graduate students and faculty members helped develop the game, and press toward a more abstract conceptualization. Rand Corporation provided me with a sheltered summer during which much of the writing was done. The National Science Foundation provided a grant which also protected large segments of time, and paid for computer and other facilities. Gudmund Hernes, Robert Harris, Alex Seidler, and other colleagues and graduate students gave valuable comments, corrections, and ideas. Virginia Bailey typed manuscripts under circumstances sometimes trying. Hetty Desterbe prepared the index. And Alan Hill of Heinemann kept

---

[3] Crozier (1964) examines such processes in a business organization in terms that easily fit with the conceptual schema developed in this book.

after me to write this book, even when it took a form quite different from that we had initially discussed. To all these people and organizations I am grateful.

James Coleman

1 Mathematics of Social Action

There are two quite different streams of work in the study of social action, both of which begin at the level of the individual.[1] The two streams of work represent fundamentally different conceptions of man. Where the ordinary lay conception of man is as a person responding to his environment in pursuit of some goal, these conceptions each recognize half of that description. The first conception explains man's behaviour as response to his environment; the second explains his behaviour as pursuit of a goal. The first searches for causal processes and determinants of behaviour, and often uses a mechanistic explanatory frame, which employs the concepts of 'forces' and 'resultant action'. It has been the implicit basis of much of the best empirical work in sociology, from Durkheim's analysis of the causes of suicide to the present.

The second conception sees man's action as goal-directed, and focuses attention less on present environmental conditions than on future desired states. Man is conceived less as a product of his environment than as the source of preferences which lead to action. This conception has been the basis of much common-sense explanation of behaviour, of some theoretical work in sociology, represented by Weber and Parsons, and of one major theoretical structure: economic theory, based upon a conception of rational economic man.

The two streams have foundations in psychological theory, where they may be termed 'stimulus-response' theories and 'purposive action' theories, respectively. A decade ago, one might have pointed to Clark Hull's work as the archetype of stimulus-response theories, and E. C. Tolman's work as the archetype of purposive action theories.

[1] These two directions of work are distinct from those, like sociological functionalism and certain parts of ecology, that begin at the level of the collectivity.

In philosophy and religion, these two perspectives sharply divide two sets of beliefs. The first is of man as a creature of his fate, whose life is determined by the forces that surround him. The second is of man as the architect of his future.

In recent years, both of these streams of work have been extended through mathematical treatment. Two rather distinct bodies of mathematical applications have developed, each of which has a certain mathematical coherence or unity. As will be evident, these two theoretical approaches do not imply wholly distinct mathematical treatments. Nevertheless, the development of mathematical models for these two conceptions of behaviour has generated distinctive types of mathematical approaches.

Although these approaches are distinct, and different mathematics is used to mirror them, there are certain similarities that flow from the fact that both approaches involve the study of social action.

Causal processes

In the mathematical treatment of causal theories, an action is described as an event with particular *outcomes*. Ordinarily, the outcome of an event is seen as putting an individual into a given *state*. Thus the result of an action is ordinarily for the individual to be in a particular state, which may differ from his prior state. For example, in the simple case, an action like voting is assumed to be an event with n possible outcomes, where n is the number of candidates. The outcome is assumed to be governed by a set of probabilities, $p_1, \ldots, p_n$, that he will cast his vote for candidate $1, \ldots, n$.

A system of action can consist either of a set of events all representing actions of a single individual, a set of events each representing an action of a different individual, or a set of events representing multiple actions of different individuals. What is problematic about an event, and requires explanation, is which outcome of the event will occur. As a consequence, many of the variations in these models concern the dependence of the event's outcome on various possible causes or determinants. Two major types of causes have been examined in the literature. First of all, events may be dependent on the outcome of prior *events*. Since events may represent one individual's actions, or those of many individuals, dependence of an event on the outcome of other events may be of two types: dependence on the state of the same individual, or dependence on the state of other individuals. It is some-times the case, in fact, that the same mathematical models may be used to represent both intra-individual dependence and inter-individual dependence.

The second major type of cause of an event's outcome is a state of the individual or the environment that does not change, or changes independently of the other events included in the system. Some of these states are the attributes or variables commonly used to account for behaviour: the individual's age, level of education, attitude, sex, family size, occupation, etc. Because these states either do not change, or change independently of events in the system, the mathematical models necessary to represent these causal processes are different from those in which events are dependent on outcomes of other events internal to the system.

Purposive action

When we turn to mathematical treatment of purposive theories, there is a somewhat different conception of action. There is still a system of events, each event with a set of possible outcomes; but the events are no longer identical to the actions. Actions of the actors in the system *control* the outcomes of events, either wholly or partially; and the action is selected through the conscious choice of the actor, choosing that action which he believes will lead to the outcome most beneficial to him. Thus the outcome of a future event does not depend directly upon the outcome of previous events, through a causal process, nor upon attributes of the individual. There is the inter-position of a conscious, rational agent (or agents), whose choice determines, partly or wholly, the outcome of the subsequent event. The actor makes his choice of actions through his perception of the consequences that particular outcomes will have for him, and his perception of the dependence of outcomes upon his actions.

Comparison between the causal theories and the purposive theories may be made more systematic by setting down the sequence of elements that comprise the conceptual framework of each. In the causal theories, the sequence is

cause → event outcome

The cause may be other events internal to the system of events under consideration, or external. The outcome is ordinarily conceived as a state of an individual or a collectivity.

In the purposive theories, the sequence is still built around event and outcome, but contains the concepts of action and consequence:

$$\text{action} \rightarrow \text{event outcome} \rightarrow \text{consequence for actor}$$

In purposive theories, there is an implicit or explicit 'look-ahead' feature, in which the actor 'looks ahead' at the expected consequences of different outcomes for him, and adjusts his action to these possible consequences. This gives rise to the essential behaviour principle of purposive action theories, the principle of utility-maximization. This principle states nothing more than that the actor will choose that action which according to his estimate will lead to an expectation of the most beneficial consequences. As such, it constitutes a 'functional' theory, in which an action is conceived to be shaped by its future consequences, rather than by prior causal factors. Further, as in other functional theories, there is conceived to be an organism that is acting homeostatically, that is, toward self-maintenance. In this case, the organism is the individual, and the homeostatic mechanism devised by economic theory is a principle of utility-maximization, or satis-faction-maximization, a principle that generates the concept of 'utility' in such theories.

Functional theories differ sharply in their *a priori* justifiability, this one appearing far more justifiable than a functional theory specifying homeostasis of a group or collectivity, because of the empirical fact that an individual as an organism does maintain a continuity of internal organization as a single actor, while collectivities of individuals are transitory, often undergo reorganization, and often do not act as a single actor.[2]

The major virtue of a functional theory is that the action principle it specifies provides an economy that allows it to make predictions with a less extensive data base than is true for causal theories. Causal theories may be regarded, in this perspective, as merely compact descriptions of empirical regularities, or 'laws', and thus require observation of such regularities before they can be formulated. The major defect of a functional theory, on the other hand, lies in its very

---

[2] It appears likely, however, that for a different branch of social science, psychopathology, such assumptions about continuity of internal organization of the individual and more generally, the conception of the individual as a homeostatic organism, should not be made. Psychopathology might profitably be viewed as the study of persons who fail to organize action toward a goal, comparable to a disorganized collectivity.

economy of data, for it is more tenuous, less fully confirmed in any specific case.

This initial comparison of these two approaches to the study of social action shows some of their similarities, together with an important difference. Although the similarities are strong, this difference has led to the use of very different mathematical approaches. Causal theory has led to the use of probability models in which the outcome of an event is conditional upon certain other event outcomes or upon certain states. Dynamics are introduced when these conditional probabilities are linked together in a chain or a process, the probability of an outcome of one event is conditional upon the state of the individual (or group), and that state itself is the outcome of a preceding event. Purposive theory has led to the use of many kinds of mathematics, all of which have in common the fact that some maximization or optimization is employed: linear algebra, systems of differential and difference equations, theory of games, linear and nonlinear programming, and others.

In this book, I will develop one direction of purposive theory, involving collectivities. But before doing that, it will be useful to give a review of some of the directions of causal theory and purposive theory in which mathematical work has been done, and to include with this review references to some of that work.

Causal theory and models of action

There are two basic conceptual frameworks of action which serve as the foundations of causally determined social action. One of these is the conception of independent events occurring with identical probabilities, which is the basis of Bernoulli trials and the binomial and multinomial distributions. The second is the conception of a continuum of time, with events occurring independently along this continuum, and with identical probabilities of occurring within any small period of time. This is the basis of the Poisson process and the Poisson distribution.

Bernoulli events and the Poisson process

The conception of a set of independent and identical trials can be captured mathematically by a very simple formulation, by which the probability of k successes in n trials may be calculated. If r is the probability of success on any trial, then the probability of success in one trial can be expressed simply (where $p_1(1)$ is the probability of one success in one trial):

$$p_1(1) = r \tag{1.1}$$

Then if we know the probability that the number of successes in $n - 1$ trials is $k - 1$, and the probability that the number of successes is k, we can calculate in general the probability of k successes on n trials:

$$p_k(n) = rp_{k-1}(n - 1) + (1 - r)p_k(n - 1) \tag{1.2}$$

With these two equations, it is possible to calculate for any n the probability of k successes. This calculation, compactly written, is the binomial distribution:

$$p_k(n) = \binom{n}{k} r^k (1 - r)^{n-k} \tag{1.3}$$

The general idea is of a sequence of independent, identical events, each with the same two outcomes. There are few social phenomena that fit these assumptions, though some physical events, such as tossing a coin, with heads and tails as the possible outcomes, do. The importance of Bernoulli events and the binomial distribution is that the conception gives a baseline model in which a distribution of an aggregate may be calculated from assumptions about individual events. It constitutes a basis to which assumptions more appropriate to social processes may be added.

When there are more outcomes than two possible (for example, as in throwing a pair of dice rather than a coin), a slight generalization of the idea of Bernoulli trials may be used. The aggregate distribution that arises from this generalization is the multinomial distribution. If there are r possible outcomes, with probabilities of occurrence $r_1, \ldots, r_s$, the multinomial distribution is:

$$p_{k_1, \ldots, k_s}(n) = \frac{n!}{k_1! \ldots k_s!} r_1^{k_1} \ldots r_s^{k_s} \tag{1.4}$$

When $s = 2$, this distribution reduces to the binomial distribution of eqn. 1.3.

A similar base to that provided by Bernoulli trials is provided by the Poisson process for a different kind of process, one operating through time.[3] In the Poisson process, an event has a probability of occurrence in each small increment of time, dt, a probability that is independent of the particular point in time, and of the occurrence of events prior to it in time. If this probability is denoted $q\,dt$, the change in probability that no events have occurred during a period of time from 0 to t can be expressed by a simple equation (where $p_0(t)$ is the probability of no events in time t):[4]

$$dp_0(t) = -q\,dt p_0(t) \qquad (1.5)$$

When eqn. 1.5 is integrated, this gives the probability $p_0(t)$, of zero events in time 0 to t as a function of the parameter q (which I will call a transition rate):

$$p_0(t) = e^{-qt} \qquad (1.6)$$

Analogous to the sequence of Bernoulli trials, the change in the probability of k events in time t can be calculated by knowledge of the probability of k and $k-1$ at time t:

$$dp_k(t) = [-qp_k(t) + qp_{k-1}(t)]\,dt \qquad (1.7)$$

From eqns. 1.5 and 1.7 can be calculated the Poisson distribution, which gives the probability of k events at time t in terms of the transition rate for a single event, q:

$$p_k(t) = \frac{(qt)^k e^{-qt}}{k!} \qquad (1.8)$$

If we think of 'outcomes' of events as in the Bernoulli trials, the *occurrence* of an event in the Poisson process is comparable to an outcome such as 'success' in the Bernoulli trials. Comparable to the multinomial generalization of Bernoulli trials is a Poisson process in which there are s types of events that can occur, each with a transition

---

[3] The formal properties of the Poisson process allow it to be used not only where the continuum over which events are independently distributed is time, but is some other continuous variable. A slight generalization allows the process to be used as well for a space of two or more dimensions. However, I will not discuss these generalizations, because they do not lead toward a dynamic process, which is of interest here.

[4] The parameter q is defined by a limiting process, as follows: If $p(\Delta t)$ is the probability of occurrence of an event in time Δt, then

$$q = \lim_{\Delta t \to 0} \frac{p(\Delta t)}{\Delta t}$$

See Coleman (1964a) for further discussion, and Cox and Miller (1965) for more precise definition of the process.

rate of $q_i(i=1,\ldots,s)$. This gives rise to a simple generalization of the Poisson process:

$$p_{k_1\ldots k_r}(t) = \frac{(q_1 t)^{k_1}\ldots(q_s t)^{k_s}\exp\{-t(q_1+\ldots+q_s)\}}{k_1!\ldots k_r!} \qquad (1.9)$$

Some temperance of expectation is appropriate about the ability of such models, or small extensions of them, to describe behaviour accurately, because these are simple models which can hardly be expected to mirror the complexities of persons' behaviour. However,

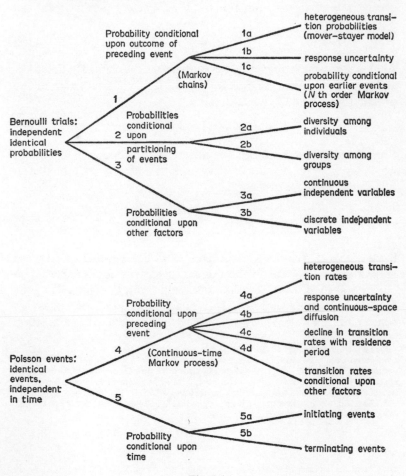

Fig. 1.1

from these two foundations, assumptions of independence and identical probabilities can be relaxed in various ways which create models which are useful for mirroring particular aspects of social action. Figure 1.1 shows the ways in which these two foundation models have been modified and elaborated to aid in the description of social action.

Extensions of Bernoulli trials

In the upper half of Figure 1.1, the upper branch (1) shows the modification of Bernoulli trials that has been most important for social and psychological applications. This is the relaxation of the assumption that the probabilities governing each event are independent of the outcomes of those events that have gone before. In the simplest case, the probabilities governing the outcomes of the event are conditional upon the outcome of the last preceding event. This is a Markov chain, and can be thought of quite simply in this way: a given outcome on the preceding event is equivalent to placing the individual in a given *state*, and the probabilities for each outcome on the next event are associated with this state. The elaboration of eqn. 1.2 in this case becomes an equation that generates the probability of being in state j after the next event (i.e. the event has outcome j) as a function of the probability of being in each state before that event. If there are s states and $p_j(n)$ is the probability of being in state j on trial n, then

$$p_j(n) = r_{1j}p_1(n-1) + r_{2j}p_2(n-1) + \ldots + r_{sj}p_s(n-1) \quad (1.10)$$

The process is defined by s equations like eqn. 1.10, for $j = 1, \ldots, s$.[5] The parameters r_{ij} are transition probabilities: the conditional probability of an outcome j on an event, given that the outcome of the preceding event was i (i.e. the preceding event placed the individual in state i). There is an $s \times s$ matrix of transition probabilities that generates a vector of state probabilities following event n, given the vector of state probabilities following event $n-1$.

The greater applicability of a Markov chain than Bernoulli trials to social and psychological processes lies in the fact that the parameters

[5] See Kemeny and Snell (1960), Bartholemew (1967), Beauchamp (1970) for exposition of the basic ideas of Markov chains in the context of social science applications.

of a Markov chain are conditional probabilities, conditional upon the 'state' of the individual. If the state is defined appropriately, and if the set of individuals over which the process is defined is fairly homogeneous, then one might expect the process to describe the movement from state to state. This sequential dependence brings a dynamic character to the system: whereas there is no particular order to the sequence of Bernoulli trials, due to their independence from one another, the sequential dependence of a Markov chain links the events in a given order. This brings the mathematical system closer to the ability to represent a dynamic physical or social process. The formal properties of the system allow deductions that give the model a considerable amount of predictive power for those applications in which its assumptions are met: the equilibrium probability distribution among states; the expected passage time (i.e. number of events) from state i to j; the expected recurrence time from state i back to state i; the probability distribution among states after a given number of events, and others.

The applications to which Markov chains have been put cover a wide range of behaviour. Probably the first was an application to vote intentions by Anderson (1954). Anderson used panel data from the 1948 election campaign to describe the month-to-month changes in vote intentions of the panel members among the three states: Republican, Democratic, and undecided. This application of the model is one of a number which have been made to the general area of attitude change, in which data from panel surveys have been used to estimate parameters.

A second area of application has been to purchase behaviour, particularly choice among different brands of the same goods. In this application, purchase of a given brand is assumed to place the individual in a state associated with that brand. Thus in this application, the states are brands, and the transition probabilities are probabilities of switching from brand to brand. The data used in fitting the models are ordinarily taken from consumer diary panels that are maintained by market research organizations. Massy, Montgomery, and Morrison (1970), review and summarize a large number of applications of Markov chains to brand behaviour in consumer purchasing.

Probably the most extensive application of Markov chains to social phenomena, however, has been in movements among occupations. Here the definition of a state appears quite straightforward: working in a given occupation.[6] There have been two kinds of applications: to intergenerational mobility (from father to son), and to intra-generational mobility (covering a given time span of five or ten years, or from initial job to current job). The transition probabilities in intra-generational mobility may cover several job changes (as in the attitude change case, but not as in the purchase behaviour case, where the data record each purchase), but nevertheless show the probability of being in job j at the second observation, given that he was in job i at the first observation. Application of a Markov chain to intra-generational mobility among occupations has been carried out by Blumen, Kogan, and McCarthy (1955), Hodge (1966) (for mobility between industries), and others. Application to father-son mobility has been carried out by Svalastoga (1959), Matras (1960), and others.

The deficient diagonal, and three extensions of Markov chains

In all these applications, a particular empirical deviation from Markov predictions occurs. This appears to have been first noted by Blumen, Kogan, and McCarthy, who found that transition probabilities estimated from movement between adjacent time periods over-predicted the amount of change between time periods that were farther apart in time. A different way of stating the deviation is that the model's predictions from transition probabilities estimated from changes between two time points give a deficient main diagonal when compared to the actual change between points more widely separated in time.

An example in a different area is shown in Table 1.1 below. A sample of housewives reported on a sequence of purchases of pancake mix, indicating which of three brands they bought. Table 1.1 shows the table of adjacent purchases, the transition probabilities estimated from that, the predicted table relating purchase t and $t + 2$, and the actual table of purchases (data from Coleman, 1964b).

[6] One of the sources of poor fit among Markov chains, however, has been in a too-simple definition of what constitutes the state. For example, the occupational mobility applications would very likely have shown better fit if the state had been defined by both the occupational title of the job and the wage category, or even merely a more precise classification of occupational titles. The problem, of course, lies in the fact that the proliferation of states requires more data for estimating transition probabilities than ordinarily exists.

12   THE MATHEMATICS OF COLLECTIVE ACTION

Table I.I

Purchases of pancake mix

		Brand at purchase t + I				Estimated transition matrix		
		I	2	3				
Brand at purchase t	I	232	55	37	324	.72	.17	.11
	2	50	213	59	322	.16	.66	.18
	3	32	56	253	341	.09	.16	.74
		314	324	349	987			

		Predicted purchase t + 2				Actual purchase t + 2			
		I	2	3		I	2	3	
Purchase t	I	178	82	64	324	218	65	41	324
	2	74	159	89	322	67	186	69	322
	3	55	84	202	341	33	56	252	341
		307	325	355	987	318	307	362	987

This problem of underpredicting the main diagonal (i.e. underpredicting the amount of stability) when the period covered by the table is greater than that for which the transition probabilities were estimated is so pervasive that it points to a general defect in Markov processes as applied to social action. In attempting to discover which of the assumptions of the Markov process is at fault, two different possibilities have been suggested. The first is that different individuals are in fact different in their transition probabilities (path 1a in Figure 1.1). Those who change states at the second observation include those with the highest transition probabilities. Those who remain include the individuals with the lowest transition probabilities. Their probability of changing states at the next observation is consequently lower than the transition probabilities estimated initially, when the volatile individuals' changes occurred. But the Markov process assumes that their probabilities are identical, and thus overpredicts their movement out of the state. In fact, so long as there is any heterogeneity in transition probabilities, the Markov process predictions will be deficient in the main diagonal when the probabilities have been calculated over a shorter period than the period for which the prediction is made. The calculated probabilities are based on the total initial set of individuals in that state which includes both those who are volatile and those who are more stable; but the later transitions are made only from the remaining set, which includes fewer of the volatile individuals.

This is the first explanation of the deficient diagonal, and it has led to various kinds of modification of the Markov process. The first of these, introduced by Blumen, Kogan, and McCarthy (1955) and further developed by Goodman (1961), is to assume two types of persons, 'movers' and 'stayers'. The movers have a certain set of transition probabilities, and the stayers never move. The estimation task then becomes one of estimating the proportion of stayers in each state, as well as the transition probabilities for the movers. Bartholemew (1967) has generalized this by assuming that all persons have transition probabilities, but there is a distribution over persons of overall rates of movement. McFarland (1970) has pursued similar directions, again assuming that transition probabilities have a distribution over persons.

A second explanation of the deficient diagonal (path 1b in Figure 1.1) is of a quite different sort. It is that there is response unreliability, which when tabulated for two points in time, masquerades as change. This can be seen intuitively as follows. Suppose the data in the upper left of Table 1.1 were produced not by change at all, but merely by unreliability of response. Thus the apparent cases of purchase of brand 1 at time 1 and brand 2 at time 2 are merely unreliability of purchase behaviour. Each individual has only a given stable *probability* of purchasing each of the brands. He makes no changes, but merely purchases at each time according to this schedule of fixed probabilities. This may be seen as a relaxation of the assumption of identical probabilities of response made in Bernoulli events, while reinstating the first assumption of independence between events.

If all the apparent changes in that table were due to each individual's use of a fixed schedule of probabilities at each purchase, then we would expect an identical table when the responses were separated farther in time. That is, there would be *no* decline at all in the main diagonal as the responses were further separated, because individuals do not change at all over time, but use the same set of probabilities at each time of purchase. Obviously, then, a Markov process, which predicts a decline in the main diagonal, would be incorrect. Now it is not true that in most social data there is *no* decline in the main diagonal; it is merely a lesser decline than would be predicted by the estimated transition probabilities. But if there is a *mixture* of response unreliability and actual change, then the data will show a decline, but not as much as predicted by the Markov model. In effect, the transition probabilities are overestimated, because they are based not only upon the actual changes, but also include the unreliability that masquerades as change. As with the heterogeneity of transition probabilities, *any* response unreliability will lead to the deficient diagonal predictions.

The extension of the Markov assumptions has not been carried out with Markov chains based on discrete events in time, but has been carried out for Markov processes continuous in time, which are extensions of the Poisson processes. The extension is carried out in Coleman (1964b) with application to purchase behaviour among brands, and has been extended to continuous movement of the transition probabilities (analogous to a diffusion process in physical chemistry) by Massy, Montgomery, and Morrison (1970).

Still a third extension of a Markov chain to attempt to correct the problem of the deficient diagonal is the use of a higher-order process. In the first-order Markov chain, the outcome of an event is conditional only on the outcome of the immediately preceding event, which is ordinarily described as having put the individual in a particular 'state'. But the conditionality need not stop there. The outcome of an event may depend upon the two, three, or N preceding events. The equation giving this conditional probability is simply an expansion of the equation for the first-order Markov process. If there are m states in the first-order process, then an Nth-order process has m^{N+1} conditional probabilities, since there are now m^N states, rather than merely m.

One way of looking at this extension is to conceive of the outcome of an event as dependent not only on the present state, but also on the past history of events for this individual. Certainly this is one way in which different degrees of 'volatility' may be distinguished among those whose current state is the same. And by redefining the state so that it is defined by the outcomes of the N preceding events, incorporating past history as part of the definition of the present state, the Nth order Markov process may be transformed into a first-order process.

One area in which Nth order Markov processes have been applied with some success is in consumer behaviour, where data often come from panels in which the same individuals report many purchases. Kuehn (1958) carried out such an examination of the purchase of particular brands of frozen orange juice, and Frank (1962) carried out a similar examination in the purchase of coffee. Goodman (1959) presents statistical tests for the Nth order Markov chain.

More recently, however, there has been less interest in higher-order

Markov chains as a way of reducing the problem of the deficient diagonal. It is generally recognized that a record of the previous actions of individuals is one of the most efficient ways of distinguishing those with different transition probabilities; but once this is done, the model appears to add little insight into the processes that govern the action. There is a direct parallel between higher-order Markov processes and higher-order extrapolation of a curve. With two prior points, a straight line can be extrapolated, using the slope given by these points. With three prior points, a rate of change in the slope can be incorporated into the extrapolation; with four, a rate of change in the rate of change, and so on. But such increasing precision in extrapolation aids very little in knowledge of the process that generated the curve, even though its predictive power might be great for short extrapolations. The higher-order Markov chain is similar, providing a kind of blind aid to predictability without any progress toward adequately mirroring the process that makes necessary the incorporation of past history into the process.

Extensions of Bernoulli trials: heterogeneity in response probabilities

In path 2 of Figure 1.1, a different extension of Bernoulli trials is represented, in which no sequential dependence is involved. In Bernoulli trials, there is the assumption that each event is governed by the same probabilities for the two or more outcomes. However, if events represent actions of individuals, then different individuals' actions may be governed by different probabilities. Or if events represent actions of individuals in different groups, then individuals within the same group may have different probabilities, differing from those of individuals in other groups. More generally, if the same individuals make more than one response, and the responses are sequentially independent, we can expect some variation in the individual's response (i.e. his underlying probability of response 1 will be less than 1 and greater than 0; but there will also be variation between individuals in their underlying probabilities of making a given response).

This kind of relaxation of Bernoulli assumptions has been carried out by Lazarsfeld (1959) in one form of latent structure analysis. A different way of relaxing the Bernoulli assumptions has been carried out by Coleman (1964a, Chapter 12).[7] In general, the models that make this relaxation of Bernoulli assumptions are designed to study the diversity among persons, and if the data are sufficient, to estimate the response probabilities of different persons. The value of these extensions lies in their ability to partition the response variation into a component due to variation within the individual, and a component due to variation between individuals.

This same extension may be applied to a partitioning of events in which homogeneity of response probability is assumed within a group, and heterogeneity between groups. This is shown as path 2b in Figure 1.1. Under this assumption, it becomes possible, when each member of a group makes a single response, to calculate the variance of the distribution of response probabilities among groups, as well as to estimate the response probability of each group (see Coleman, 1964a, Chapter 14).

Both of these extensions, shown in Figure 1.1 as path 2a and path 2b, illustrate relaxing of the identical-probability assumptions of Bernoulli trials, while maintaining the sequential independence assumption. They are not generally useful for social applications as are Markov chains, because they reflect static distributions rather than changes, but do provide a way of mapping some aspects of social structure.

Extensions of Bernoulli trials: outcomes dependent on other factors

Neither of the preceding extensions of Bernoulli trials constitutes a causal process in which other factors are introduced to explain the

[7] In this approach, calculations are carried out as follows: assume that individual k has a stable probability v_{ik} of giving response i. Then the expected proportion of individuals giving response i is

$$p_i = \frac{1}{n} \sum_{k=1}^{n} v_{ik}$$

The observed proportion giving response i can be regarded as an estimate of p_i. The expected proportion giving response i twice is

$$p_{ii} = \frac{1}{n} \sum_{k} v_{ik}^2$$

The observed proportion of individuals giving response i twice is an estimate of p_{ii}. The variance of the distribution of v_{ik} is then $p_{ii} - p_i^2$, and the observed proportions can outcomes of events. However, other work, represented in path 3, has provided such an extension. In that work (which ordinarily treats only events with two outcomes), the probability of a positive outcome is seen as a function of other states of an individual (path 3b), or on his position on one or more continuous variables (path 3a). The approach has been to introduce a linear decomposition of the probability of a positive outcome, or of some function of that probability. Three models have been widely used, all with the following linear form, where $f(p)$ is a function of the probability of a positive response:

$$f(p) = a + b_1 x_1 + \ldots + b_n x_n \qquad (1.11)$$

where $x_1, \ldots, x_n$ are either discrete attributes representing states (1 if he is in the state, 0 if not), or values of continuous variables, showing his position on those variables.

Three functions of p have been widely used as functions to be linearly decomposed according to eqn. 1.11. These are, together with the terms associated with their usage:

$f(p) = p$ (regression analysis with 0–1 dependent variable;
$\qquad\qquad\qquad\qquad\qquad$ linear decomposition) (1.11a)

$f(p) = \log p$ (logit analysis) (Thiel, 1969, Goodman, 1971) (1.11b)

$f(p)$ defined by:

$$p = \int_{-\infty}^{\log f(p)} N(0,1)\,dx \quad \text{(probit analysis) (Finney, 1964)} \quad (1.11c)$$

This last is a transformation that is motivated by the following idea: p is the probability of success, and $\log f(p)$ is an underlying variable such that probabilities of success are normally distributed along it. Thus the cumulative probability of success as $\log f(p)$ increases is given by the cumulative normal distribution.

Each of these functions has certain virtues and faults. The virtues of letting $f(p) = p$ lie in the simplicity, the convenient interpretability of the resulting coefficients, and its usability at the individual level in regression analysis. The faults lie in statistical problems (the variance

---

be used to estimate this variance. Similarly, for responses i and j, the observed proportions can be used to estimate the covariance $p_{ij} - p_i p_j$. If a particular form for the distribution of v_{ik} is assumed, then the likelihood distribution for a given individual given one or two (or more responses) can be calculated. See Coleman (1964b) for such calculations in application to purchase behaviour.

of p varies widely along its range), and the possibility that values outside the range $(0, 1)$ might be predicted by the model. The probit analysis advantages lie in the reasonableness of the interpretation in the applications for which it was used (biological assays, in which the independent variables were dosages of drugs); its disadvantages lie in difficulty of calculation and in statistical testing.

Logit analysis appears to have the greatest net advantage. It has good statistical properties, with a variance approximately constant over the range of p, and calculation is not difficult. Its primary disadvantage appears to lie in the lack of simple interpretability of the coefficients in the linear equation.

Logit analysis and regression analysis with 0–1 dependent variable have been used primarily in the analysis of responses in surveys, in which some dependent action is to be explained by independent states and variables viewed as causal. Probit analysis has been used primarily for examining the effectiveness of drugs or combinations of drugs, with the dependent response being probability of being killed (or cured), and the independent variables being dosages of drugs. It has been used in a few cases (Farrell, 1954, Tobin, 1955) where probability of purchase is the dependent response, and income is the principal independent variable.

This last direction of extension of Bernoulli trials, introduction of independent variables, can be seen as another way of allowing heterogeneity of response probabilities. However, in contrast to paths 2a and 2b, where the heterogeneity is merely described, here it is accounted for in terms of other properties of the individuals.

Altogether, these extensions of Bernoulli trials show well how a very simple model of action that does not fit social behaviour at all can be extended by relaxation of certain assumptions and substituting new assumptions, to provide models that are very useful in the analysis of social action. As the next section will indicate, a similar development has taken place with the Poisson process.

Extensions of the Poisson process: continuous-time Markov process

The particular importance of the Poisson process and its extensions for social applications lies in a property of all stochastic processes that are continuous in time. A Poisson process defined as the occurrence of *either* of two independent events a or b is described simply by the sum of the two parameters for the separate processes, $q = q_a + q_b$. For a process that occurs at discrete points in time, such as Bernoulli trials, this is not true. The probability of either of two independent events a or b is $p_{a \cup b} = p_a + p_b - p_a p_b$. But in a process continuous in time, the probability of an event a in an infinitesimally small increment of time dt, $q_a dt$, is itself an infinitesimally small quantity. Thus the probability of either event a or b in the infinitesimally small increment of time dt, is

$$q \, dt = q_a \, dt + q_b \, dt - q_a q_b \, dt \, dt \qquad (1.12)$$

and the last term, involving $(dt)^2$, can be neglected, giving $q \, dt = q_a \, dt + q_b \, dt$, or $q = q_a + q_b$.

This virtue of a Poisson process is particularly important in sociology, for certain social processes can thus be defined as the sum of the individual processes, if the individual processes are independent. For example, from an individual's probability per unit time, q_i, of going to a cinema, we can not only calculate the probability of his going 0 times, once, twice, etc., over a given period of time, but if we know the q's for other persons as well, and their attendance is independent of his, we can calculate the probability that there will be 0, 1, ..., attendees at a cinema simply by use of a q which is the sum of the individual q_i's. For purely individual processes as well, this additivity is valuable: if we know that the Poisson probability per unit time toward going to the cinema due to factor 1 is q_1, and that due to factor 2 is q_2, and these impulses are independent, then the total parameter q due to both factors is simply $q_1 + q_2$.

There are various elaborations of the Poisson process that are particularly appropriate both for sequential dependence of actions in an individual's behaviour (such as occurs in operant conditioning) and for social dependence of one individual's action upon that of another, as occurs in diffusion of an innovation. All these elaborations require removal of the assumption of sequential independence of events, and this leads directly to the continuous-time Markov process. The idea is much the same as with the extension of Bernoulli trials to a Markov chain: the outcome of one event places an individual in a particular state, and the probabilities of new events depend on that state. In extending the Poisson process, the comparable change is this: the (spontaneous) event places the individual in a new state in which his changes are governed by a new parameter (or set of parameters if he can move to various states from the new state). In this extension, the transition rates which move the individual to a new state will be denoted q_{ij}, from state i to state j. Let us suppose that when the individual is in state 1, there are two independent processes, governed by transition rates q_{12} and q_{13}, into states 2 and 3. The rate of decline in probability of being in state 1 due to each of these two independent processes (assuming no transitions back into state 1) is, following the same principles as for the Poisson process:

$$\begin{bmatrix} \text{change in} \\ \text{probability of} \\ \text{being in state 1} \end{bmatrix} = - \begin{bmatrix} \text{probability of} \\ \text{going from state} \\ \text{1 to state } j, \\ \text{given residence} \\ \text{in state 1} \end{bmatrix} \cdot \begin{bmatrix} \text{probability of} \\ \text{being in state 1} \end{bmatrix}$$

$$dp_1(t) = -(q_{12} + q_{13})\, dt p_1(t) \tag{1.13}$$

Similarly, in state 2 there are two independent processes, governed by transition rates q_{21} and q_{23}, and in state 3, two processes governed by transition rates q_{31} and q_{32}. There is an increase in the probability of being in state 1 occurring through two of these four processes, governed by q_{21} and q_{31}. Altogether, the change in probability of being in state 1 is simply the sum of four independent processes:

$$\frac{dp_1(t)}{dt} = -q_{12} p_1(t) - q_{13} p_1(t) + q_{21} p_2(t) + q_{31} p_3(t) \tag{1.14}$$

The continuous-time Markov process is thus defined by the various sub-processes, which can be collected as in eqn. 1.14 into those expressing the overall rate of change of the probability of being in each state—in this case, three equations of the form of eqn. 1.14, giving the rate of change in p_1, p_2, p_3. Obviously, such a process generalizes to any number of states.

The continuous-time Markov process and the discrete-time Markov chains obviously have much similarity of structure. In each, there are states, probability distributions defined over these states, and constant probabilities of transition from state i to state j, independent of past events other than the one which placed the individual in state i. The single difference is that, in the discrete-time case, all the probability of transition is compressed into fixed equally spaced time points, while in the continuous-time case, the probability is spread evenly over the time line. At any point in time, the probability of transition is zero, and it is only by integrating $q\,dt$ over an interval of time that a non-zero probability of change arises. The similarity of these two processes can be further seen through the following relationship: A continuous-time Markov process gives[8] equations of the following form for the probability of being in state j at time t as a function of the probability distribution over states at time 0:

$$p_j(t) = r_{1j}(t)p_1(0) + \ldots + r_{kj}(t)p_k(0) \qquad (1.15)$$

where the parameters $r_{ij}(t)$ are functions only of the transition rates, q_{ij}, and t. These parameters are identical to transition probabilities in a discrete-time Markov chain where the time points of transition are t units of time apart, that is, a discrete-time process with transition probabilities equal to $r_{ij}(t)$. Thus we can say that a continuous-time Markov process can generate a discrete-time Markov chain with given time interval t between observations.[9]

This correspondence indicates something about the conditions that should dictate the choice between a discrete-time model and a continuous-time model for describing a process that is actually continuous in time. If the underlying process is believed to be discrete at intervals corresponding to the observation points, or if it is not, but all observations are equally spaced in time (such as waves of interviews of a panel of individuals, one month apart in time, or daily observations on individuals), and if the q_{ij}'s are not of intrinsic interest for theoretical reasons, then a discrete-time chain, with its simpler mathematics, may be used. If neither of these two conditions holds, then a continuous-time model should be used.

It should be clear, then, that it is not merely the nature of the process governing the events or actions that dictates the model to be used in describing the process, but also the nature of the observations and the use to which the model is to be put. Spontaneous actions occurring

---

[8] The equation through which it does so is the integral of the system of eqn. 1.14 over time period 0 to t. Expressed in matrix form, this integral is $P(t) = P(0)e^{Qt}$, where $P(t)$ is the vector of state probabilities at time t, and e^{Qt} is a matrix defined in a generalization of the definition of e, as the infinite series,

$$I + Qt + \frac{(Qt)^2}{2!} + \frac{(Qt)^3}{3!} + \ldots,$$

and Qt is the matrix with elements $q_{ij}t$.

[9] It is not the case that any discrete-time Markov chain can be generated by an appropriate continuous-time process. Heuristically, those discrete-time chains that cannot be generated by a continuous-time process are those in which the equilibrium distribution is approached through a damped wave, rather than approached asymptotically.

continuously through time can be mirrored by a discrete-time model if the only record of those acts is periodic observations of the state of the individual resulting from the most recent act, and if the only interest is in projection into the future. Much of our interest here, however, is in a development of the appropriate theoretical structure underlying a set of observations, and for this, a continuous-time process is usually an appropriate first step, providing the transition rates q_{ij} as elements to be explained in more complex theoretical model.

Applications of continuous-time Markov processes have not been as numerous as applications of Markov chains, because of the more direct estimation of transition probabilities r_{ij} than of transition rates q_{ij} from the data. It is primarily in their further extensions, which are simpler and more direct than with Markov chains, that they have been especially used. However, where the observation points can mask two or more changes that have occurred in an intervening period (as in occupational mobility or in attitude change), the continuous-time process does allow a more direct mirroring of the process than does a discrete Markov chain. Bartholemew (1967) has used the process in studying occupational movement, and Coleman (1964a) has used it in studying attitude change.

The deficient diagonal: response unreliability

The problem of predictions of deficiencies in the main diagonal of cross-tabulations has been attacked by use of continuous-time processes as well as by use of discrete chains. The general statement about these is that the extensions are simpler and more natural with the continuous-time process, but that no striking advantages arise from its use. Bartholemew (1967), in his generalization of the mover-stayer model to a model with a continuously distributed parameter expressing the rate of change, found it straightforward to do so by use of a continuous-time process. The extension involving response uncertainty with an underlying Markov process was developed with the continuous-time model, although it was subsequently possible to express the model in terms of transition probabilities, as a discrete-time model. I will not discuss either of those extensions here, since the ideas underlying them were discussed in an earlier section.

The extension to an Nth order Markov chain provides an opportunity to show one difference between the approach with a discrete-time model and the approach of a continuous-time model. The Nth order discrete-time chain with m states has m^{N+1} conditional probabilities, rather than m^2, as does the first-order chain. Each of these probabilities can be directly estimated with $N+1$ observations on a sample of individuals assumed to be governed by identical parameters. One could, given those transition probabilities, estimate the transition rates that would have generated them. However, with the continuous time model, it is possible to capture much of the substantive idea behind the Nth order process by a much simpler and more parsimonious model. The idea ordinarily behind the Nth order process is that the longer an individual is in a state, the less likely he is to leave it. But there is no natural function of the transition probabilities that can express this. However, with the transition rates, there are two natural functions that capture this idea. If q_{ij} is the transition rate from state i to state j, then these two functions are:

$$\frac{dq_{ij}(t)}{dt} = -aq_{ij}(t) \qquad (1.16)$$

$$\frac{dq_{ij}(t)}{dt} = -\frac{a}{t}q_{ij}(t) \qquad (1.17)$$

In the first of these, the transition rate continually declines in proportion to its existing size. In the second, the transition rate declines, but more rapidly at first, and less rapidly as time in the state continues.

With several observations on the same persons, it is possible to estimate the q_{ij}'s for different length inter-observation periods, and then examine how well eqns. 1.16 and 1.17 account for the kind of changes in $q_{ij}(t)$ that are observed. What is perhaps most useful is that one is not as constrained by the particular data at hand: with an Nth order process, one must assume that nothing about the history before the $N+1$ observations affects the individual's rate of movement. However, with either eqn. 1.16 or eqn. 1.17 in a continuous-time process, information for estimating a can be obtained from as few as three observation points on the sample. With an Nth order Markov chain, this would limit the model to a second-order chain; but with the use of eqn. 1.16 or eqn. 1.17 in the continuous-time process, the historical effect is not limited to that time span. (It is useful to note here that Morrison (1967) has modified Markov chains to incorporate the idea of reduced probabilities of change as duration of residence is longer, and Ginsberg (1972) has examined the applica-

2

tion of semi-Markov processes to migration, in a further generalization.)

In general, however, the benefits of the continuous-time process for handling the problem of the deficient diagonal are not extremely great. The same general strategies are available for the discrete-time chain and the continuous-time process.

Dependence of transition rates on other factors

One important extension of the continuous-time process that has had no counterpart in the discrete-time chain is the introduction of explanatory factors to account for the transition rates themselves (path 4d in Figure 1.1). With Bernoulli trials, the causal variables and states have been introduced to explain the outcome of the event (see eqn. 1.11) but not to explain the transition probabilities. Here, however, they are introduced to explain the transition rates themselves. This involves a decomposition of q_{ij}, which has taken either of two forms:

$$q_{ij} = a + b_1 x_1 + \ldots + b_n x_n \qquad (1.18)$$

$$\log q_{ij} = a + b_1 x_1 + \ldots + b_n x_n \qquad (1.19)$$

The linear decomposition has been exposited in a number of publications (Coleman, 1964a, 1968, 1970) and the log linear decomposition has been exposited by Rubin (1972) and Coleman (1973b). By introducing the explanatory variables into the transition rates themselves, it becomes possible to use the model both in the analysis of change, as a dynamic model, or in the analysis of cross-sectional data, under certain assumptions of aggregate equilibrium. With data obtained from continuous observations, for example, the *duration* of residence in the state may be used to estimate q_i (the total transition rate out of the state), since the expected duration of residence in a continuous-time Markov process is $1/q_i$. Thus the reciprocal of the duration or $-\log$ (duration) may be used as dependent variable in a regression equation for estimating parameters in eqn. 1.18 or eqn. 1.19. Sorensen (1972) has carried out such analysis, using transition between jobs as the dependent variable, and various characteristics of the individual and the job presently held as the independent states or variables.

Another application of this decomposition of transition rates has been in the analysis of change in two or more interdependent attributes.

Transition rates for change in one attribute are made a function of the state of the individual on the other attribute(s). When the parameters are estimated by use of panel data, they show the degree of dependence of each attribute on each other attribute. McDill and Coleman (1963) have applied this to the analysis of change in college plans and membership in the leading crowd in high school.

In the analysis of cross-sectional data, under assumptions of aggregate equilibrium, the decomposition of q_{ij} according to eqns. 1.18 and 1.19 gives the same two models as the decomposition of response probabilities in the extension of Bernoulli trials, in eqn. 1.11a (regression analysis with dichotomous dependent variable) and eqn. 1.11b (logit analysis). Rubin (1972) uses these two decompositions with a wide variety of survey data, and concludes that the log linear decomposition of eqn. 1.19 gives somewhat better fits to the data than does the linear decomposition. Adding this to the better statistical properties of the log linear decomposition presents a rather strong case for the use of this decomposition rather than the linear one. However, when the analysis is carried out in the form of least squares estimation with observations at the individual level so that the observed value of the proportion p is always 0 or 1, then only the linear model can be used.

Transition rates dependent on numbers of preceding events

A general class of extensions of the Poisson process consists of models in which the transition rate depends on the number of prior events. Because of the additivity of transition rates in independent processes, this dependence can take an especially simple additive form. In a simple extension, the transition rate from state i (in which i actions have been carried out) to state $i + 1$ might be:

$$q_{i,i+1} = \alpha + \beta i \qquad (1.20)$$

where α is the transition rate when no actions have been taken, and β is the addition to $q_{i,i+1}(i)$ for each action having been taken.

Two types of applications have been made: applications to repetitive acts of the same individual (in which each action adds another component to the transition rate), and to acts of other persons (in which each other person's action adds a component to the transition rate). The first is psychic contagion, and areas of application have been to accidents, absences from work, and similar repetitive actions of an individual which may increase the likelihood of the next action. The second is social contagion or diffusion, and areas of application have been voting, adoption of a new practice, marriage, riots, and others.

A variety of specific models have been devised to mirror particular situations, with forms varying from eqn. 1.20 and constructed to fit the structure of the particular situation. Despite the general applicability of models that stem from this foundation, each model must be structurally appropriate to its area of application, making different models applicable to different situations. Some of these may be found in Hernes (1972), Coleman (1964a), Bartholemew (1967) and Spilerman (1971).

Initiated and terminating processes

There have been several types of evidence that transition rates in a continuous-time process change in systematic ways, and are not constant, as required by Markov process assumptions. The most frequent is that in many instances, the rate of change out of a state seems to decline as the length of time in the state increases (path 5a in Figure 1.1). For example, the probability of returning a mail questionnaire or a coupon from a magazine declines over time, in what appears as an exponential decay. Or as another example, the rate of leaving a job is greatest for those who have just taken the job, and seems to decline over time.[10]

All the examples in which there appears to be a systematic decline in transition rates through time are of the sort suggested by the examples above: they are processes initiated by an external stimulus event. The decline in the transition rate can be usefully conceived as a decay in attention to the stimulus with the passage of time after its occurrence.

This can be conceived as a generic kind of social process, a process that is initiated by a cause which is then removed—as in a mechanical system when an initial velocity is imparted to a particle by a force acting at a point in time. Panel studies of decision making, attitude change, and consumer behaviour in response to such events have been called 'impact studies'. The question that arises is what kind

[10] This could be due to heterogeneity among individuals (some are 'movers' and others are 'stayers', or some are more volatile than others), or it could be due to actual changes in transition rates as a function of the length of time on the job.

of model of change correctly expresses the changes that occur in the probability of response through time.

It is very likely not useful to conceive of a simple generic process of decline in transition rates that will be useful for all empirical situations. Yet there is one simple model that appears to fit certain circumstances. This is an exponential decay in the transition rate, according to the equation:

$$\frac{dq(t)}{dt} = -aq(t) \qquad (1.21)$$

which after integration gives a transition rate $q(t)$ as a function of two parameters:

$$q(t) = q_0 e^{-at} \qquad (1.22)$$

where q_0 is the transition rate at the time of the initiating event, a gives the rate of decline, and $q(t)$ is the transition rate at time t after the initiating event. Hernes (1971) has used this model to describe the decline in marriageability from the point of first eligibility.[11] Sorensen (1972) shows that this model describes well the decline in rate of changing jobs as age increases. Sorensen goes beyond this and argues that 'psychological time' is such that, as persons grow older (with birth the initiating event in this application), they act more slowly, and any transition rate characterizing their action declines according to eqn. 1.21. McGinnis (1968) has also studied situations of residential mobility in which there appears to be a decline in transition rate (i.e. probability per unit time of moving residence) as a function of the period of time since the last move. He, however, has left the process quite general, without specifying a functional form for the decline in transition rate.[12]

[11] The total transition rate for an individual includes another component as well: the pressure from others to get married, according to a kind of social diffusion process. If P is the proportion of the cohort married, then in Hernes' model, the transition rate is $Pq_0 e^{at}$.

[12] This creates an interesting possibility: if in general, the transition rate declines in this way with age, but it also declines over time after having been subject to an initiating event, then there are two declines: a long-term one, dependent on age, and superimposed upon that, a decline from a specific initiating event. For example, transition rates for job changes might be subject both to the long-term decline in transition rates, and the short-term decline consequent upon the event of taking the job. This decline can be modelled rather simply, because of the additive property of transition rates:

$$\frac{dq}{dt} = -a_1 q(t) - a_2 q(t)$$

or

$$q(t) = q_0 \exp\{-a_1(t + \theta) - a_2 t\}$$

where a_1 is the decline due to age, a_2 is the decline due to a specific event, θ is the age when that event takes place, and t is the period of time since that event. In such a case, we would expect a_2 to be much larger than a_1.

This decline of transition rates after an initiating event, for which there is some general evidence, is identical to eqn. 1.16, which was introduced in an earlier section to account for this decline in transition rates in a continuous time Markov process. It may be that this dependence of q on time in social applications is a very general phenomenon, and should, rather than the Markov assumption of constancy in transition rate, be used as the baseline assumption. But all this awaits further exploration in social applications of stochastic processes.

Another general kind of social process which appears to create changes in transition rates is a process that has a specific terminal point in time (path 5b in Figure 1.1). An election is such an event, and changes in attitude before the election would be such a process. Another more esoteric example is a kind of auction that was held around the eighteenth century in England: bidding could occur until a candle flickered out or until sand had passed through a sandglass three times—and the last bid before this terminating event was the bid taken. Observations suggest that in such processes terminated by an event at a predetermined time, transition rates *increase* over time in a systematic fashion. Again the question is, what model correctly accounts for the observed data; and again, it is likely that different models are appropriate for different specific applications. But an exponential growth shows a good fit in a variety of empirical situations, and it may be that the buildup of attention to a forthcoming event acts by a reverse of the process of declining attention to a past event. If this is the case, and if the transition rate at the time of the event (measured from an arbitrary starting point) is $q(\tau)$, then the transition rate at an earlier time t is found by decrementing q backwards in time from time (r), following the same model as expressed in eqn. 1.21 and 1.22:

$$q(t) = q(\tau)e^{-a(\tau-t)} \tag{1.23}$$

and if we designate the value of q when $t = 0$ as $q(0)$, then this reduces to:

$$q(t) = q(0)e^{at} \tag{1.24}$$

These two forms of change in the process contrast to those stable processes in which there is no change in transition rates over time. Although there are numerous other ways in which transition rates may change, due to external and unpredictable events, the two extreme cases of initiated processes and terminating processes seem frequent enough to warrant special attention along with the usual treatment of constant or stable processes.

These two situations of initiation and termination appear to offer clear possibilities for experimental studies. The psychological mechanisms of change are not clear, but they could be classified by detailed experimental investigation. The underlying mechanisms appear to be related to attention, and if the processes through which attention declines following an event or builds up prior to one can be uncovered, a fairly general process of augmentation and decay can probably be described mathematically. This is an excellent example of a stage of social science in which the contribution of specific experimental work to theory is clear and straightforward.

The various extensions of the Poisson process indicate something of its versatility and the promise it holds for mirroring social and psychological phenomena. Together with extensions of Bernoulli trials, these extensions seem to provide the appropriate mathematical framework for social action in a causal—as distinct from purposive—framework. Altogether, a very promising foundation for the mathematical study of action in a causal framework has been created over the past ten years, to which both theoretical and empirical work can make well-defined contributions.

Purposive action theory

Purposive action theory is based on a model of individual choice, in which the choice is made in the anticipation of consequences. Because this book as a whole is devoted to developing a branch of purposive action theory, I will leave until Chapter 2 a more extended discussion of the direction in which work in purposive action has gone.

However, for comparison with causal models of action, it is useful to list the branches of development of purposive action theory, for comparison with Figure 1.1. The starting point for purposive action is what economists describe as individual choice under certainty. But if this is viewed within a framework comparable to that described in the preceding section, it is individual action, exercising control over the outcome of an event, when the consequences of the possible outcomes are known and are fully under the control of the actor.

This starting point has been elaborated, in statistical decision theory and in game theory, in two directions (see Figure 1.2). First (path 1), uncertainty is introduced between the individual's action and the outcome of the event which has consequences for him. By translating that uncertainty into risk, i.e. environmental actions with given or assumed probabilities, statistical decision theorists have developed the theory of rational behaviour under risk. The elements of this theory are briefly described in Chapter 2.

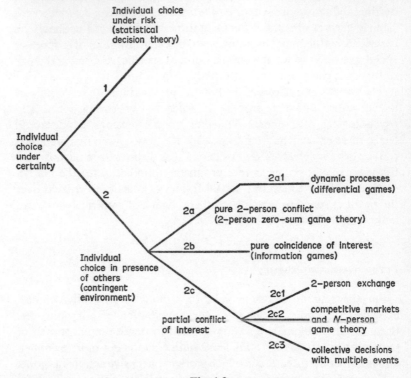

Fig. 1.2

Path 2 involves a different type of relaxation of the assumption that the outcome of events is fixed by the individual's action. In place of an uncertain nature, the individual is faced with strategic others, who like himself are interested in maximizing their gain. The basic theory for this kind of environmental contingency has been begun by Von Neumann and Morgenstern in the theory of games. The principal results in that theory have been in two-person games of pure conflict, where interests of the two players are irrevocably opposed (path 2a in Figure 1.2). In Chapter 2, a brief description of some of these results is given, and games of pure coincidence of interest (path 2b) are mentioned as well. One of the extensions of zero-sum-two-person games has been the introduction of time and continuous movement of each player, in a development termed differential games (Isaacs, 1965, Kuhn and Szego, 1971). This work, originally begun for the study of problems of capture and pursuit in war, and now converging with control theory in engineering, appears to be fruitful for a considerably wider range of social processes than those to which it has been applied.

For most of social, political, and economic life, however, interactions with others involve partial conflict of interest (path 2c), rather than pure conflict or pure coincidence of interest. One form of such interaction, two-party exchange (path 2c1) serves as the basis of a large portion of economic theory. More difficult problems lie in systems of two-party exchange of private goods in a competitive market (path 2c2); still more difficult are problems of collective decisions, in which a collectivity must make a choice between two (or more) alternatives, though different members may have different preferences (path 2c3 in Figure 1.2). This necessitates the development of a theory of collective decisions based on individual preferences, and this book contributes to such a development. The problem requires use of both elements from statistical decision theory and game theory, and thus cannot be regarded as purely an elaboration of the theory of choice in contingent environments, as shown in Figure 1.2. That is, in some cases, environments that are in fact contingent can be regarded as fixed, independent of his action, thus allowing a considerable simplification of the mathematical treatment. It was this simplification which the classical theory of perfectly competitive markets made, and it is this simplification that needs to be withdrawn when considering markets that are oligopolistic or monopolistic.

In the next chapter, development and elaboration of the concept of rational action is reviewed in order to locate the work in collective decisions to which the remainder of the book is devoted.

2 Concepts of Rational Action

In causal models of social action, the structure of action is character-ized by events and outcomes. In the form of action in which the event is imposed from without, as in empirical situations with events such as an election or a question in an attitude questionnaire, and as represented mathematically by extensions of Bernoulli events, the individual's action constitutes the outcome of the event. It is the pattern or structure among these outcomes that is problematic. In the form of action in which the individual spontaneously acts at some point in time or space, represented mathematically by extensions of the Poisson process, it is the action itself that constitutes the event and the outcome.[1] It is both the timing of the actions and their pattern or structure that is problematic.

In order to develop models of purposive behaviour, two further characteristics of events must be described. That is, if an individual acts purposively, then this implies two things: that he expects various possible outcomes of an event to have differing consequences for him, and that the actions available to him must have some effect on the outcomes. If the first of these conditions did not exist, he would have no reason to act to affect the event's outcome, because it would make no difference to him. If the second did not exist, his action would be futile, because it could not affect the outcome.

Purposive action is, in effect, action taken in the context of a control system, the control system being the actor. As in any such control system, there must be a closed loop between action and consequence,

---

[1] In the correspondence between Bernoulli events and the Poisson process, an infinitesimally small period of time dt becomes the event, and the outcome corresponding to success on a trial is dependent upon $q\,dt$, the probability of an individual's taking an action in this period of time. In the general use of continuous-time models, however, it appears most reasonable to describe the action itself, occurring at some point in time, as the event and outcome.

i.e. some information feedback from the consequence by means of which the action may be modified. Thus, while the structure of action in causal models can be described in terms of one-way sequences of relationship, from cause to event outcome, there is a closed loop in a system of the sort under consideration here. There is action-event outcome-consequence, and a final link, which is the 'purposive' portion of the link, or the 'guidance system', from consequence back to action, so that the action taken is *affected* by the consequences, just as the consequences are in turn affected by the action. This may be interpreted in at least two ways, which at a superficial level of analysis are different, though they are likely the same at a deeper level. First, the actor has a 'look-ahead' mechanism, so that he anticipates the consequences of the action, and it is these expected consequences that affect the action. Or, second, the actor in a continuing sequence of action-and-consequence alters his action on the basis of the consequences of preceding actions, so that it is in fact the consequences of preceding actions that affect the consequences of future action. At a deeper level of analysis, these may be the same, because his anticipation of future consequences is certainly based on past experience with similar action in similar circumstances.

Either of these ways of interpreting rational behaviour may be expressed by a closed-loop sequence, in which we think of the following interdependence between the actor and his environment:

(1) The actor makes a decision, selecting among actions.
(2) Action implementing the decision.
(3) Outcome of event, partially controlled by actor's action.
(4) Consequence of outcome for actor.
(5) Information about consequence goes to affect next decision.

Diagrammatically, the sequence can be expressed as shown in Figure 2.1. The absence of arrows from outside does not mean that each step in the sequence is affected only by those shown in the diagram; indeed, what makes the action problematic is that the consequences of his action for him may depend also on other elements in the environment.

A variety of different models of action have been used as the basis for purposive action by different social scientists. The most common in use among sociologists is the means-ends scheme with which Talcott Parsons began his theoretical work (1937). In effect, in this model, an actor's goals or ends are established outside the framework of rational action (except in so far as they are means to broader goals), and rational or purposive action consists in the selection of those means that the actor believes will most efficiently (implicitly meaning at least cost, though costs are ordinarily not an explicit part of this theoretical perspective) lead to the goal.

A second theoretical framework for purposive action is due to a set of authors best represented by a Polish logician, Tadeusz Kotarbinski, which is labelled praxiology.[2] Praxiology is essentially the science of efficient action, or the science of directed action. The general works in praxiology have both the virtues and faults of generality.

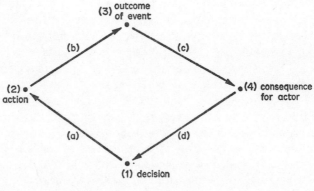

Fig. 2.1

They are designed to cover a very wide range of individual and social action, including conflict and collective action, but like the very general work of Talcott Parsons toward such theory, have limited their theoretical developments mainly to classification schemes.

A third direction of work, which the praxiologists see as a portion of praxiology, is the theoretical framework on which micro-economics is based, a framework that has been used and extended in the theory of games. This theoretical framework is at the opposite pole from that of Parsons and the praxiologists in its simplicity, for it contains in its use for classical micro-economic theory only one concept, 'preference', and one principle of action, that of choosing the most preferred action. In its further developments, in statistical decision theory or in theory

[2] Tadeusz Kotarbinski (1965). Other works relevant to this approach are Ludwig von Mises (1949); and Emanuel Lasker (1907).

of games, it contains a more restrictive concept of 'utility' replacing preference, a more restrictive principle of action, maximizing utility, replacing the principle of choosing the most preferred action, and an additional concept as well, the subjective probability (as held by the actor) of a given action leading to a given outcome.

This theoretical framework has the virtues and faults of a simple theory. It is subject to development in mathematical form, as is exemplified by the mathematical form of those theories which are based on it. The faults have been the limitation of the theories that stem from it to restricted areas of action, either to individual action in a known and non-contingent (i.e. non-social) environment, or to limited social processes, principally the process of mutually beneficial exchange. This is illustrated not only by economic theory, but by those broader social theories that have been recently developed from this perspective, theories based wholly on mutually beneficial exchange processes and on individual efficient action in a non-contingent environment.[3]

This framework of theory has not been successfully applied to situations of non-voluntary or coerced action, and the concept of power has no place in it. Thus many social and political processes lie outside its range. Nor does the general idea of goals and means find very good expression in the theory, since the principle of utility maximization does not provide algorithms by which sequences of action may be constructed to lead toward a given goal. It is less compatible with the heuristic ideas of means as paths toward a goal than are some theoretical approaches on which guidance and tracking systems are based.

Of the various approaches to a theory of purposive action, the simple approach on which economic theory is based appears to provide the soundest foundation, despite its limitations. I will attempt to build the foundation of a social theory, including power relationships, collective action, and other social phenomena, using this framework and the various extensions of it that have been developed in recent years.

Before beginning on this task, however, I want to clarify the role of 'rationality' in the present work. Confusion always arises in the

---

[3] These 'exchange theories' in sociology are best exemplified by George Homans (1961), Peter Blau (1964), and John W. Thibaut and Harold H. Kelley (1959). These theories may be described as heuristic rather than formal for they are not developed in mathematical form. The work of Thibaut and Kelley, however, follows quite closely the formal framework of game theory and utility theory.

discussion of rationality and utility theory about whether action is to be regarded as rational by definition, or instead, the theory is regarded as empirically descriptive and thus empirically disconfirmable. The confusion ordinarily arises from not distinguishing carefully the theoretical framework as a logical—that is tautological—framework and its empirical application.

In the tautological theoretical framework itself, there exist formal relations between elements of the theory; in a theory with the concept of utility and the action principle of maximizing utility, an individual actor always and invariably takes that action which maximizes his utility subject to the constraints he faces. Thus in the theory, the action may be taken as a primitive, and the utility defined in terms of it; that is, the utilities associated with a set of outcomes may be defined as a set of numbers which, when associated with the outcomes, are consistent with the action taken (still in the formal theory) under the principle of maximization of utility.[4] Alternatively, the utilities of outcomes may be taken as the primitive, and the action a defined term, consistent with these numbers under the utility-maximization principle of action.

All this is in the formal theory itself. In its application, it may be used in either of two ways. The first is the way all theories are used, that is, as an empirically disconfirmable theory of behaviour. If it is so used, then there are two alternative points at which the theory may be linked to reality at the individual level, corresponding to the alternative primitives in the system: either by assigning numbers to utilities on the basis of *a priori* assumptions of the observer about the utilities of different outcomes to the actor, or by taking as given only the actor's action, and assigning numbers to utilities in such a way that they are consistent with this action under the action principle of utility-maximization. Unless the observer merely wants to test his *a priori* judgement about the utilities actually held by the actor, rather than testing the theory itself, the second approach is the correct one. The testing of the theory then comes in examining the consistency of the actor's behaviour under the given assignment of numbers, because the actor may behave in such a way that no assignment of numbers as

---

[4] For action in certain kinds of situations, for example when the action leads to a given outcome with certainty, then the set of numbers compatible with the action is unique only up to an order relation. More generally, depending upon the specific characteristics of the action principle, the numbers assigned to outcomes as measures of utility will have differing degrees of uniqueness. This will be discussed in a subsequent section.

utilities is consistent with the behaviour.[5] If such inconsistencies of behaviour arise, then the structure of the theory itself, and not merely the assignment of utilities to outcomes, must be revised. The experience with regard to the various forms of utility theory (utility under certainty, and utility under risk) is mixed; it is clear that it does not perfectly conform to behaviour, but it is not clear whether this is merely a matter of adding complexities to the theory (in the way that friction from air resistance must be added to the simple model of falling bodies to predict correctly the trajectory of a body in air), or a more fundamental revision of the very structure of the theory.[6]

There is an additional complicating factor in this theory, due to the fact that it does not contain a principle through which utilities change over time. Thus it is often possible to rescue the theory from disconfirmation merely by regarding the utilities as having changed, and making new assignments consistent with the new behaviour. Obviously, however, if such rescues are carried out universally, without some rule of constraint, then the theory is useless.

A second and quite different use of the theory of rational action is a special and unusual one, not found for other, non-purposive theories. It is sometimes assumed to be a correct description of efficient behaviour, and used as a calculating device for determining what action to take when utilities are given. This use is most often found in application of linear programming to production, distribution, and inventory problems, when the empirical criterion by which utility maximization is achieved (such as lowest money cost) is easily specifiable. This use, however, as a guide to action is limited to precisely those cases, and it is probably wiser to consider this use as outside the realm of theory, but merely use of the same mathematical maximization procedures when a criterion is given.

Rational action under varying circumstances

Rationality under certainty for single events

In application of the paradigm of action–event outcome–consequence, there are various circumstances that lead to different concep-

---

[5] The simplest example of this is in the theory of rationality under certainty, in which the actor's behaviour implies only a preference ordering among outcomes. But he may prefer A between A and B, prefer B between B and C, but then prefer C between A and C. Insofar as he does so, the theory is fundamentally incorrect, and must be fundamentally revised.

[6] Recent experimental work in choice behaviour by Tversky (1972) suggests that a more fundamental revision may be necessary.

tions of rationality. As the circumstances of action, and the resulting definition of rationality, become more complex, the question of whether the definition is appropriate becomes much more problematic. This has been most evident in disputes over the best principle of action in various forms of game theory.

In describing the conceptions of rationality under various circumstances, I will make use of the existing theories of rationality derived from classical micro-economics, statistical decision theory, and game theory. I will, however, be selective in my use of these frameworks, particularly that of game theory, utilizing only those conceptions of rationality that I regard to be useful for social theory.

The simplest form of rationality is that on which classical economic theory is based, that is, 'rationality under certainty'.[7] In this form, there is a determinate relation between the actor's action and the outcome of the event, to which is (determinately) associated a given consequence. Classically, this consequence was described as having a given utility for the actor. However, in rationality under certainty, it is sufficient to specify a preference order among the possible consequences.[8]

This principle of rationality under certainty is in effect a principle of consistency of behaviour. Rationality at this level implies that faced with a choice of actions, each of which leads to a particular known outcome, an individual will choose in such a way that he can be said to have a consistent preference ordering for outcomes. That is, if when confronted with the choice between A_1 (leading to outcome a_1) and A_2 (leading to outcome a_2), he chooses action A_1, and if when confronted with the choice between A_2 and A_3 (leading to outcome a_3), he chooses action A_2, then he also chooses A_1 when confronted with the choice between A_1 and A_3. Thus his behaviour obeys the principle

[7] Gary Becker (1962) has shown, however, that a considerably weaker principle of behaviour than that of maximizing utility or even consistency of preference among different goods can explain the indifference maps with isoclines convex to the origin, on which micro-economic theory of demand depends. The principle is essentially one of consistency of behaviour, together with the assumption that more of a good is preferred to less (the latter being part of the definition of a good).

[8] In the case of rationality under certainty, many authors prefer not to use the term utility at all, since it is not necessary to say that the individual maximizes anything, but merely that he expresses preferences that can be arranged in a consistent order. To use that approach has the greater elegance of parsimony, and would be preferable in the present case except for the value of maintaining a consistent conceptual framework across the various conditions of action. Nothing is lost by using the concepts of utility and maximization so long as it is recognized that the assignment of numbers to outcomes as utilities in such circumstances would be constrained only by the order relation among the numbers, and no properties other than their order relation would be subsequently used in prediction. See Uzawa (1959) for a formal definition of such preference systems.

of transitivity which is implied in the concept of ordering. It is possible to associate some number with his preference for a_1, and call this the utility of outcome a_1 to him, so long as only the order properties of these numbers are used subsequently. For any numbers may be assigned to outcomes a_1, a_2, and a_3, so long as the number assigned to a_1 is larger than that assigned to a_2, which in turn is larger than that assigned to a_3. Thus if any numbers can be assigned, within the constraint of a fixed order among them, any further properties of the relations between the numbers so assigned have no referent in behaviour.

Rationality without full control of outcome, in a non-contingent environment [9]

The second level of rationality is one in which there is a single modification of the paradigm described above. The determinate relation between the actor's action and the outcome of the event is changed to a non-determinate one. In Figure 2.1, arrow (b) no longer fully determines the outcome. It is assumed that the individual can and does associate probabilities of each outcome conditional upon each of the action alternatives open to him; and here, in contrast to the preceding case, these conditional probabilities are not all zero or one. He then selects that action which gives him the greatest expected utility. (Here as elsewhere the theory is very limited, assuming that the action alternatives are predetermined; it provides no algorithm for him to seek out new action alternatives, nor any other way of exploiting his environment beyond choosing among the action alternatives open to him. Thus he is treated as a more passive actor than one might hope would be the case in a theory of purposive action. However, at the present time I see no way of eliminating that passivity in any systematic way.)

It is useful to see how this second level of rationality operates, through use of a specific example.

A student, Tom, comes to class one day and hears the instructor say, 'You may decide whether or not to take the final examination in the course. If you do not take the exam, your course work will fully determine your grade. If you do take it, the final exam will fully

---

[9] This section is not intended to give a full introduction to the concept of rational behaviour under risk, but only an overview to provide a perspective for later sections, and particularly Chapter 3. For a more extensive introduction to the concept, and statistical decision theory within which it was developed, see Luce and Raiffa (1957), Chapters 2 and 13.

determine your grade.' Tom has course work which he estimates will give him a B or a C. He feels if he takes the exam, he could get an A, B, C, or D. What should he do?

Clearly, Tom should do what his best judgement suggests. If he knew what grade he would get on the basis of class work and what grade he would get on the examination, he would have no problem. He would be in a situation of choice under certainty, and would choose whichever gave him the preferred grade. But the situation is more complicated. The theory of utility under risk would say that Tom's rational judgement is formed in this way:

(1) He has a given subjective probability of getting a B and a C on the basis of his current work. Suppose, for the example, those are .6 and .4 respectively.

(2) He has a given subjective probability of getting an A, B, C, and D on the test. Suppose, for the example, these are .3, .3, .3, .1, for A, B, C, D respectively.

(3) For him, the grades have relative values or utilities. Suppose, for the example, that the relative gain he would experience by getting a C rather than a D is 4, the gain from a B relative to a C is 3, and the gain from an A relative to a B is 2.

(4) Finally, his judgement of the better action is based on the benefits or utilities he would experience from each outcome under each action, weighted by the probability that each would occur. This would give him an 'expected benefit' or 'expected utility' for each action, and he would choose the action that gave him the higher expected utility. In the present case, the benefits or utility he would experience under the two actions are (first, let the benefits or utility of getting a D be denoted as u_d. Then $u_c = u_d + 4$, $u_b = u_d + 7$, and $u_a = u_d + 9$):

If he chooses not to take the examination:

$$\text{expected utility} = .6(u_d + 7) + .4(u_d + 4) = 5.8 + u_d$$

If he chooses to take the examination:

$$\text{expected utility} = .3(u_d + 9) + .3(u_d + 7) + .3(u_d + 4) + .1(u_d)$$
$$= 6.0 + u_d$$

Thus if these are Tom's underlying utility differences between grades and subjective probabilities, the theory predicts that he would choose to take the examination. Whatever the value of u_d, $6.0 + u_d$ is greater than $5.8 + u_d$.

There is, of course, the problem of where the subjective probabilities and utility differences came from in an example like this. Numbers like these can only arise as a compact way of summarizing the results of numerous experiments in which Tom was confronted with choice alternatives. Then the final choice alternative described in the calculation above is merely a testing of the consistency of his behaviour. If such previous experiments had not taken place, then the theory still states that he acts according to underlying subjective probabilities and utilities, though they are unknown. The choice he makes here would not be predicted, but would be one datum to be used with others, in inferring these values.

Several points should be made about this definition of rationality under broadened circumstances. First, the situation may be described as one in which the actor has, through his action, only partial control of the outcomes of the event. The remaining control is held by an external environment as another actor whose action is not contingent upon his own, nor upon the utilities various consequences have for him. Such an environment I will describe as a non-contingent environment, and will regard it as outside the system of action under consideration. The paradigm is enlarged to show dual control over outcome of the event:

$$\begin{array}{c} \text{action of actor} \searrow \\ \qquad\qquad\qquad \text{event outcome} \to \text{consequence.} \\ \text{action of environment} \nearrow \end{array}$$

The second point is that, under some conditions, the actor may not have a basis for estimating the conditional probabilities of the environment's action, but finds himself in an environment of pure uncertainty about those probabilities (though no uncertainty about the structure of action, knowing that the environment will act non-contingently). It is ordinarily assumed that a condition of uncertainty is transformed by the individual into a condition of risk, by attaching conditional probabilities to outcomes in the absence of past experience.[10]

The third point is that rationality under risk implies considerably stronger assumptions about utilities than does rationality under certainty. It implies that the assignment of numbers to consequences as utilities of these consequences for the individual is constrained much more narrowly than in the case of rationality under certainty. Here the

[10] See Savage (1954). For a review of various treatments of uncertainty, see Luce and Raiffa (1957) Chapter 13. The only way an actor can behave if he is to be consistent with the theory of utility under risk, is to attach a set of probabilities to each of the possible outcomes under each of the actions he might take.

number is constrained within a set of transformations that carry it into another number differing only by a positive scale constant and an additive constant, these constants being the same for all outcomes. The resulting utility scale may be regarded as a cardinal scale (i.e. subject to transformations by only a positive scale constant) of the differences between utilities associated with pairs of outcomes. Rationality under risk implies also an assignment of numbers as subjective probabilities that have the properties of probabilities (all are non-negative, and they sum to one).

It is the movement from rationality under risk to the next level of rationality that the first social context of action arises. It is also in this expansion of the definition of rationality that the definition of what is in fact rational becomes more open to question. The conjunction of these two developments occurs because it is in a social context of action that each actor faces a contingent environment, and thus must base his action in part upon expectations about the other's action. And it is such expectations or assumptions that might reasonably differ.

Rationality in the presence of a strategic other[11]

John von Neumann and Oskar Morgenstern (1947) extended the concept of rationality beyond the two conditions described above, rationality under certainty and rationality under risk. In this extension, behaviour is carried out in the presence of a strategic other, whose behaviour is contingent upon his expectations about what one will do. Thus in order to act rationally in this case, one must have a basis for generating expectations about what the other might do.[12] The work initiated by von Neumann and Morgenstern has its most solid grounding for a particular situation in which an actor faces a strategic

[11] As in the preceding section, I will make no attempt to give a full introduction to the concept of rationality in the presence of a strategic other as developed in the theory of games. Besides von Neumann and Morgenstern, there are several good introductions to the theory of games of pure conflict ('2-person, zero sum' games). Luce and Raiffa (1957) give a comprehensive and clear exposition of numerous aspects of game theory; Rapoport (1966) gives a good introduction to 2 person zero sum games.

[12] In purposive behaviour theory, a distinction may be made between rational behaviour in the sense of intention to act most efficiently toward a goal, and rational behaviour in the sense of accomplishing that intention. These have been termed methodical and factual rationality by some praxiologists. As the environment becomes increasingly complex, it is less and less possible to devise an unchallengeable procedure for realizing rational intentions. As a consequence, in the higher reaches of rationality, there are many contenders for the position of most efficient action. Recognizing this, it will sometimes be necessary to truncate the calculation rule (this will be particularly true in collective decisions) to allow a definition of rationality that can be in fact calculated.

other: for single events, and under conditions of pure conflict of interest.

The framework of rationality is extended in this circumstance to a situation in which the actor chooses an action, a second actor chooses an action, and the outcome is contingent upon both actions—with the sole extension beyond rationality under risk being that the second actor is now known to be acting contingently, in expectation of what one might oneself do. Neither actor knows the other's action before acting himself, but anticipates what the other might do, and also knows the other is anticipating his action. The diagram used before is now extended to become

action of actor A ↘
↗ event outcome ⟨
action of actor B ↗

consequence to actor A
↗ ⟨
consequence to actor B

This diagram suggests what in fact turns out to be the case: that in devising control systems (or rules of action), each actor must now look at the *relation* between the consequences for the two actors, and that this relation becomes the crucial factor not only in deciding upon a course of action, but even in devising a principle of action.

Pure conflict of interest for single events

The first case, which itself divides into two parts as will be evident later, is that in which there is pure conflict between the consequences to actor A and those to actor B. This is the case in which, among all the possible outcomes, the preference order of B among the outcomes is exactly the inverse of the preference order of A.[13] Numerous situations which involve the division of some good between two parties are like this. In this situation of pure conflict of interest, actor A's assessment of his own best action in the face of B's is considerably simplified: in carrying out an assessment of what is best for him, and an assessment of what is best for the other, he need consider in a situation of pure conflict of interest only a single set of utilities (or preferences, for all that exists at this point is a preference order among outcomes): what is better for him is worse for the other, for all possible comparisons between outcomes.

Besides the relation between consequences, the other crucial element

[13] In the theory of games, this was termed a zero-sum game by von Neumann and Morgenstern, a heuristically appealing, but unfortunate choice which suggests an interpersonal comparison of utility for which the theory of games provides no basis. In some aspects of the theory of games, however, an implicit and hidden introduction of interpersonal comparison does occur as Shapley points out (1967).

in the actor's strategy is an assumption made by each actor about the kind of strategy to be used by the other. The assumption that von Neumann and Morgenstern use, and the assumption that will be accepted here, is a reflexive one, that the other actor is the same sort of creature that I am. Having made such an assumption, it then follows that the only rational strategy on my part is a strategy that assumes that his strategy is such that it would be the same as mine if he were in my place. For if it were rational for me to assume otherwise, then it would be rational for him, as a creature like myself, to assume otherwise about me; but then his assumptions would be wrong; thus mine must be wrong as well.

Von Neumann and Morgenstern devise a principle of action by considering two hypothetical games, which under certain circumstances lead to the same outcome: a 'minorant' game for A, in which A moves first, and actor B responds, and a 'majorant' game for A in which B moves first and A responds.

The result of those considerations is this: Suppose I am actor A. Then if there is an action of mine in the minorant game (say A_i) which leads actor B, in maximizing his utility under my action A_i, to a response (say B_j), such that the same action B_j of his in the majorant game leads me, in maximizing my utility under action B_j, to response A_i, then that pair of actions, A_i, B_j, is the rational strategy for both.[14] This derives from the fact that each may equally well think of minimizing the other's utility as maximizing his own. In the minorant game, A recognizes that B will choose an action, after his, which maximizing B's utility, minimizes his own. Suppose u_{kl} is the utility to A of an outcome resulting from action A_k and B_l. Then if A takes action k, B will take that action B_h which minimizes u_{kl}. B_h is that action such that

$$u_{kh} = \min_l (u_{kl})$$

Recognizing this, A will choose that action which maximizes the minimum utility he would receive under any action of B. This strategy might be written: A_i is that action such that

$$u_{ij} = \max_k \min_l (u_{kl})$$

[14] See von Neumann and Morgenstern (1947), Section 14.2. An important assumption in this framework of ideas is that if there were sequential actions as in the majorant and minorant games, an action by the first to move does not change the set of actions available to the second actor, or change the utilities associated with any outcome. If that were the case, then a first move might be advantageous. As it is, it confers no advantages, only costs through disclosure of one's move before the other chooses his.

Similarly, in the game where he acts second, he simply maximizes his utility under B's choice h:

$$u_{ih} = \max_k (u_{kh})$$

If B's consideration in the game where he acts first leads him to choose (by way of maximizing the minimum utility he can get under a subsequent action of A) the same action B_j that he will choose in acting second after A has chosen A_i which will maximize A's minimum utility, then the pair of actions A_i and B_j constitute the rational strategy for both.

These principles of action may be examined concretely by considering two games as shown in Table 2.1. In this table, the utilities to actor A for each outcome are listed below the diagonal, and those for actor B are listed above the diagonal.

Table 2.1

		Actor B		
		B_1	B_2	B_3
	A_1	70 / 3	10 / 9	80 / 2
Actor A	A_2	90 / 1	50 / 5	30 / 7
	A_3	20 / 8	60 / 4	40 / 6

(a)

		Actor B		
		B_1	B_2	B_3
	A_1	90 / 1	70 / 3	10 / 9
Actor A	A_2	40 / 6	50 / 5	30 / 7
	A_3	20 / 8	60 / 4	80 / 2

(b)

The games are to be played only one time, and under the condition that neither actor knows the other's action until after he has taken his own. There are several points to be noted about both games. First, both are games of pure conflict, since in each, the nine outcomes are ordered inversely for the two actors.[15] This is so even though the utilities for actor B are ten times as large as the utilities for actor A. It is only their inverse order of preference that leads this to be a game of pure conflict.

A second point to be noted is that for neither actor in either game is one of the actions dominated by another. An action is dominated by a second if under any condition, no matter what the other actor does, the second is a better action than the first. This condition does not hold for any of the actions of either actor.

If I take the perspective of actor A, and consider first the minorant game, in which I must act first, I must take that action which maximizes the minimum I will receive (since after my action, actor B will take the action which maximizes his own return, thus minimizing my return). Consider game (a) first. If I take action A_1, B will take B_3, giving me a return of 2. If I take action A_2, B will take B_1, giving me a return of 1. If I take action A_3, B will take B_2, giving me a return of 4. Thus action A_3, which maximizes my minimum return at 4 (and gives actor B a return of 60), is the action I would take in such a game where I acted first.

In the majorant game of game (a), where I act second, I see that if actor B takes action B_1, my best response is A_3, giving me a return of 8. If actor B takes B_2, then my best response is A_1, giving me a return of 9. If actor B takes B_3, my best response is A_2, giving me a return of 7. Thus I know that actor B will take the action which minimizes this return (since, given that the game is pure conflict, that action maximizes his return), which is action B_3, giving me a return of 7 and him a return of 30. Actor B in effect is acting to minimize the maximum of my return (though this is only coincidence, since in a game of pure conflict, actor B's minimizing of A's maximum return is actually maximizing his own minimum return).

Similar considerations hold for the analysis of game (b). In the minorant game, under action A_1 my minimum is 1, under A_2, my minimum is 5, and under A_3 my minimum is 2. Thus action A_2 maximizes my minimum return at 5, leading actor B to take action B_2, and giving him a return of 50, and is the action I would take. In the

---

[15] I assume for the present that only pure strategies (definitely choosing one action) are allowed, and not mixed strategies (choosing a probability mixture of two or more actions). The latter case will be considered briefly below.

majorant game, if B takes action B_1, I respond with A_3, giving me 8; if he takes action B_2, I respond with A_2, giving me 5; and if he takes action B_3, I respond with A_1 giving me 9. Thus his best action is B_2, giving him a return of 50 (and me a return of 5).

These results of actor A's examination of the majorant and minorant games are shown in Table 2.2. The returns to actor B are shown as well, though these need play no part in my consideration.

This analysis of the two games shows a fundamental difference between them. In game (b), both the majorant and minorant games give the same outcome (and actor B's analysis would show the same, since a majorant game for actor A is minorant for B, and vice versa). Von Neumann and Morgenstern argue that in such a game, this is the equilibrium, since the return to actor A should be no greater than the return he gets in the majorant game, and no less than he gets in the minorant game. Since the return is the same in both these games, that return is the one point fulfilling such a condition. This point, in which the maximum of the row minima equals the minimum of the column maxima, is called the 'saddle point' of a game.

Table 2.2

	Game (a)				Game (b)			
	A's action	B's action	Return to A	(Return to B)	A's action	B's action	Return to A	(Return to B)
Minorant game (plays first)	A_3	B_2	4	(60)	A_2	B_2	5	(50)
Majorant game (plays second)	A_2	B_3	7	(30)	A_2	B_2	5	(50)

In game (a), there is no such equilibrium or saddle point. The actions of each in the majorant and minorant games differ, and the returns of the two games differ. All that can be said at this point is that actor A's return will not be below 4 nor above 7, and B's return will not be above 60 or below 30, if both play rationally (that is, actor A choosing A_2 or A_3, and actor B choosing B_2 or B_3).

John Harsanyi (1966) has expressed this strategic consideration, which leads to the solution of games with a saddle point, by use of the concept of 'best reply': if there is in the set of action-alternatives of A and B an action A_i which is the best reply of A to an action B_j which is the best reply of B to action A_i, then this pair of actions leads to a unique outcome,[16] and is the rational strategy for both.

[16] All outcomes with identical consequences are considered to be the same outcome.

The concept of rationality in the presence of a strategic other involves considerably more complex considerations than that of the concept of rationality under risk, merely by the addition of a single contingent other in place of the non-contingent action of the environment, giving a hint of the heights of complexity to which rationality might arise in complex social situations. There is also a weakness in this concept that arises from his assumptions about the behaviour of the other: as von Neumann and Morgenstern argue, perhaps the 'most reasonable' assumption he might make about the other is that the other is calculating as he does; but perhaps he should instead assume that there is a probability distribution of the other's strategies around this most reasonable or most likely strategy, *not* assuming with probability one that the other actor will act rationally.[17]

In addition, the von Neumann and Morgenstern assumption implies that one has no information about the other (because information would modify one's assumption that the actor is the same sort of creature, using identical strategic considerations).

Secondly, there is a difference among actors related to this that a more sophisticated theory would take into account. It is a difference in different actor's purposive mechanisms, in the degree to which they 'react' to immediately preceding events without using a broad base of experience and without extrapolating from other situations, rather than 'calculate' by using such extrapolations, in carrying out action. This difference also exists among different types of actions for the same individual, for in some situations an individual will 'react', and in others he will 'calculate' in planning his action. This difference has led some observers of behaviour to describe action as either *expressive* action, without a goal and merely expressing an internal tension, or *purposive* action, directed toward a goal. It is probably more useful to think of different degrees of complexity in the purposive mechanism by which an individual controls his action, and to attempt to describe

[17] Such a development of the theory of rational behaviour in the presence of a strategic other would be an interesting one. In it, the von Neumann–Morgenstern principle would be a special case, in which that probability distribution had zero variance. It is interesting to note that if this assumption on the part of actor A led to a probability distribution of actions on his part that is identical to that which actor B, under similar assumptions about him, assumed he would make, those two probability distributions would be the distributions that formed a stable rational pair under this definition of rationality. However, the utility achieved by such a pair of probability distributions in a game with a pair of best replies in the Harsanyi sense would necessarily be the same as that achieved by the pair of best replies—for otherwise, one player could improve his expected outcome merely by moving to his best reply in the Harsanyi sense. The same statement could not be made, however, about games without a pair of best replies.

the nature of these purposive mechanisms.[18] It is interesting to note also that the same difference is found in guidance systems of different complexity. Some, which have the capability to use only a very limited kind of information, will be able to 'seek out' a target only under a very narrow range of situations, while others will be able to do so in the presence of quite unusual circumstances. (See Isaacs, 1965, Kuhn and Szego, 1971, Starr and Ho, 1969).

The von Neumann–Morgenstern theory takes into account none of this, by use of the single simple assumption on the part of each actor about the other: that he is identical to me. This implies use of the minimax criterion for choice of an action. However, even with the fact that this concept of rationality is more tenuous than the preceding ones, it does not suffice for all cases of single-event pure conflict in the presence of a strategic other. Under some circumstances such as game (a) above, there is not a pair of best replies, and this strategy will not suffice.

To deal with this situation, one can imagine other modifications of the concept of rationality. One way of approaching the question is to look at the problem in the following way: In any game of pure conflict, if one considers a sequence of 'virtual' actions $A_{i_1}B_{j_1}, A_{i_2}B_{j_2} \ldots$ in which each responds to the other by maximizing his utility under the constraints imposed by the other, there comes finally to be a repeating cycle, which may include all the actions of each, or some subset of the actions of each. When this subset contains only a single action of each, then each has a best reply to the other's best reply, the game has a saddle point, and the definition of rationality stated earlier holds. If not, then there are several possible definitions that follow the same spirit. First is von Neumann and Morgenstern's definition, which is for each actor to construct an action that is a probability mixture of those in the cyclical set, weighted to produce a 'combined best reply' to the other's 'combined best reply'. They show that such a probability mixture based on considerations of double-contingency is always possible and produces a unique outcome. The strategy is a minimax mixed strategy.

In the minimax mixed strategy, each actor chooses that probability

[18] A general framework of theory within which such investigations might well be carried out is servomechanism control theory, for this theory describes such systems governed by control devices that utilize information feedback to modify future actions. In addition, information processing systems, as realized in computer programming, ordinarily contain such control mechanisms that use the consequences of past actions to modify future ones. In recent work (see Starr and Ho, 1969), there has been a convergence of the theory of differential games and control theory.

mixture of actions that makes his expected return unaffected by the other's action. Von Neumann and Morgenstern showed that in any game of pure conflict without a saddle point, but with linearly related utilities of outcome for the two actors (exemplified by game (a) above)[19] actor A can achieve a return which the other cannot reduce, of u_A^*, a return which limits the other to u_B^*; that actor B can achieve a return which the other cannot reduce, of u_B', limiting actor A to u_A'; and that $u_A^* = u_A'$ and $u_B^* = u_B'$. That is, by playing a mixture of strategies that makes his return independent of the other's action, he can achieve as a minimum that utility which is the maximum to which the other can limit him. The price he must pay in this case is more severe than in the saddle-point game: his optimal strategy, by making his return independent of the other's action, limits his maximum return to the best minimum he can achieve, no matter how irrational the other's action. But this new definition of rationality in situations where no pair of best responses exists has other implications that are even more questionable. For illustration of one, consider first a game where a pair of best replies does exist. Then if actor B does not take this action, actor A by playing his best reply gains more than if actor B had played his best reply. Thus the best replies are self-enforcing: an actor who moves away from the best reply is punished for doing so. But as indicated above, this does not occur when using a minimax mixed strategy in games without a pair of best replies. In order to exploit actor B's misplay, then actor A must himself play a non-optimal strategy. Consequently, we can ask in what sense is actor B's 'non-optimal' strategy truly non-optimal? For it to harm actor B, then actor A must also play a non-optimal strategy, and suffer the chance of being hurt below his optimal-guaranteed minimum. Consequently, a so-called non-optimal action of actor B either has no ill consequences for him (if actor A plays his optimal mixed strategy), or acts as a lure (if actor A does not play his optimal strategy), allowing actor B to suffer only a temporary loss and then make a large killing.

The answer to this may be that the von Neumann solution is appropriate only for single plays of a game, since each player makes no use of information about any previous plays of the other player, and von Neumann and Morgenstern do argue this. By this argument, the mixed strategy is a rational play even for a single game, since it anticipates the action of the other. But if this is the case, why not carry this

[19] In both games (a) and (b), utility to A plus 1/10 utility to B always equals 10.

anticipation even further into an anticipation of lures and counter-lures? Perhaps the only answer is that this leads us into a morass from which we cannot extricate ourselves. But this is hardly a justification for the von Neumann mixed strategy.

The concept of rationality that leads to a mixed strategy has the important virtue of constituting a direct extension of the concept of rationality in a game with best replies. It has the serious fault of assuming that utility differences of different outcomes for an individual not only be cardinally measurable, but that the utilities of the two actors be related by a linear transformation $u_b = c_1 + c_2 u_a$, where c_2 is negative, and that each actor not only acts in terms of his own cardinal utilities but also correctly assumes those of the other to be a linear transformation of his own. This is not what is ordinarily meant by interpersonal comparison of utility, because the absolute magnitudes of the two utilities are irrelevant to the outcome. It means merely that a 'mixed outcome' can be constructed between two or more existing outcomes by a probability mixture of them, and that for all such mixed outcomes, the two actors' preference orderings continue to be in inverse order, and the game remains one of pure conflict when such mixed strategies are allowed.

Another concept of rationality in such a situation without best replies would be a probability mixture among those actions that are within the cyclical set, which weights them with equal probability. Still another is to pick that action or probability mixture within the cyclical set that maximizes one's expected utility under the assumption that the other is carrying out a probability mixture in which he weights all of his actions in the cyclical set equally. Note that in both these concepts of rationality the actor assumes that the other is using a *different* strategy than he is himself using. But they have the virtue of not making any assumption about the relation between the two actors' utilities beyond the inverse ordering assumed in selecting the cyclical set.

Altogether, it is quite clear that the specific assumptions about the utilities of outcomes to another person and their relation to one's own affect not only the parameters used in a given strategy, but even the very form of the strategy. In general, it can be said that if one can assume that the other's utilities for outcomes are inversely related to one's own (and can assume that the other makes such an assumption as well), then a pure minimax strategy is best if it leads to a pair of best replies; and if one can assume further that the other's utilities for probability mixtures of outcomes is inversely related to one's own, then a minimax mixed strategy is best. But that assumption of inverse relation of probability mixtures requires a linear relation between the two actors' utilities, an assumption with no basis for behavioural confirmation.

One must then say, I think, that the definition of rationality in pure conflict in the case where there is not a pair of best responses is less satisfactory than in the case where there is. But it is not this case that I wish to pursue, and will merely note this caveat before moving to games of coincidence of interest and partial conflict of interest.

Rationality in the presence of a strategic other with pure coincidence of interest

In a game where there is perfect coincidence of interest, the only problems that can arise are problems of co-ordination. That is, if our interests coincide perfectly, then the only problem is that of co-ordinating our actions so that each of us receives the maximum utility that he can. Any failure to realize maximum gains is due to a failure of communication.

Now in some situations in society, the pursuit of rational action is accomplished by having *two types* of actions, that is, a channel of communication in order to inform the other and be informed by him, and the consequential action itself. The communication channel is used to establish co-ordinate action in this situation. In many situations, however, one communicates only by the consequential action itself. Schelling (1960) presents a number of examples of cases where one communicates only through his action. (For example, if you were planning to meet someone at noon in New York City, and you had neglected to fix a meeting-place, where would you go to maximize your chance of meeting the other?)

Some insights into the way information may affect one's assumptions about the other's strategy may be gained by considering a game of pure coincidence of interest in which one must communicate through one's action alone. In this case, information must be transmitted by means of successive plays in the game. For illustration, consider a game with outcomes and rewards at a single move shown in Table 2.3. In this game, both actors receive a reward (worth u_1 to actor A and u_2 to actor B) if they both carry out action 1 or both carry out action 2. But they receive nothing if one carries out action 1, and the other action 2. In this game, it is equally to my interest, if I am actor A, to obtain the outcome resulting from A_1, B_1 or from A_2, B_2. Similarly, it is equally to the B's interest to have either of these outcomes. But without some information transmission, neither of us will be able to achieve either of these outcomes, though there is perfect coincidence of interest. In everyday life, it is perhaps most closely realized by two persons passing on a narrow path. If I go to my left and he to his right, we block each other. If the reverse is true, we still block each other. If we both go to our right, or both go to our left, we pass. What is the rational action for each of us, to minimize the expected delay in passing, in the absence of prior conventions such as passing on the right?

Table 2.3

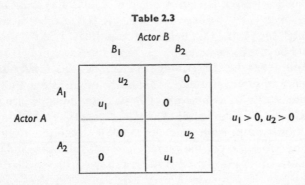

Obviously, since the situation is wholly symmetric, and in a single play of a game there will have been no past transmission of information, there is no basis for rational action in a single pair of actions. It is necessary to carry out a sequence of action to make rationality possible.

Each of us wants to use his actions for two purposes:

(1) to transmit information about subsequent play to the other actor; and

(2) to respond to the information transmitted by the other on previous plays.

If I used my actions only to transmit information about subsequent action, then I would maximize information transmission by merely taking the same action every time. The other actor would in this way have maximum information about my next act.

But if I were to act in this way, and the other were to act in this way as well, then unless we chose co-ordinating actions (A_1, B_1 or A_2, B_2)

on the first move, we would never reach the rewarding pair of actions. This results from the fact that each of us is using his action only to transmit information about his own play, and neither is responding to the other. In the everyday example, this is represented by a man who first moves to the left and then remains there, independent of the other's action. Such an action is rational only if he believes the second actor will use his actions wholly for the second purpose, to respond to the information transmitted by the first. Under such an assumption, an absolutely fixed choice, which transmits the maximum information, is rational.

But such an action would hardly be rational if I assumed the other actor would act as I do. Thus if I define my action as 'rational', and ask what would be the expected outcome if the other actor acted 'rationally', then I find that unless we co-ordinated on the first move, we would be blocked forever.

It appears that the only strategy that can be considered rational in the absence of prior information about the other, is one that gives a maximum return if I assume the other will use the same principles of action as I do. This implies that I neither concentrate wholly upon the information–transmission role nor wholly upon the response-to-information role. Co-ordination requires both following and leading, and if both of us lead or both of us follow, no co-ordination will result.

In view of this, it is useful to examine possible strategies heuristically, to determine their rationality.

First, assume that I take *random* actions, using a mixed strategy that leads me to choose A_1 half the time and A_2 half the time. This strategy would totally defeat my purpose, for it would fulfill neither the information–transmission role nor the response role.

Secondly, assume that I use the same mixed strategy, but to transmit information without fixating on a single action, I *alternate*, choosing A_1 and then A_2 in a fixed sequence. This strategy has the appearance of greater flexibility than the fixed strategy of choosing the same action each time, but it is worse. It is no more responsive to the other's action, and thus could lead to an endless impasse. And it is less efficient in transmitting information than is a pure strategy of the same action each time.

Thirdly, assume that I follow absolutely the preceding action of the other, using my action wholly to respond to information from the other. If I were to do this, and he were to do the same, then both of us would be following a non-existent leader, and co-ordination again would not be achieved.

Fourthly, consider a strategy in which I choose with probability x to follow my own previous action, and probability $1 - x$ to maximize my return assuming the immediately preceding action of the other. That is, with probability x I act in the role of leader, and probability $1 - x$ in the role of follower. With this strategy, two questions arise: does it, under any condition, provide a higher expected return than the other strategies; and if so, what value of x will maximize the return?

The characteristics of this strategy can be seen by examining the first three moves. The first move, with actions A_1 and B_1 taken with probability $\frac{1}{2}$ gives each of the four possible outcomes with the following probabilities:

Outcome

11   (A_1, B_1): $\frac{1}{4}$ utility u_1 and u_2
12   (A_1, B_2): $\frac{1}{4}$ 0 utility
21   (A_2, B_1): $\frac{1}{4}$ 0 utility
22   (A_2, B_2): $\frac{1}{4}$ utility u_1 and u_2

The probability of outcome 11 or 22 is $\frac{1}{4} + \frac{1}{4} = \frac{1}{2}$. If outcome 11 or 22 has been achieved, that same outcome will persist on subsequent moves, since following one's previous action and following the other's immediately preceding action give the same action. Thus in terms of Markov chains, outcomes 11 and 22 are 'absorbing states', whatever the value of x. If the outcome is 12, then with probability x actor A will carry out A_1 and with probability x actor B will carry out B_2. This means that with probability x^2 the next outcome will be 12; with probability $x(1 - x)$, it will be 11; with probability $(1 - x)x$, it will be 22; and with probability $(1 - x)^2$ it will be 21. A similar distribution of probabilities occurs if the first outcome is 21.

The table of conditional probabilities of outcomes on the next move, given each possible outcome of the first move, is shown as Table 2.4.

Table 2.4

	Next outcome			
	11	12	21	22
11	1	0	0	0
First outcome 12	$x(1 - x)$	x^2	$(1 - x)^2$	$(1 - x)x$
21	$(1 - x)x$	$(1 - x)^2$	x^2	$x(1 - x)$
22	0	0	0	1

3

The selection of an x to maximize the expected return is equivalent to selection of an x that will maximize the probability of moving to either state 11 or 22. For either state 12 or 21, this probability is $2x(1 - x)$, and it is maximized when $x = 0.5$. Thus in this wholly symmetric case, the maximum utility may be achieved by following one's own action with probability 0.5, and following the other's action with probability 0.5. Stated otherwise, maximizing utility implies a probability mixture of leader and follower actions, each being used with probability 0.5. It is interesting to recognize that the conditional probabilities of Table 2.4 are like those in a Markov chain, and the shift from considering an optimal strategy on a single-play game to an optimal strategy which utilizes information from the preceding play is like the shift from Bernoulli trials with unconditional probabilities to a first-order Markov chain with conditional probabilities. Table 2.4 can be considered a matrix of transition probabilities, and one could use it as such to calculate the expected reward for particular values of x on each trial. For example, the probabilities of being in state 11 or 22 (the rewarded outcomes) by move are as shown in Table 2.5 for $x = .5$, $x = \frac{1}{3}$ (or $\frac{2}{3}$), and $x = 1$ (or 0). The second row of Table 2.5 shows the serious defect of acting always as leader or follower, while the third row shows results of a strategy in which either the leader or follower role is played two-thirds of the time. The first row shows results of the optimal strategy.

Table 2.5
Probability of receiving reward by move 1, 2, 3, 4, or 5

	Move				
	1	2	3	4	5
$(x = .5)$	.5	.75	.875	.938	.969
$(x = 1.0$ or $0)$	.5	.5	.5	.5	.5
$(x = \frac{1}{3}$ or $\frac{2}{3})$	.5	.722	.846	.913	.952

It is possible to conceive in this context of a 'pure strategy' in a different sense from the idea of pure strategy in single-play games. A pure strategy here would be a strategy with the probability of acting as leader equal to 0 or 1, which means that conditional probabilities of action are 0 or 1. In the single-play game, a pure strategy meant that the probability of A_i was 1.0 for some i, 0 for all others. Here, the pure strategy means that the probability of A_i *given* A_i on the last move, or given a particular B_j, is 1.0. A mixed strategy in the present sense means the conditional probabilities are less than 1: the actor acts both as leader and as follower.

The optimal strategy employed in this game at the present level of analysis is one in which each actor selects a probability mixture of 0.5 of being follower and 0.5 of being leader. A strategy which carried the analysis to a deeper level would be to allow this probability itself to change over time as a function of the other's tendency to take the leader or follower role, or to bias the probability of taking the leader's role to begin with, to inform the other that one was taking the leader or follower role. The first of these deeper-level strategies could be described as a sensitivity to the other, or following the other, at a deeper level—a sensitivity not to his preceding action, but to a conditional probability inferred from it. The second could be described as leading the other in a deeper sense than before: informing the other that one is not likely to change one's action or is quite ready to change one's action.

These deeper-level strategies begin to sound somewhat more like the actual considerations that persons use in social situations—not only where there is complete coincidence of interest, but also where there is conflict of interest (where the use of one deeper-level strategy or the other may have differentially beneficial consequences to the two parties). Psychological research, in fact, suggests that persons differ in general in their sensitivity to cues from others and to internal cues, a difference corresponding to differences in such deeper-level strategies.

Just as a Markov chain could be used to describe the first-level strategy of a leader-follower mixture, it is likely that an appropriate extension of a Markov chain or Markov process could be used to describe the deeper-level strategy. That, however, is tangential to the problems of this book, and will not be pursued here.

Rationality in the presence of a strategic other with partial conflict of interest for a single event [20]

The concept of rational behaviour under the above conditions remains very limited indeed. Most social situations, for example, involve not pure conflict of interest, nor pure coincidence of interest,

[20] There has been much recent work on games of partial conflict of interest ('non-zero sum' games), especially in connection with development of the foundations of the theory of markets, perfect and otherwise, in economics. For a collection of some contributions, see Shubik (1964). For more general work in this aspect of theory of games, see the various papers of John Harsanyi (e.g. 1966, 1967, 1968). There has also been empirical work in particular kinds of such games, especially the Prisoner's Dilemma. See Rapoport and Chammah (1965).

but partial conflict, in which some subset of outcomes is better for both actors than are any of those outside the subset, but among that set, some are better for one actor, while others are better for the other. Where it is possible through the joint actions of both to realize a subset of outcomes preferable to both, then we can say that the actions taken by both will lie within that subset. Thus the others can be ignored, and if it is a situation of pure conflict within this subset, a minimax strategy can be chosen. But it is often not possible to reduce the game to one of pure conflict, as the familiar example of a prisoner's dilemma game indicates. The prisoner's dilemma game derives its name from a dilemma confronting each of the two separated prisoners in jail for a joint crime: If he testifies implicating the other, but the other does not, he will go free and the other will receive a maximum sentence. If both testify against the other, they will both receive sentences less than the maximum. If both hold out, they will both receive sentences on a minor charge in the absence of evidence on the major charge. The situation might be described by a diagram such as that shown in Table 2.6.

Table 2.6

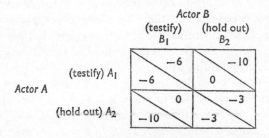

Here the order of preference of A for outcomes is $A_1 B_2$, $A_2 B_2$, $A_1 B_1$, and $A_2 B_1$. The order of preference of B is $A_2 B_1$, $A_2 B_2$, $A_1 B_1$, and $A_1 B_2$. In this case, the least preferred outcome for A is the most preferred for B, ensuring that no subset of mutually preferred outcomes can be found.[21] Yet outcome $A_2 B_2$ (both holding out) is preferred to

---

[21] As von Neumann and Morgenstern point out, an n person game of partial conflict can be converted into an $n + 1$ person game of pure conflict (or zero-sum, as they term it) with nature as a passive player. In a three-person game, coalitions are always possible, and in this case, an implicit coalition can occur either between A and B, A and nature, or B and nature—or, if both take action 1, a non-coalition solution will occur. Von Neumann and Morgenstern claim to have treated fully such games, but their treatment does not cover this game, in which prior agreements are not possible, and there is no redistribution of the spoils by the coalition partners, both of which conditions are assumed by them.

$A_1 B_1$ (both testifying), so that their interests are not wholly in conflict. Using the analysis developed for games of pure conflict, we would see that action A_1 dominates A_2, and B_1 dominates B_2. Thus in those terms, rational action on the part of each would lead to $A_1 B_1$—a worse outcome for both than $A_2 B_2$. All that can be said about such a game is that it *is* individually rational to take an action which, taken together with the others' actions, leads to an outcome that is less beneficial to both than could be achieved by them had there been some co-ordination. More generally, for a single event with partial conflict of interests not reducible to a situation of pure conflict, there has been no satisfactory concept of rationality devised beyond that for pure conflict.[22]

Rationality in the presence of a strategic other with multiple events

When there are multiple events in the system of behaviour under consideration, rather than single ones, three important possibilities arise that enormously complicate matters. The first of these is transmission of information, as indicated in the case of pure coincidence of interest discussed earlier. For example, it appears that often a player in a prisoner's dilemma game will take the action corresponding to A_2 or B_2 in Table 2.6 above, to communicate to the other player that he is willing to co-operate.

The second new process is that of taking information communicated intentionally or not by the other's action on past events, and modifying one's behaviour on the basis of it. In games of pure coincidence of interest, this will be of mutual benefit; in other games, it may be to the harm of the other player. More generally, the outcome of past events may be useful to the actor in any situation, ranging from pure conflict of interests to pure coincidence of interests, when the outcome is not solely under the control of his action, to infer either the pattern of action of a non-strategic environment, or the strategy used by a strategic other.

A third new possibility in the case of multiple events is that of using one's control over an action in more creative ways than merely to take action to affect that outcome. In particular, one may be able

[22] Anatol Rapoport, who has studied prisoner's dilemma games extensively, from both theoretical and experimental directions, argues that such a concept of rationality has been found for the prisoner's dilemma. But the concept requires a referee to examine the first player's choice, and thus changes the game in important ways. See A. Rapoport, 1967. In other respects, Rapoport's article provides an excellent introduction to the various concepts of rationality under increasingly complex environments, as discussed above.

to use control over an event in which the outcomes have for him little utility difference, in order to affect the outcome of an event in which the utility differences among outcomes are great. The major way in which this is carried out in social and economic life is exchange. If use of goods he possesses is conceived as one event over which an actor has full control, and use of other goods that he does not possess is conceived as a second event over which he has no control, then if the use of the second goods has more utility for him than use of the first, he can attempt to exchange his control over the first for control over the second, by exchanging ownership or physical possession. If he can find another actor who owns the second goods and has reverse preferences, he may be able to effect an exchange.

Similarly in social life, much social activity can be described (as indeed some of it has been described) as exchange of control over one event for control over another. In political processes as well, much activity of legislators can be described as implicit agreements to give up a vote on one issue in return for a promise to aid in a similar future circumstance, or in some cases for a vote on another issue or for another event of utility, such as appointment to a given committee. Explicit exchange is only one of several kinds of actions that are possible to increase one's utility in the case of multiple events occurring over time. The importance and general ubiquity of exchange in social life, however, is sufficient to suggest that by the introduction of multiple events, the theory of purposive action comes to a level that makes it potentially interesting as a theory applicable to social phenomena. It is this, of course, which allows the theory to have been used in economic analysis.

Having described in a loose fashion the various levels of the concept of rationality as they have been developed, I will describe in the next chapter more precisely the characteristics of the systems of action I propose to investigate. These systems will contain a number of actors and a number of events, and are designed to constitute abstract representations of systems of action found throughout social, economic, and political life.

3 Collective Actions

Definitions

A first view of the nature of the systems of action to be considered here can be obtained from the following set of definitions of elements of the system:

(D1) There are one or more *actors* in the system at hand, n actors in general.

(D2) There are one or more *events* in this system, m events in general. In some cases, events will be assumed to be ordered in time; in other cases, their time order is neglected.

(D3) Each event has two or more *outcomes* that may occur.

(D4) Each actor may take *actions*, which will exercise partial or total control over an event, affecting or determining its outcome.

(D5) Each actor has a set of *subjective probabilities* associated with each action and outcome. These will be labelled $p_{i_0 j_k}$, and are actor j's subjectively held conditional probabilities of the occurrence of outcome i_0 of event i given action j_k of actor j. That is, $p_{i_0 j_k} = \Pr_j i_0 | j_k$.

(D6) An actor j has (subjective) *total control* over an event i if for each outcome i_0 there is an action j_k such that $p_{i_0 j_k} = 1.0$. An actor j has (subjective) *partial control* over an event if for some outcome i_0 of the event, there is a pair of actions j_k and j_h such that $p_{i_0 j_k} \neq p_{i_0 j_h}$.

(D7) Partial control over an event may be exercised by an agent outside the system whose actions are assumed to be governed by a fixed probability distribution, independent of any actions taken by members of the system. Events for which this is the case will be said to be partially controlled within the system; otherwise an event is fully controlled within the system.

(D8) Each outcome of each event has a given *utility* for each actor.

Utilities are properties both of an actor and an outcome, and will be labelled u_{i_0j}, the utility of outcome i_0 for actor j. References to the event will be deleted except when necessary for clarity. When an individual holds complete control over an event, it is possible from his behaviour only to infer a preference ordering among the outcomes. However, in the general case, when he does not hold total control, it is possible to infer from his behaviour utility differences between pairs of outcomes, since his action is based on the expected utility of particular actions, as discussed earlier. Since we will be dealing with the general case, we will assume the individual has utilities for outcomes, and that utility differences for different outcomes of the same event are defined up to a transformation of scale.

(D9) An event j is *consequential* for an actor j if for some pair of outcomes i_0 and $i_{0'}$, $u_{i_0j} \neq u_{i_{0'}j}$.

Action-principle: Besides these definitions, there is a single action-principle which governs the actions of the actors in the system: Each actor chooses those actions which maximize his utility given the environmental context created by the events, the other actors, and the fixed agent external to the system. The action-principles he uses are basically those discussed earlier, except that in some cases of greater complexity, certain assumptions will be made to reduce the problems of efficient action to manageable proportions.

Structural definitions

It will be principally the structure of relations between events and actors that is of concern here. To give an idea of the forms of structure that can occur, and to provide terms to be used in further treatment, the following definitions of structural aspects of the system will be useful:

(D10) *Individual control* of a single event occurs when there is only one actor in the system who exercises any control over the event. *Independence of control* in a system occurs when not more than one actor exercises any control over a given event, i.e. when all events are under individual control. That is, for all outcomes i_0 of an event i, if for an actor j, $p_{i_0j_k} \neq p_{i_0j_h}$ for some pair of actions j_k and j_h, then for all other actors, j', $p_{i_0}j'_k = p_{i_0}j'_h$ for all pairs of actions j'_k and j'_h.

(D11) *Individual consequence* for a single event implies that the event is consequential only for a single actor. *Independence of consequence* in a system occurs when all events have individual consequence, that is, when outcomes of each event have different utilities for only one actor: if for actor j, $u_{i_0 j} \neq u_{i_0' j}$, then for all other actors, j', $u_{i_0 j'} = u_{i_0' j'}$, for all pairs of outcomes i_0 and i_0'.

(D12) In a system where there is not independence of consequence, each event can be described by the subset of actors for whom the event is consequential. These will be described as the *affected actors* of this event, or the affected set.

(D13) In a system where there is not independence of control, each event can be described by the subset of actors who have control over the event. These will be described as the *controlling actors* for the event, or the controlling set.

(D14) If the set of affected actors includes the set of controlling actors for a given event, this event is said to be *internally controlled*. If the set of controlling actors includes the set of affected actors, the event is said to be *internally consequential*. If the event is both internally controlled and internally consequential, then the set of controlling actors is identical to the set of affected actors, and the event is said to be *co-ordinated*.

(D15) In a system with independence of consequence (or independence of control), and in which all events are co-ordinated, then each event is under the partial or total control of only a single actor, and is consequential for that actor alone. In such a system, actors will be described as *independent actors*.

(D16) If one or more of the affected actors of event k is a controlling actor of event i, then event i is said to be *contingent* upon event k. If two events are contingent on one another, they are said to be *mutually contingent* events. If event i is not contingent upon k, then i is said to be independent of k. If each event in a set is independent of all others in the set, they are said to be independent events.

(D17) If one or more of the events for which actor j is a controlling actor is consequential for actor h, then actor h is said to be *dependent* upon actor j. If two actors are dependent on one another, they are said to be *interdependent*.

(D18) If actor h is dependent upon actor j who is dependent upon actor k, and h is not dependent upon k, then h is said to be dependent upon k at order 1. Generally, if h is dependent upon k through a minimum chain of s other actors, h is said to be *dependent upon* k *at order* s.

(D19) If event j is not contingent upon event k, but is contingent upon an event i which is contingent upon k, then j is said to be contingent upon k at order 1. Generally, if j is contingent upon k through a minimum of s other events, j is said to be contingent upon k at order s.

(D20) If neither of two events is contingent upon each other at order s for all $s \leqslant m - 2$, then the events are not contingent upon each other at any order, and are said to be *separable*. The set of events can be divided into separable subsets.

(D21) If neither of two actors is dependent upon each other at order s for all $s \leqslant n - 2$, then the actors are not dependent on each other at any order, and are said to be *isolated* from one another. Each member of the set of controlling and affected actors for a subset of events separable from a second is isolated from each of the actors who are controlling and affected by the second subset of events. These actors are thus separated into *isolated sets* of actors by the separability of events into separable sets.

These structural terms allow description of various kinds of social organization. An economic market of private goods in which the use of an item of goods is an event, and ownership of these goods constitutes control of that event, is a system with independence of control and independence of consequence. For an event whose outcome is determined by a collective decision, such as in a legislature, the members of the legislature are the controlling actors, and those constituents and the legislators themselves affected by the outcome are the affected actors. Such an event is internally controlled but not internally consequential. In a jury decision which has consequences only for a defendant, the jurymen are the controlling actors, and the event is individually consequential. The event is neither internally controlled nor internally consequential. When a judge makes a decision affecting only a defendant, the event is individually controlled and individually consequential, but not co-ordinated. When an executive in a bureaucratic organization makes a decision affecting the employees, the event is individually controlled but not individually consequential, and the employees are the affected actors. When a set of electors votes an executive out of office, the electors are the controlling actors, and the event is individually consequential, but not internally consequential (unless the executive is himself one of the electors).

These definitions of structural aspects of the system provide useful ways of perceiving such a system, but constitute in themselves only special cases, and are not analytically useful. To provide a more generally useful framework requires a return to the basic definitions 1–9, and the development of such a framework from them. This will be the first task of this chapter.

A framework for collective action

To give a more general approach to the description of structure among actors and events, it is useful to simplify the perspective toward individual events. First, only events which have two outcomes, 1 and 2, will be treated. These outcomes will ordinarily be interpreted as passage or failure of a proposed collective action, such as a bill in a legislature. The term 'collective action' evokes imagery of a collectivity itself as an actor, composed in some fashion of the individual members as actors. I do not want to introduce formally such transition between levels at this point, but merely draw attention to the fact that an outcome of an event, partially controlled by each of a set of individual actors, will be described as an action or inaction of a collectivity of which these individual actors are members.

The second simplification of the perspective toward individual events concerns the idea of 'control' of an action. For many purposes, it would be useful to be able to specify the individual's degree of control of an event independent of the actions of others. The definition of partial control over an event by actor j [(D6) above] suggests that this might be possible, for it defines partial control of an event by actor j as the existence of two actions k and h such that for some outcome i_0 of the event, $p_{i_0 j_k} \neq p_{i_0 j_h}$. Note that because of the restriction to two outcomes, this implies that for the other outcome, the probabilities differ also, and by the same amount. Because of this, in subsequent notation, the subscript for outcomes will be dropped, and whenever subjective probabilities of outcomes are explicitly used, they will refer to outcome i_0, which will ordinarily be interpreted as a positive outcome in a decision for a collective action. If there is total control of the event by individual j, then by definition (D6), there are two actions k and h such that $p_{i j_k} = 1$ and $p_{i j_h} = 0$, or $p_{i j_k} - p_{i j_h} = 1$. At the other extreme of no control, for every pair of actions k and h, $p_{i j_k} - p_{i j_h} = 0$.

This suggests that a reasonable measure of the 'degree of control' of actor i over an event is given by the maximum difference in the probability of outcome 1 that he can induce through carrying out one action rather than another. Thus if we label the control of actor j over an event i as c_{ij}, then according to this definition,

$$(D22) \qquad c_{ij} = \max_k p_{ij_k} - \min_k p_{ij_k}$$

Furthermore, since it is not rational for the individual to exercise less than his maximum potential control over event i, all actions other than the two which maximize and minimize p_{ij} may be neglected. We may thus think of the degree of control c_{ij} as the increment in probability of outcome 1, Δp_{ij}, that actor j can achieve or prevent for event i. It is tempting to interpret these two actions in a collective decision as a positive and negative vote; however, there are complications to this interpretation, as we shall see shortly.

There is one difficulty in the formulation that results from these considerations. The subjective probability of an outcome, given that he carries out a particular action, has been presented as if it were not conditional upon the actions of other actors. But such unconditional subjective probabilities are valid only in the second level of rationality, rationality under risk, where the outcome is partially controlled by a non-strategic environment. As the preceding chapter noted, rationality in the presence of others cannot use such unconditional subjective probabilities. In the presence of strategic others, an actor does not have a fixed set of probabilities associated with each of their possible actions, as he does for a non-strategic external environment. Their actions are contingent upon their estimate of what his will be. Thus he cannot estimate a subjective probability of each outcome for each of his possible actions in so simple a fashion.

However, it is possible to specify a degree of control in a single collective decision between two alternatives, where each actor has one vote, if we accept certain assumptions. It is evident that it is always in his interest to cast a positive vote if he is in favour of a positive outcome. That is, there is no possibility of strategy for him or for the other actors. As a consequence, he can treat them as he would the external environment, and estimate the probability that his vote would be deciding. As a simple example, assume a three-person group with a majority rule, in which A estimates that B and C will both vote positive with probability .5. Thus his estimate of the environment he faces is that it will have $m = 0$ positive votes with probability .25, $m = 1$ positive vote with probability .5, and $m = 2$

with probability .25. The increment in probability of positive outcome that his vote makes is thus

$$\Delta p_{1j} = p_{1_1} - p_{1_2} = (p_{1_1|0})(\Pr\{m = 0\}) + (p_{1_1|1})(\Pr\{m = 1\})$$
$$+ (p_{1_1|2})(\Pr\{m = 2\}) - [(p_{1_2|0})(\Pr\{m = 0\})$$
$$+ (p_{1_2|1})(\Pr\{m = 1\}) + (p_{1_2|2})(\Pr\{m = 2\})]$$
$$= (0)(.25) + (1)(.5) + (1)(.25)$$
$$- [(0)(.25) + (0)(.5) + (1)(.25)]$$
$$\Delta p_{1j} = .5$$

That is, half the time he can control the outcome, under the assumptions he makes about the external environment. Note, however, an apparent paradox: actors B and C would also each calculate, using the same reasoning, that he could control the outcome half the time. Thus according to these calculations, the total control over this collective decision is 1.5 rather than 1.0. The resolution of this paradox requires a deeper consideration of the concept of the 'external environment' that each of the actors is using. Each actor is assuming in effect that he casts the final vote; that the environment, consisting of the others, acts, and then he acts. But this assumption is obviously not valid, for each of the three cannot be last. If we reconsider, and ask what is the control that each exerts over the collective decision when he is in each of the three possible positions, then the following calculations hold for A (and for B and C as well, with labels changed):

Position of A	Probability of m positive prior votes			Probability of casting deciding vote
	$m =$ 0	1	2	
1	1	0	0	0
2	.5	.5	0	.5
3	.25	.5	.25	.5

Since actor A has a probability of $\frac{1}{3}$ of being in each of the three positions, then his probability of casting the deciding vote is $\frac{1}{3} \times 0 + \frac{1}{3} \times .5 + \frac{1}{3} \times .5 = \frac{1}{3}$.

The end result of this examination is that in the case when an individual is in the presence of other actors, then even when strategic behaviour is irrelevant (as in the case of voting on a single event with two outcomes), it is necessary to calculate Δp_{ij} with the greatest care, taking into consideration not only the possible configuration that others' actions might present to him, but also, since he is also part of their environment, the various positions in the total sequence of actions that he may occupy.

It turns out that when this is done, then in a collective decision with a simple majority vote, when he makes the assumption that each will vote positively with probability $\frac{1}{2}$, his probability of determining the outcome or degree of control is $1/n$, where n is the total number of actors. The general formula for calculating his degree of control when he estimates that the other actors have probability p of voting positively can be found by extracting one term from n binomial distributions, one binomial distribution for each position in the voting sequence that he may occupy, that is, position 1, 2, ..., n. In these binomial distributions, there will be 0, 1, ..., $n-1$ votes prior to his, and his vote will be the deciding one if (assuming n to be an odd number) $(n-1)/2$ of these have been cast in favour. The probability of this is of course zero unless at least $(n-1)/2$ others have already voted.

The term to be extracted from each of the binomial distributions when r others have preceded him in voting is:

$$\frac{r!}{\left(\frac{n-1}{2}\right)!\left(r-\frac{n-1}{2}\right)!}p^{(n-1)/2}(1-p)^{r-(n-1)/2}$$

Each of these positions in the sequence occurs with probability $1/n$, so that the calculation of his degree of control is the sum of these terms multiplied by $1/n$:

$$c = \frac{1}{n}\sum_{r=\frac{n-1}{2}}^{n-1}\frac{r!}{\left(\frac{n-1}{2}\right)!\left(r-\frac{n-1}{2}\right)!}p^{(n-1)/2}(1-p)^{r-(n-1)/2}.$$

It is useful to note that in the case where $p = \frac{1}{2}$, this measure of degree of control reduces simply to $1/n$, for the quantity under the summation sign sums to 1.

When n is even, in order to maintain symmetry between positive and negative outcomes, we assume the decision rule is such that when the vote is $n/2$ positive, an unbiased coin is tossed to determine the outcome. In this case, the actor in question can cast the deciding ballot half the time when $n/2 - 1$ votes have been cast in favour, and half the time when $n/2$ votes have been cast in favour. This would lead to a modification to include a second summation with $n/2$ replacing

$(n-1)/2$, and each of the two summations multiplied by $\frac{1}{2}$. In the case where his estimate of p, the others' probability of casting a positive vote, is $\frac{1}{2}$, this gives a control of $1/n$ as in the case where n is odd.

In order to examine structural variations in collective actions, the use of the concept 'degree of control', of actor j over event i, c_{ij}, in events that involve joint or collective action will be assumed to imply a particular kind of decision rule, which allows leaving aside the problems of the conditionality of Δp_{ij} upon actions of other actors.[1]

This decision rule may be termed a 'probabilistic decision rule'. The rule is as follows: if there are n voters, and n_1 of them cast a positive vote, then a random device with n possible outcomes is used to determine the decision. If any one of the first n_1 of the n outcomes occurs, then the collective decision is positive; otherwise, the decision is negative. Or a random number is drawn from a rectangular distribution between 0 and 1, and if the number is less than or equal to n_1/n, the collective decision is positive.

With such a decision rule, the effect of one actor's vote on the outcome is always $1/n$ if he has one vote to cast. If he casts the vote positively, the increment in probability of passage is always $1/n$, independent of the other voters' actions. Thus his degree of control can always be specified independently of others' actions.

This rule generalizes to the situation where an actor may have any number of votes, or any fraction of the total control over the collective action.

Although the restriction to a probabilistic decision rule is a serious one, it allows the examination of other aspects of collective decisions; and it has the virtue that it is a perfectly conceivable—and on many counts, desirable—decision rule, even though it is not used in practice in any collective decisions of which I am aware.

To carry out the examination of structural variations in collective decisions, it is useful to apply two descriptive matrices to a collectivity: a matrix representing the structure of control of actors over events, and a matrix representing the structure of consequences of events for the actors.

The matrix C of control over an event is an $m \times n$ matrix with elements c_{ij} representing the control an actor j has over an event i. The sum of control of an event, over all actors in the system, is equal to 1

---

[1] However, for a discussion of the situation when Δp_{ij} cannot be considered independent of others' actions, see Coleman (1968) where change in Δp_{ij} with changes in the commitments of others is examined.

if the event is fully controlled within the system, less than 1 if it is partially controlled from outside, that is,

$$\sum_{j=1}^{n} c_{ij} \leqslant 1$$

The control matrix constitutes one of three principal elements of the *constitution* of the system, for the constitution determines the control of actors over events, as embodied in the control matrix. A second element of the constitution is the rules by which various events are decided (e.g. majority decision rule in a collective decision), which is here assumed to be a probabilistic decision rule. A third element is the structure of decisions among subsets of the collectivity (e.g. committees) that are necessary to determine an action for the collectivity as a whole.

The determination of the amount of control over an event held by each actor is straightforward in many cases: in a decision made by a single actor, for example in an executive position, that actor has complete control over the event, $c_{ij} = 1.0$. In a legislative decision in which each actor has one vote, if there are n legislators, each legislator has $1/n$ of control of the event, i.e. the passage of the bill.

In other situations, the specification of control over the event is more problematic—for example, when passage of a legislative action consists first of its passage within committee, and then of its passage in the larger legislature, the committee members obviously have more power over the passage of the bill than do the other members, but just how much more? The answer requires us to distinguish carefully between different elementary events that in conjunction result in an overall final outcome. In this example, there are two such events, not one, and two would appear in the matrix: the committee decision, and the overall legislative decision. In the column of the matrix representing the committee decision, every member of the committee would have control $1/n_1$ if n_1 is the committee size; and in the column representing the legislative decision, every member of the larger legislature would have control $1/n_2$ if n_2 is the size of the legislature.

In certain complex cases such as this, it will be necessary to recognize explicitly the fact that certain events are directly conditional upon the outcomes of others. This recognition will take the form of a third matrix showing the conditionality of events upon other events—as, in this case, the final legislative action is jointly conditional upon the committee action and the legislative action. This conditionality of some events upon the outcome of others constitutes the third principal element of the constitution of the system. However, introduction of this conditionality will be deferred for the present, and we will consider events which are linked to one another only through the actors they affect and are controlled by.

The matrix representing the structure of consequences for the actors includes, as indicated earlier, a specification of definition 3 given above: the number of outcomes of each event will be restricted to two. This is particularly useful in considering the action of the system (or of different actors or collectivities within it), because one outcome represents action of the actor or collectivity, and the other represents failure to act. In most collective decisions, for example, only a single proposed action is considered at one time. It is voted on and accepted or rejected before another action is considered.

In such two-outcome events, the utility of the outcome representing action on event i for actor j is $u_{i_1 j}$, and the utility of the outcome representing no action is $u_{i_2 j}$. The 'utility of the action', relative to the status quo, is $u_{i_1 j} - u_{i_2 j}$, which may be a positive number (if the action is more beneficial than the status quo), or a negative number (if the action is less beneficial than the status quo).

The scaling of these quantities $u_{i_1 j} - u_{i_2 j}$ (or of the $u_{i_k j}$ from which they are derived) is undetermined, because there is no basis for an interpersonal comparison of utility, which such scaling would imply if the subsequent utility differences are aggregated over different actors j. Thus we will do two things: scale each actor's utility differences so that the sum of their absolute values over all events in the system equals 1.0—this makes the values of y_{ji} relative measures of utility differences for the actor; and aggregate over actors only with explicit recognition of the implications for interpersonal comparison of utility.

The utility differences, scaled in this way, will be designated by y_{ji}:

$$(\text{D23}) \qquad y_{ji} = \frac{u_{i_1 j} - u_{i_2 j}}{\sum\limits_i |u_{i_1 j} - u_{i_2 j}|}$$

These quantities y_{ji}, which will be termed *relative utility differences*, are positive if actor j favours the collective action on event i, negative if he opposes it. Their absolute values sum to 1.0 over the events in the system; and the greater the absolute value, the greater the difference this collective action makes for him.

The scaling of utility differences y_{ji} so that $\sum_i |y_{ji}| = 1$ allows for a simple interpretation of the meaning of the resulting numbers. If $|y_{ji}|$ is labelled x_{ji}, then x_{ji} may be described as his *interest* in the event, using the term 'interest' in a way consistent with its common meaning. The interest of an actor in an event is the difference that its outcome will make for him, or the importance of the outcome for him. The scaling which makes x_{ji} sum to 1 over all events i is a scaling such that x_{ji} is a measure of the *proportion* of j's total interest in this system that is in event i. Thus each actor's total interest in the system of events is scaled to 1, and x_{ji} is his relative interest in event i.

Formally, interests, x_{ji}, are defined as follows, in terms of the relative utility differences, y_{ji}:

(D24) $$x_{ji} = |y_{ji}|$$

and

$$\sum_i x_{ji} = 1.0$$

Since interests represent the absolute values of the relative utility differences, a second quantity, the direction of interests, may be defined to represent the sign of the utility differences, s_{ji}:

(D25) $$s_{ji} = \operatorname{sgn} y_{ji}$$

The value of breaking apart y_{ji} into two parts, one for the absolute value, and the other for the sign, is that the actor carries out two kinds of actions in increasing his utility, first gaining as much control as possible over those events that matter most to him (i.e. for which he has high interest), and second exercising that control, through voting for example, in the direction that will increase his utility.

The measures of relative interest may be used to describe the structure of the system through a matrix X with entries x_{ji}. Such a matrix shows the distribution of each actor's interest in events, just as the matrix of control C shows the distribution of control over events.[2]

Use of these two matrices in conjunction can illustrate the structural definitions 9–15 given earlier. Those definitions described events in terms of the coincidence of control and consequences in the same subsets of the total set of actors. Since c_{ij} represents the fraction of

---

[2] Although the conceptual scheme allows the possibility that part of the control over an event is held from outside the system of actors explicitly included, I will examine here only those cases in which total control is held by the actors explicitly included. Thus in this examination,
$$\sum_j c_{ij} = 1$$

control of event i lodged in actor j by the constitution, and x_{ji} represents the fraction of j's interest in event i, then the product of these two, $x_{ji}c_{ij}$, represents the fraction of his total interest that he controls through event i. The sum of this product over all events gives the total fraction of his interest that he controls.

It is, of course, through control of those events which interest him that he is able to achieve his purposes, that is, to maximize his utility. For in order to maximize his utility he must do two things: first, gain control over those events that interest him, and secondly, exercise that control in such a direction that the outcome he favours occurs.

If we define z_{jk} to equal the sum of $x_{ji}c_{ik}$, that is,

$$z_{jk} = \sum x_{ji} c_{ik} \tag{3.1}$$

then the quantity z_{jj} is the fraction of his interest that he controls, or the fraction that he controls of the events that affect him. Rationality for him consists in acting so that this quantity is as near as possible to 1.0, if there is any way in which he can affect it.

The quantity off the diagonal of the product matrix is z_{jk}, the fraction of j's interest that is under the direct control of k. This may be described as actor k's amount of direct power over j, for it constitutes the degree to which j's interests depend upon the actions of actor k.

Altogether, then, the product matrix $Z = XC(= \{z_{jk}\})$ represents a relation of control and dependence among actors. Its entries sum to 1 across each row, and a given row shows the distribution of control of j's interests among the various actors of the collectivity.

The same operation can be performed by aggregating over actors, though with careful attention to the implications of this for interpersonal comparisons of utility. If the quantity $c_{ij}x_{ji}$ is aggregated over actors j, the resulting quantity (which may be labelled w_{ii}) is the overall fraction of control over event i that is interested in i. The off-diagonal element, w_{ik}, is the fraction of control over i that is interested in k. The effect of aggregating over actors is to count equally the 'interested control' of an event, independent of the particular actor in which the fraction of control and the quantity of interest are located. The matrix $W = CX(= \{w_{ik}\})$ thus embodies the structure of relations among events, just as the matrix Z embodies the structure of relations among actors. The various structural characteristics of the system given in definitions 10 to 21 above can be described by reference to these matrices. Table 3.1 presents matrices of control and interest, C and X, for seven events and eight actors, exhibiting several structural variations. Included in the table are the product matrices Z and W, showing the structure of relations among actors and events.

Event 1 is individually controlled and individually consequential, and thus both the event and the actor are totally independent of the remainder of the system. Actor 1 and actors 2–8 are isolated sets of actors, and events 1 and 2–7 are separable. Event 7 is individually controlled (by actor 7) but not individually consequential. Actor 7 is shown by Z to have an interest only in events under his control, but

Table 3.1

			C Actors									X Events					
		1	2	3	4	5	6	7	8		1	2	3	4	5	6	7
	1	1	0	0	0	0	0	0	0	1	1	0	0	0	0	0	0
	2	0	.4	.6	0	0	0	0	0	2	0	.8	.2	0	0	0	0
	3	0	.7	.3	0	0	0	0	0	3	0	.5	.5	0	0	0	0
Events	4	0	0	.4	.6	0	0	0	0	4	0	0	0	.7	0	.3	0	Actors
	5	0	0	.2	0	.2	.2	.2	.2	5	0	0	0	.3	.3	.3	.1
	6	0	0	0	.2	.8	0	0	0	6	0	0	0	.3	.4	.3	0
	7	0	0	0	0	0	0	1	0	7	0	0	0	0	0	0	1
										8	0	0	0	0	1	0	0

		$Z = XC$									$W = CX$					
	1	2	3	4	5	6	7	8		1	2	3	4	5	6	7
1	1	0	0	0	0	0	0	0	1	1	0	0	0	0	0	0
2	0	.46	54	0	0	0	0	0	2	0	.62	.38	0	0	0	0
3	0	.55	.45	0	0	0	0	0	3	0	.71	.29	0	0	0	0
4	0	0	.28	.48	.24	0	0	0	4	0	.20	.20	.42	0	.18	0
5	0	0	.18	.24	.30	.06	.16	.06	5	0	.10	.10	.12	.34	.12	.22
6	0	0	.20	.24	.32	.08	.08	.08	6	0	0	0	.38	.24	.30	.08
7	0	0	0	0	0	0	1	0	7	0	0	0	0	0	0	1
8	0	0	.2	0	.2	.2	.2	.2								

also to have control over events that are of interest to actors 5, 6, and 8. Event 5 is contingent on event 7 through actors 5 and 7 who have interests in event 7, and partial control over event 5; and event 6 is contingent on event 4 through actors 4 and 5. Event 2 is controlled by actors 2 and 3, and affects the same actors, so that it is a co-ordinated event, as is event 3. Actors 2 and 3 and events 2 and 3 nearly form an isolated set, except for the partial control of actor 3 over events 4 and 5. As a result, Z shows that actors 2 and 3 are dependent only on each other, but that 4, 5, 6, and 8 are dependent on actor 3; and W shows that those who control events 2 and 3 have interest only in these events, but that events 4 and 5 are partially controlled by an actor or actors with an interest in both events 2 and 3.

The structures of relations among events and among actors are shown in Figure 3.1. Each directed line from an actor or an event to another actor or event shows the dependence of the second on the first. Figure 3.1(a) shows the structure of relations among actors, and is taken from Z; Figure 3.1(b) shows the structure of relations among events, and is taken from W. These figures show the isolation of actor 1 and event 1, the autonomy of actor 7 and event 7, and the joint autonomy of actors 2 and 3 (no arrows leading toward the pair, except from each other), and the joint independence of events 2 and 3 from the other events.

These structures of relations among actors and events provide the basis for theories that can show the functioning or malfunctioning of the system. For this structure consists of a set of actors each of whom is attempting to maximize his utility, according to the principle of purposive behaviour described in the preceding chapter. I have not yet indicated what actions are possible in order to realize one's interests; these depend on the rules of the system. The realization of one's interests arises through an increase in the quantity $\sum_i x_{ji} c_{ij}$, that is, an increase in the proportion of one's interests that he can control. Thus one action in the realization of interests lies in establishing the constitution or ground rules of a social system, increasing one's control as much as possible. This occurs in socio-political systems in the formation of constitutions, and in less formalized systems in the establishment of initial rights and obligations. It can be observed in the attention paid to initial definitions of what is 'legitimate' when long-term relations, such as husband-wife relations, are established.

Here, however, I will take as given the initial constitution or agreed-upon structure of direct control. Thus I will take as given the matrix C as well as the matrix of interests X. Once such a structure is established, the principal activities of actors in attempting to realize their interests consist of actions through which they gain effective control over events they are interested in, through giving up effective control over events they are not interested in. In economic activities, this consists of an explicit exchange of control; in other areas of life, including political activities, it consists of less explicit exchange of control, often based on informal agreements.

Only when control is explicitly exchanged, through the physical

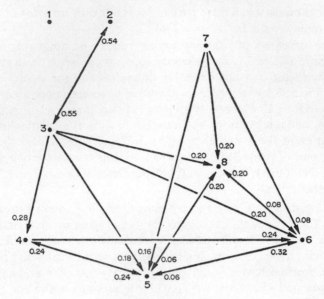

(a) Relations among actors

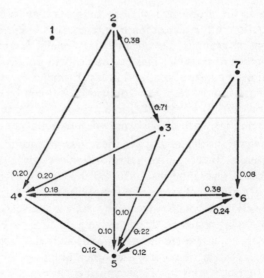

(b) Relations among events

Fig. 3.1

transfer of ownership, can a fully developed market emerge, in which there is further transfer of ownership, with full negotiability and the emergence of a market price for control over each event. However, even in systems which fall short of such full negotiability, approximations to a price system often develop, for individuals are concerned to gain as much control as possible over those events that interest them, and thus have an interest in giving up as little control as possible over those events they do control in return for a given amount of control over those events that interest them.

Because such approximations to a market system do emerge in a highly interdependent social system, I will develop a system of action in which a perfect market is assumed. In the first and simplest approach to this system of action, individual actors will be concerned simply to increase their control over those events that interest them, and will pay no attention to the direction of interest of other actors. In a subsequent treatment, individuals will also pay attention to direction.

The general idea from which we will begin is that, for control of each event (say event i), there will be a demand which consists of the control of other events held by those who are interested in event i, and thus willing to offer that control in return for control over i. There will also be a supply of control over event i made available by those whose interest in that event is below their interest in the control for which they can exchange this control. From such demand and supply will emerge in a perfect market an equilibrium price or value for control over each event.[3] It is possible to define more precisely this equilibrium in a system of the sort described above. Equilibrium exists when demand for control over an event equals supply of control over the event, for all events. The adjustment occurs through modifications in the value or price of each event, which will be represented by v_i for event i. That is, equilibrium occurs when the *value* of all demand for control over the event equals the *value* of all supply of control.

The value of control over an event depends upon the interests of powerful actors, i.e. actors with many resources, in the event. Obviously, if many actors with large amounts of resources are interested in the event, then its value will be high, because the effective demand is high: actors are both interested in it and have resources with which to pay for it.

---

[3] There are conditions under which no equilibrium price will develop. However, in accordance with the general plan to deal with simplest cases first, I will not investigate these until it becomes necessary to do so.

Supply of control over the event consists of the value of all control that exists in the system for that event, that is, if S_i is the supply of control over event i,

$$S_i = \sum_j v_i c_{ij} \tag{3.2}$$

and when all control is within the system, as assumed here, $\sum_j c_{ij} = 1$, then

$$S_i = v_i \tag{3.2a}$$

Thus the value of the total supply of control over i is simply the value or price of i, v_i.

Demand for control over i may potentially occur from all those who are interested in the outcome of i, that is, all those actors j for whom $x_{ji} > 0$. Since the total demands that each actor in the system can make depend on his constitutional control of events with high value, it is useful to conceive of these as his total resources. His total constitutional resources can be measured in terms of his proportion of constitutional control of events, with each event weighted by its equilibrium price or value. If individual j's total resources are labelled r_j, then

$$r_j = \sum_i v_i c_{ij} \tag{3.3}$$

where v_i is the value or price of control over event i. These values will be measured relative to one another, with the total value in the system equal to 1. Thus equation 1 gives the proportion of the total value in the system over which actor j has control. This total set of resources held by an individual may be described as his power to realize his interests in this system. Power expressed in this way is not a relational concept between two individuals; it is a scalar quantity, representing the fraction of the total value in the system over which he has constitutional control.

If individual j is to maximize the product of his interests and final control, that is, maximize $\sum_i x_{ji} c_{ij}^*$, where c_{ij}^* is his final control after exchanges, then he should buy control over that event for which the ratio of his interests to the event's value, x_{ji}/v_i, is maximum. For each unit of value that he gives up, he can realize the greatest increment in interests through exchanging it for control over that event for which the ratio x_{ji}/v_i is maximum.

If he behaves this way, he will be acting in such a way as to maximize his utility in the system. However, for the present, we will assume a somewhat different behaviour, and then later discuss its relation to maximization. We assume that if his resources are $v_k c_{kj}$ summed over all events k, he allocates those resources over events i *proportional to* the ratio x_{ji}/v_i, rather than only for that event for which x_{ji}/v_i is maximum. Thus his final control over event i, c_{ij}^*, will be

$$c_{ij}^* = \frac{x_{ji}}{v_i} \sum_k v_k c_{kj} \qquad (3.4)$$

or the value of his final control over event i will be eqn. 3.4 multiplied through by v_i,

$$v_i c_{ij}^* = x_{ji} \sum_k v_k c_{kj} \qquad (3.4a)$$

The total demand for control over event i will be this demand summed over all actors j. If D_i is the demand for i then

$$D_i = \sum_j x_{ji} \sum_k v_k c_{kj} \qquad (3.5)$$

Equilibrium occurs when $D_i = S_i$ for all events i, or, from eqns. 3.2 and 3.5,

$$S_i = D_i$$

$$v_i = \sum_j x_{ji} \sum_k v_k c_{kj} \qquad (3.6)$$

Equation 3.6 is the fundamental equation of the static system, and it is useful to consider it at some length. First, it should be noted that, in eqn. 3.5 and eqn. 3.6, there is for the first time an aggregation of interests over actors. This constitutes an explicit interpersonal comparison of utility or interests, for it adds interests of actors j weighted by a quantity $\sum_k v_k c_{kj}$. This 'weight' for each actor's interest constitutes an interpersonal comparison based on the resources of each actor in the system, since his resources, r_j, are $\sum_k v_k c_{kj}$. This concept is the one concept of interpersonal comparison of utility which has operational, as opposed to ethical, meaning. It is a measure of just how the constitution of the given social system, in endowing him with particular amounts of control over events, has given him the power to realize his interests, and thereby weighted his interests according to their importance in determining outcomes in this system.

Lloyd Shapley (1967) has described, in game theory, two concepts of interpersonal comparison of utility which, under certain equilibrium conditions, coincide. These concepts, unlike the classical idea of interpersonal comparison of utility based on 'how strongly' different persons feel about something, are very similar to the one produced by the present theory, for they are based on the actual positions that different players achieve in a game.

An implication of this interpersonal comparison is that it is not given *a priori*, but is dependent on the particular constitution of the system, that is, the rules which govern this system.

Equation 3.6 allows the calculation of the set of values or prices v_i if the structure of interests X, and the structure of control C, are known. If there are m events, there are $m - 1$ independent equations of the form of eqn. 3.6 which can be solved to find the equilibrium values, v_i.

The equations may perhaps be most easily solved in matrix form. Let $V =$ the row vector with elements v_i, and let $W = CX$ as in Table 3.1. Then $V = VW$, or $0 = V(W - I)$. Now because of the dependence of one v_i upon the others, define $V^* = \{v_i^*\}$ where $v_i^* = v_i/v_m$. Dividing by v_m gives $0 = V^*(W - I)$. This may be written as $0 = V^*(W^* - I) + Y$, where W^* is W with the last row and column deleted, and Y is a row vector with elements $v_m^* w_{mi}$, or simply w_{mi}. Transposing Y gives $-Y = V^*(W^* - I)$, and right-multiplying by the inverse of $W^* - I$ gives $-Y(W^* - I)^{-1} = V^*$. Then since $v_i = v_i^* v_m$, and $\sum v_i = 1$, we have $\sum_{i=1}^{m} v_i^* v_m = 1$, and $v_m = 1/\sum_{i=1}^{m} v_i^*$. Then v_i may be found by $v_i = v_i^* v_m$. Equation 3.3 may be used to find r_j, the resources or power of each actor j. The system may alternatively be solved for r_j by substituting eqn. 3.3 into eqn. 3.6 to obtain an equation in r_j, x_{ji}, and c_{ij}. If the product matrix W or Z is separable into two distinct submatrices, as in Table 3.1 (1 vs. 2–8 in Z, or 1 vs. 2–7 in W), then the two submatrices should be analysed separately, since they are wholly distinct systems. No comparisons of value or power can be carried out between such totally independent systems.

It is useful to derive these equations from a dynamic system in which the value or price of each event adjusts downward if supply exceeds demand and upward if demand exceeds supply, until equilibrium values are reached for all events. One way that this might be conceived concretely is by a kind of dual auction in which prices are set for each event and then adjusted in slow degrees until the demand and supply are equal for each issue.

Mathematically, we may write m equations in which the rate of change of v_i is proportional to the difference between the amount of value offered as demand for control of i and the supply of value of i,

$$\frac{dv_i}{dt} = k(D_i - S_i) \qquad (3.7)$$

As the value of i increases, the demand for i decreases and the supply increases, so that when $D_i = S_i$ for all i, the values are at equilibrium.

We shall assume that actors generate supply of control over i and demand for control over i as indicated earlier, and expressed below:

(1) At all points in time, each actor has a total demand for i, expressed in units of value, equal to the same fraction of his total resources as his interest in i is of his total interests. That is, his total demand for i is $r_j x_{ji}$, where r_j is his current power.

(2) His current holdings of i have a value $v_i c_{ij}$.

(3) Consequently, his excess demand, or market demand, for i is his total demand minus his current holdings, or $r_j x_{ji} - v_i c_{ij}$. If this quantity is positive, it is a demand placed in the market, i.e. an offer of that amount of value (which consists of control over other events) for i at the current price, v_i. If this quantity is negative, it is a supply of i placed in the market, i.e. an offer of that amount of control over i at the current price, v_i.[4]

When these offers to buy control over i and offers to sell control over i are added over all individuals, they constitute the total demand minus supply of i at current prices. Thus eqn. 3.7 becomes

$$\frac{dv_i}{dt} = \sum_j r_j x_{ji} - \sum_j v_i c_{ij}$$

$$= \sum_j r_j x_{ji} - v_i \qquad (3.8)$$

---

[4] This market procedure may be made slightly more realistic by recognizing that his total demand for i does not include that value which he already owns as control of i. Thus his excess or market demand, $r_j x_{ji} - v_i c_{ij}$, may be written

$$x_{ji} \sum_k v_k c_{kj} - v_i c_{ij} = x_{ji} \sum_{k \neq i} v_k c_{kj} - (1 - x_{ji}) v_i c_{ij}$$

The last expression says in effect that his excess demand is a fraction x_{ji} (his fraction of interest in i) of his value held in *other* events minus $1 - x_{ji}$ (his fraction of interest in other events) times the value he holds in event i. This more realistic way of expressing the relation does not affect it, for this would still give eqn. 3.8.

When demand and supply are equal, then $dv_i/dt = 0$, and eqn. 3.8 reduces to the equilibrium value of eqn. 3.6.[5]

The problem of maximization

The theory of collective decisions provides a market solution for collective decisions in which actors have resources and interests, and can exchange those resources in a free market. However, there are several kinds of assumptions that keep the theory from conforming to conditions of real collective decisions, even when an open market in votes exists. One of these is the probabilistic decision rule, which is nowhere found in practice. But perhaps the most serious problem is that the actions implied on the part of the actor are not those which maximize his expected gain in interests, but rather actions in which he allocates his resources proportionally to the expected gain in interests. If, in contrast, he were maximizing his expected increment in interests, he would choose the one issue that would benefit him most for a given unit of resource input, and concentrate all his resources on that issue. Since his costs for issue i, in terms of resource inputs, are measured by the current price or value, v_i, of the issue, the increment in interests per unit resource input is measured by x_{ji}/v_i. Thus the principle of maximizing expected gain is one which dictates that he use all his resources, r_j, to control issue i, where i is the issue such that

$$x_{ji}/v_i = \max_k (x_{jk}/v_k)$$

This assumes, of course, that his resources r_j are not sufficient to extend beyond control of issue i, that is, it assumes that $r_j \leqslant v_i$. If this is not the case, then he is in the position of a monopsonist, who

[5] There is a point of questionable rationality in the market activity described above. This is the fact, mentioned earlier, that each actor divides his total demand (that is, his total resources) according to the fraction of interest he has in each event. Rationality would appear to dictate that he use his resources solely to gain control of that event for which the ratio of his interest to the current price is greatest. In that way, each unit of value spent will have maximum effect in increasing one's control over his interests. If the system is a large one and interest in events is distributed independently, then the distribution of maximum interests for individuals with a given amount of resources should be approximately the same as the overall distribution of interests, thus giving the same result obtained here. However, this remains a point of difficulty in the model as it stands, particularly when the number of actors and number of events is small. In certain cases, the equilibrium values will be the same if actors attempt to gain control of the event with greatest interest relative to price, but in most cases, the equilibrium values will differ somewhat. The question of maximization vs. distribution is discussed in the next section.

may find strategic behaviour, in withholding part of his demand to lower the price, to his advantage.

The difference between the maximization outcome and the proportional-distribution outcome can be illustrated by a two-actor, two-event system, with control and interest matrices as shown in Table 3.2.

Table 3.2

	actor 1	actor 2		event 1	event 2	
event 1	1	0	actor 1	x_{11}	x_{12}	$x_{11} + x_{12} = 1$
event 2	0	1	actor 2	x_{21}	x_{22}	$x_{21} + x_{22} = 1$
	control			interest		$x_{12} > x_{11}, x_{21} > x_{22}$

Using eqn. 3.6 and solving for v_1, we have

$$v_1 = x_{11} v_1 c_{11} + x_{11} v_2 c_{21} + x_{21} v_1 c_{12} + x_{21} v_2 c_{22}$$

$$= x_{11} v_1(1) + x_{11}(1 - v_1)(0) + x_{21} v_1(0) + x_{21}(1 - v_1)(1)$$

$$v_1 = \frac{x_{21}}{1 - x_{11} + x_{21}}$$

Let us suppose further that not only is each actor more interested in the event controlled by the other, but also actor 2's difference in interests is greater than that of actor 1's, for example, that $x_{11} = .4$, $x_{12} = .6$, and $x_{21} = .8$, $x_{22} = .2$.[6] Then solving for v_1 gives

$$v_1 = \frac{.8}{1 - .4 + .8} = .57.$$

Use of eqn. 3.2 shows the following configuration of values and power:

$$r_1 = .57 \qquad v_1 = .57$$
$$r_2 = .43 \qquad v_2 = .43$$

[6] This may appear to be an illegitimate interpersonal comparison of utility, but is not. These numbers could be estimated by a lottery offer following the von Neumann–Morgenstern procedure. For example, actor 1 could be confronted with the following offer: 'With probability p you will have to perform your task, and actor 2 will not; with probability $1 - p$ actor 2 will have to perform his task, and you will not. Do you accept this offer?' This offer is repeated for various values of p. At the value of p at which actor 1 is exactly indifferent to the offer, $p = x_{12}$ and $1 - p = x_{11}$. A similar experiment with actor 2 would establish the values of x_{21} and x_{22}. Note that these experiments involve no interpersonal comparisons at all, only the comparison of each actor's relative strength of interests in event 1 and event 2.

If each exchanges partial control over actions as described above, each actor will come to have $c_{ij}^* = r_j x_{ji}/v_i$ of control of each issue i. This becomes

$$c_{11}^* = .4 \qquad c_{12}^* = .6$$
$$c_{21}^* = .8 \qquad c_{22}^* = .2$$

As these numbers show, actor 1 comes to have greater control of events than actor 2 because his ratio of interests in the other's action relative to his own is less than that of actor 2.

The extent to which each realizes his interests in this case is given by $\sum_i x_{ji} c_{ij}^*$, for actor 1, $.4 \times .4 + .6 \times .8 = .64$, and for actor 2, $.8 \times .6 + .2 \times .2 = .52$. These realized interests cannot be directly added, however, because actor 1 has greater power in the system, and thus for aggregating interests to examine the 'aggregate realized interests', actor 1 must count more heavily than actor 2: realized interests = $.64 \times .57 + .52 \times .43 = .59$. Thus of a total possible realized interests of 1.0 in any system, this procedure produces a realized interest of .59.

However, if in fact both actors are attempting to maximize their interest, the outcome described above will not be the outcome. We know only that actor 2 will attempt to gain *full* control of event 1, so long as the exchange rate is higher than 2:8 (that is, so long as he has to give up less than 8 units of control over event 2 for every 2 units he gains over event 1); and that actor 1 will attempt to gain full control over event 2, so long as the exchange rate is lower than 6:4 (that is, so long as he has to give up less than 6 units of control over event 1 for every 4 units he gains over event 2). Since it is easily possible to meet these constraints (for example, by an exchange ratio that is 1:1), the full exchange will be consummated, until the resources of one or both are exhausted. If, for example, the exchange rate were 1:2, actor 2 would give up all his control over event 2 in return for .5 control over event 1. As in any bargaining process, the outcome is not determined uniquely. We know only that the exchange rate will be somewhere between 2:8 and 6:4, and that exchange will proceed until resources of one or both are exhausted.

It appears, then, that the 'solution' given by eqns. 3.1 and 3.2 is not in fact a solution, because it does not result from maximization behaviour on the part of actors. Furthermore, there may not be a unique solution when each is attempting to maximize, because if one or more actors is in the position of monopsonist or monopolist, then without some further specification about the bargaining procedure, there is no means by which a determinate price is arrived at.[7]

Nevertheless, it is possible to give an interpretation to the system in which resources are allocated proportionally to interests, which does make the solution identical to that of maximizing actors. If each actor j in the system is not conceived as a single actor, but rather as a set of sub-actors each of whom has the same pattern of control (so that all sub-actor's control vectors are identical, and their sum is the control vector shown in the matrix for actor j), then the 'proportion of interests in issue i' can be interpreted as the proportion of actors who have this issue as their sole interest. Heuristically, one can see that maximizing behaviour will produce proportional allocation of resources, that is, dividing up the total power of the actor j, p_j, according to x_{ji}, since x_{ji} represents the proportion of the power of actor j that is in the hands of those sub-actors who are interested solely in issue i.

The way this is manifested in the preceding example can be illustrated by assuming that there are ten actors in the system as a whole, five in each of the two explicit actors in Table 3.2. If we make these sub-actors explicit, the matrices of control and interest are as shown in Table 3.3.

Table 3.3

	Control actors											Interest Events	
		1	2	3	4	5	6	7	8	9	10		1	2
Events	1	0	0	0	0	0	.2	.2	.2	.2	.2		1	0
	2	.2	.2	.2	.2	.2	0	0	0	0	0	2	1	0
												3	1	0
												4	1	0
											Actors	5	0	1
												6	1	0
												7	1	0
												8	0	1
												9	0	1
												10	0	1

---

[7] It is certainly possible to specify such a procedure, which will give a determinate price even in the case of two parties. A non-strategic procedure most compatible with the frame of reference under discussion here is that each places on the market all his resources as demand for the one issue which gives him greatest expected gain in interests. In the 2-actor case under examination here, this will result in equal power for each, and equal value for the two issues. On the other hand, one reasonable interpretation of the differing interests of actor 1 and actor 2 is a difference in the rate at which they will place on the market the resources they hold in order to gain control of issues that benefit them more. This possibility will be discussed further in Chapter 5.

In this system, actors 1–5 each have .2 control over action 2 and actors 6–10 each have .2 control over action 1. Of actors 1–5, four out of five, or .8, have sole interest in event 1, while one of five, or .2, has sole interest in event 2. Of actors 6–10, two out of five, or .4, have sole interest in event 1, while three of five, or .6, have sole interest in event 2.

If this market system is solved by assuming that each actor is maximizing, and placing all his resources on the market for the one issue that concerns him, the solution in terms of value of issues and power of actors is identical to the proportional solution (according to eqns. 3.4 and 3.5) of the system with two actors, shown in Table 3.2. More generally, a system which replaces each actor j who has interests divided among different issues by a set of n_j actors, each of whom has $1/n_j$ of the control of actor j on each issue, and total interests in only one issue, so that the proportion of interests of the set in issue i equals x_{ji}, will give the same solution under the maximizing action principle as will the original system under the proportional-allocation principle. Further, with x_{ji} as the proportion of actor j's interests in issue i, then consider a system which replaces actor j by m actors, labelled $j_1, ..., j_i, ..., j_m$, if there are m events, with sub-actor j_i having a fraction x_{ji} of j's control over each event (so that his control over event k is $x_{ji} c_{kj}$). This system, under the principle of maximization of interest, will give the same result as the original system under the proportional-allocation principle of eqn. 3.6. This alternative system can be conceived as an interpretation of the original one, in that the original actor represented a set of actors having identical control but differing interests, with x_{ji} as the proportion of them with sole interests in i.

This interpretation provides a better basis of justification for the solutions arrived at in eqn. 3.6. It still provides no basis for describing an individual actor's maximization behaviour when in fact he does have varying amounts of interest in various issues. When he does have varying amounts of interest in different issues, then his maximizing behaviour will lead him to attempt to gain control of an issue that is second most important, when gaining control of the most important is too costly.

There is finally another interpretation of the system that allows the proportional-allocation principle to be interpretable as maximizing behaviour of a single individual. If an individual is viewed as not having constant interests at all times, but rather interests varying over time, we can regard the proportions x_{ji} as the *proportion of time* that issue i is his sole interest. The system is in effect like that of Table 3.3, except each of the actors 1–5 represents one-fifth of original actor 1's time, and each of the actors 6–10 represents one-fifth of original actor 2's time. In this interpretation, actor 1 and actor 2 are always acting to maximize expected gain in interests, but the interests vary over time so as to give Table 3.3 as the time distribution of interests.

These results cannot be regarded as wholly satisfactory, because they require an interpretation of interest, x_{ji}, that is different from its derivation in terms of utility differences for the individual. However, having noted this discrepancy, it is nevertheless useful to see that the proportional-allocation principle can be interpreted as maximizing behaviour, either by assuming the 'actor' to be in fact a set of several actors with identical control, or by assuming that x_{ji} represents a fraction of time for which issue i is of sole interest to actor j.[8]

It is useful to note that there are some ways in which the maximization principle appears to have serious faults. If there are more events than actors, some events must have zero value, even though some actors have some interest in them. But then these zero-value events will be a 'best buy' for any individual with non-zero interests in them, leading him to withdraw his demand for another event, to make a demand for this. But then that other event, or at least some other, must then have zero value, leading to an oscillation of values.

Also, there would appear to be some 'reasonable' basis for distributing one's resources over more than a single event, despite the fact that the dictates of rationality under conditions of risk or uncertainty lead to such action. This last consideration indicates that if on common-sense grounds it does appear more reasonable to distribute one's resources over several events, then the assumptions made earlier that define the environment confronting each actor are awry in some respect, and a modification of these assumptions would lead to a distribution of efforts. This question remains to be studied, however, and for the present this discrepancy can only be noted. It is useful to note that in the proposed procedure leading to a distribution of efforts proportional to x_{ji}/v_i, a coalition of two actors would behave identically to the two individual actors acting alone, whereas in the procedure in which each actor concentrates on a single event, a coalition of two

[8] The system as described is equivalent to a system in private-goods exchange in which the price-elasticity of each good is -1.0, and the income elasticity is 1.0. See Coleman (1972) for discussion of such a system.

4

would in general behave differently than the two acting alone, con-
centrating all its efforts on the event that brings a highest return to the
more powerful of the two. In neither case, of course, is there any overall
gain from such a coalition, under the assumed probabilistic decision
rule. It may, of course, be that it is the existence of other decision rules
in real life, such as a majority rule, that leads to the 'more reasonable'
distribution of efforts over more than one event.

The probabilistic decision rule

A second defect of this theory is its necessity for a decision rule of a
type that is almost never used in practice.[9] As I indicated earlier,
with any other decision rule, a simple matrix of control as in the model
is not an adequate description of the complexities of control, because
one's control depends on the actions of another member of the
collectivity. For example, with a majority rule, if over 50 per cent of
the collectivity favours an issue, then all positive votes beyond 50
per cent, and all negative votes, have no control of the collective action
at all. There has been a measure of control devised which could be
used with any decision rule, the Shapley measure of value of a game,
adapted by Shapley and Shubik (1954) as a measure of degree of
control over collective decisions.[10] But although this is a very reasonable measure of control, its use here would be an *ad hoc* procedure.
Its use would be justifiable only if it could be shown that in some sense
(necessarily a weaker sense than with a probabilistic decision rule),
individual j's action can increment the probability of a positive
outcome by an amount Δp_{ij}, equal to the Shapley–Shubik measure of
power or control for j, modified as indicated previously. For the present, I will only note that any attempt to adapt this model to decision
rules other than a probabilistic one requires careful attention to the
concept of control on which the control matrix is based.

However, if we assume such attention has been given, there remains
another problem attendant on adapting the theory to a decision rule
other than the probabilistic one. This is the fact that in the process of
vote exchanges it comes now to make a difference just how much

[9] There appear to have been cases in primitive societies in which all members of a
group individually make their choice, and then one member is chosen by lot, and his
choice governs. This is formally the same as the probabilistic decision rule used in this
chapter.
[10] For an alternative measure of control which is a modification of the Shapley–
Shubik measure, see Coleman (1971, 1973), and Rae (1969).

sentiment there is for an issue, and how much against. With the probabilistic decision rule, interest in an event would be manifested in the price or value of the event, so long as there was any difference of direction of interest on the event. This would be ensured merely by the fact that any member who had control over some of an event that he wished to sell could threaten to vote against the remainder of the collectivity, merely to ensure that its value is maintained. All that is necessary is such a threat, and on every issue, it is to at least one member's interest (that member who wishes to sell control over i) to make such a threat if there is otherwise unanimity on the event.

In the final chapter, I will indicate ways in which the theory might be modified to allow for non-probabilistic decision rules. Before that, however, the next chapter examines various concepts that derive from the theory, and presents a number of examples of its application.

4 Further Concepts and Applications

The theory introduced in the previous chapter is applicable to a wide range of collective actions. In this chapter, I want to illustrate a few of those applications. First, however, it is useful to examine several other concepts that are derivative from the theory.

Additional concepts

The first and simplest of these is the outcome of an event. The outcome of an event in the basic theory is probabilistic: it is positive with probability equal to the final control of those actors who favour a positive outcome. If q_i is the proportion of final control held by those actors, then the probability of passage is q_i.

If s_{ji} is the sign of utility differences of actor j for event i, and c_{ij}^* is his final control over event i, then $c_{ij}^* s_{ji}$ is the increment or decrement in probability of passage due to his vote. The total probability of passage is 0.5 plus half the sum of these increments and decrements over all actors. Since the probability of a positive outcome and the proportion of positive votes for event i are both designated by q_i, then the calculation of both is directly carried out by use of c_{ij}^* and s_{ji},

$$q_i = 0.5 + 0.5 \sum_j c_{ij}^* s_{ji} \qquad (4.1)$$

In the case of a non-probabilistic decision rule, we can consider a general decision rule in which a positive outcome occurs if the proportion of votes cast in favour is greater than a particular value, q_i^*. In a majority rule, $q_i^* = 0.5$. This decision rule can be written,

$$\delta_i = 1 \text{ if } q_i > q_i^*$$
$$= 0 \text{ if } q_i < q_i^* \tag{4.2}$$

where δ_i represents the outcome, with the value of 1 if the outcome is positive, and 0 if it is negative. (If $q_i = q_i^*$, then an arbitrary rule must be introduced to determine the outcome.)

A second general concept that derives from the model is the actor's realization of interests. It is possible to calculate just how fully this system satisfies each actor's interests, since we know the final control and the outcome. However, two quite different things can be meant by his satisfaction of interests. First, the degree to which he, through his own power, is able to realize his interests; and second, the degree to which his interests are realized by the actual outcome of the events. The first of these pays no attention to the outcome, and shows only the expected realization of interests through his own power. This realization of interests through his own power is defined as the increment in probability of desired outcome through his vote, multiplied by his interest in that event, over all events. If c_{ij}^* is the final control that he possesses over event i, and we assume that with probability 0.5 this control would be cast in the desired direction if he did not hold it, then his expected interest in the absence of any action by himself is 0.5, and the increment in expected interest due to his actions is $0.5 \sum_i x_{ji} c_{ij}^*$. This means that his total expected realization of interests, considering only his own actions, is $0.5 + 0.5 \sum_i x_{ji} c_{ij}^*$, and the increment due to his own actions is

$$a_{jj} = 0.5 \sum_i x_{ji} c_i^* \tag{4.3}$$

where a_{jj} is the increment in expected realization of interests by actor j, considering only his own actions. In the basic theory, c_{ij}^* is the ratio of his interest in i to the value or price of i, times his power, $c_{ij}^* = (x_{ji}/v_i)r_j$. It at first appears that c_{ij}^* can be greater than 1.0 by this definition, for if he has all his interest in event i, and the price of i is low relative to his power, then c_{ij}^* would be greater than 1. However, the fallacy in this argument lies in the fact that v_i is in part determined by his power, r_j; if all his interest lies in event i, then v_i will be equal to r_j even if no other actor has an interest in i, and greater than r_j if another actor does have interest in i. More generally, the minimum value of the event i, when no other actor has an interest in i, is $r_j x_{ji}$, as shown by eqns. 3.6 and 3.3. This ensures that the upper limit of c_{ij}^* is 1.0.

For the basic theory, eqn. 4.3 may be expanded by substituting for c_{ij}^*, its equivalent, to give:

$$a_{jj} = 0.5 \sum_i x_{ji} \frac{x_{ji}}{v_i} r_j$$

$$= 0.5 r_j \sum_i \frac{x_{ji}^2}{v_i} \qquad (4.4)$$

This equation shows explicitly the dependence of his realization of interests upon three things:

(a) His power, r_j.

(b) The value of the events that interest him, which depends on the interests of others with power in those same events, driving up the value of those events.

(c) Also, under certain conditions, his realization of interests depends on their concentration, since the sum of x_{ji}^2 over i will be larger the more concentrated x_{ji} on a few events. However, this is true only if his resources r_j are not a major source of the price of event i. For if he is the only actor interested in each of the events in which he has an interest, then for each of those events, $v_i = r_j x_{ji}$, and in eqn. 4.4, a_{jj} becomes equal to 1.0, independent of his distribution of interests. If, however, his power is only a partial determinant of v_i for the events in which he has an interest, then for a given distribution of interests among other actors, he realizes more of his interests the more concentrated they are. Example 2 will show the way in which his realization of interests depends on his concentration of interests.

It is useful to consider what concentration of interests means when the interpretation of each actor is that of a set of actors having identical control, each with all interests concentrated on a single event, and proportional in numbers to x_{ij} (see Chapter 3). In this interpretation, concentration of interests means a larger proportion of the whole (the whole represented by actor j) having interests that are alike. Thus the effects of concentration of interests are to make each of these sub-actors who make up explicit actor j realize a greater portion of his interests, because of the benefits he receives from other sub-actors' actions. Their actions provide for him external economies. Each realizes a greater portion of his total interests, because the efforts of other sub-actors are directed in the same way as his own efforts. Thus in this interpretation with sub-actors, all of whom are maximizing in gaining control of the single event they have interest in, the concentration of interest at the level of the actor provides external economies from the point of view of the sub-actor.

The second sense in which the actor's interests are satisfied introduces for the actor what was just discussed for the sub-actor: the external economies due to the actions of other actors. For the basic theory, his expected realization of interests is the sum of his interests times the probability of action in the direction he favours. If a_j is his expected realization of interests through all actors, then

$$a_j = \sum_i x_{ji} q_i + \sum_h x_{jh}(1 - q_h)$$

where the first sum, over index i, covers all those events in which he favours action ($s_{ji} = +1$), and the second sum, over index h, covers all those events in which he opposes action ($s_{ji} = -1$). This may be simplified and put into a single sum by substituting for q_i and q_h from eqn. 4.1 (and for c_{ij}^* in eqn. 4.1), and introducing the sign s_{ji}, of his own interests:

$$a_j = 0.5 + 0.5 \sum_i \sum_k \frac{r_k}{v_i} s_{ji} x_{ji} s_{ki} x_{ki} \qquad (4.5)$$

This equation contains a sum of product terms of his signed interest times others' signed interest, weighted by the ratio of the actor's power to the issue's value, r_k/v_i. This shows that his expected realization of interest depends on the coincidence of his interest with that of others, considering both size and direction of interests. If his interests coincide highly with those of others, then their actions constitute for him external economies; if his interests are opposed to theirs, their actions constitute for him external diseconomies. The increment to his expected realization of interests from his own action is the set of terms under the summation signs in eqn. 4.5 for which $k = j$, and since $s_{ji}^2 = 1$, this reduces to eqn. 4.4. This suggests the possible utility of an analogous quantity, a_{jk}, the increment (positive or negative) to j's expected realization of interests due to actor k, which is the set of terms under the summation signs in eqn. 4.5 for a particular actor k. Then eqn. 4.5 can be written

$$a_j = 0.5 + 0.5 \sum_k a_{jk} \qquad (4.6)$$

where all terms in which $k \neq j$ are external economies or diseconomies he experiences at the hands of others in the system. From this quantity a_j for actor j, his expected realization of interests, we can calculate the total expected realization of interests of the collectivity, as the sum of a_j weighted by the power of the actor, r_j,

$$a = 0.5 + 0.5 \sum_i \frac{\sum_j \sum_k r_j r_k s_{ji} x_{ji} s_{ki} x_{ki}}{\sum_j r_j x_{ji}} \qquad (4.7)$$

The form of this equation shows that the realization of interests of the collectivity depends on the coincidence of weighted interests of the members.

It is worth while to note here Shapley's (1953) concept of the value of a game, and its relation to the present considerations. Shapley notes that the value of a game to an individual is what he can expect to get out of it, which in turn is his contribution to all possible coalitions of which he is a member. Leaving aside Shapley's formal calculation of value, which is not relevant to the present theory, we can see that a_j, the individual's expected realization of his interests, is what might be described as the value of the collectivity (as defined by the control, interest, and sign matrices) to him. It is this quantity, in comparison with what he might realize outside that collectivity, that should govern his decision to enter or remain in this collectivity. That is, if he is to maximize his expected utility, he must choose that system in which the expected realization of interests, a_j, is greatest.

A final general concept that derives from the theory is the power that the collectivity as a collectivity exhibits with regard to event i. Heuristically, the idea is this: v_i shows the value of event i, which is the sum of the interests of all actors, weighted by their power. If that interest is all in the same direction, then the collectivity has this amount of power to exert toward the environment on this event. If it is half in one direction and half in the other, the collectivity has no power remaining to exert toward the environment. In some applications, where the collective action is merely a decision that is automatically implemented, this is not important. In others, however, where the collective action constitutes a joining of forces collectively to implement collective interests, it is important.

The directed power of the collectivity on event i is the unopposed weighted interests in i:

$$b_i = \sum_j r_j x_{ji} s_{ji} \qquad (4.8)$$

where b_i is the directed power of the collectivity on event i. The maximum magnitude of b_i is v_i, and its sign is positive or negative as the weighted interest favouring the action or those opposing the action are greater. The total power of the collectivity, where its maximum power is 1, is simply the sum of the absolute values of b_i over all events i. The maximum is realized when all s_{ji} for an event i are of the same sign, for all i.

List of concepts in the theory

For reference purposes, it is useful to list several concepts that derive from the theory, both those discussed in the preceding chapter, and those that have been introduced above.

(1) Quantities assumed to be given:

Constitutional control of actor j over event i, c_{ij}, where $\sum_j c_{ij} = 1.0$, and $c_{ij} \geqslant 0$, for all actors j and events i.

Relative utility differences of actor j for event i, y_{ji}, where $-1 \leqslant y_{ji} \leqslant 1$, for all actors j and events i.

Interest of actor j in event i, x_{ji}, for all actors j and events i, defined as the absolute value of y_{ji}; $x_{ji} \geqslant 0$, and $\sum_i x_{ji} = 1.0$.

Direction of interest of actor j in event i, s_{ji}, for all actors j and events i, defined as the sign of y_{ji}.

(2) Quantities derived from the analysis:

Value of control over an event in a vote market, or simply value of an event, v_i. In the basic theory, equilibrium value is the sum of interests in the event, weighted according to the power of the actor with those interests; $v_i = \sum_j r_j x_{ji}$.

Power or resources of an actor in the system, r_j. In the basic theory, power is the sum of control over events, weighted by the equilibrium value of that event: $r_j = \sum_i v_i c_{ij}$.

Final control of an actor j over event i, c_{ij}^*. Final control is control at equilibrium, which depends on actor j's power, on his interests in i, and on the value of i. In the basic theory, final control is defined as $(x_{ji}/v_i)r_j$. As with constitutional control, $c_{ij}^* \geqslant 0$, and $\sum_j c_{ij}^* = 1.0$.

Outcome of an event. In the basic theory, the probability of a positive outcome, q_i, is equal to the proportion of final control held by those actors who favour a positive outcome, or equivalently, equal to 0.5 plus half the control exerted by those who favour a positive outcome and minus half the control exerted by those who favour a negative outcome, i.e. $q_i = 0.5 + 0.5 \sum_j c_{ij}^* s_{ji}$.

Increment in expected realization of interests due to his own actions, a_{jj}. This increment (from a baseline of expected interests of 0.5) is merely the sum of half the product of his final control on event i times his interest in i, over all events i, that is, $a_{jj} = 0.5 \sum_i x_{ji} c_{ij}^*$.

Increment in expected realization of interest due to external effects of actor k's action, a_{jk}. This increment is the product of k's final control, the sign of the direction in which it will be cast, j's interest and the sign showing its direction, or $a_{jk} = 0.5 \sum_i s_{ji} x_{ji} c_{ik}^* s_{ki}$.

Expected realization of interest for actor j is 0.5 plus the increments and decrements from all actors, $a_j = 0.5 + 0.5 \sum_k a_{jk}$. This is the expected value of the collectivity to him.

Total expected realization of interests for all actors is the sum of a_j weighted by the power of j, $a = \sum_j a_j r_j$.

Directed power of the collectivity on event i, b_i, is that part of the value of event i, v_i, which is unopposed. It is calculated as the sum of weighted signed interests, $b_i = \sum_j r_j x_{ji} s_{ji}$.

Total power of the collectivity is the sum of the magnitudes of power on each event i, $b = \sum_i |b_i|$.

Examples of applications

Example 1 : A simple legislature

In a simple ideal-type committee or legislature of n members, each member has $1/n$ of the control of each decision in the collectivity. If each decision is regarded as an event, and if the collectivity members have differential interests in different events, then there will be exchanges of control through a vote market. An example of such a distribution of interests in a collectivity is given in Table 4.1, and the structure of relations among actors and among events is shown in Figure 4.1.

Table 4.1

	Interests x_{ji} with signs s_{ji}						Control c_{ij}					
	1	2	3	4	5		1	2	3	4	5	6
1	−.4	−.3	−.15	−.1	−.05	1	$\frac{1}{6}$	$\frac{1}{6}$	$\frac{1}{6}$	$\frac{1}{6}$	$\frac{1}{6}$	$\frac{1}{6}$
2	1.0	0	0	0	0	2	$\frac{1}{6}$	$\frac{1}{6}$	$\frac{1}{6}$	$\frac{1}{6}$	$\frac{1}{6}$	$\frac{1}{6}$
3	−.4	.4	−.1	.1	0	3	$\frac{1}{6}$	$\frac{1}{6}$	$\frac{1}{6}$	$\frac{1}{6}$	$\frac{1}{6}$	$\frac{1}{6}$
4	.1	.2	.3	−.2	−.2	4	$\frac{1}{6}$	$\frac{1}{6}$	$\frac{1}{6}$	$\frac{1}{6}$	$\frac{1}{6}$	$\frac{1}{6}$
5	.2	.2	−.2	−.2	.2	5	$\frac{1}{6}$	$\frac{1}{6}$	$\frac{1}{6}$	$\frac{1}{6}$	$\frac{1}{6}$	$\frac{1}{6}$
6	.4	.1	.15	.3	.05							

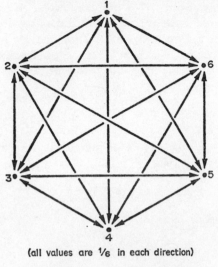

(all values are ⅙ in each direction)

(a) Relations among actors (= XC)

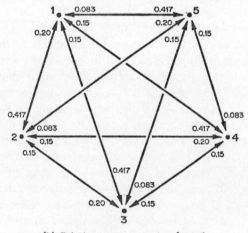

(b) Relations among events (= CX)

Fig. 4.1

As Figure 4.1 shows, in this special case, each legislator has equal amounts of direct control over every other actor. However, different events have different amounts of direct dominance over other events. The dominance of each event in a simple legislature can, as Figure 4.1 shows, be expressed as a general property, independent of the object event. In this case, event 1 has a dominance of .417 over all others; event 2 has a dominance of .2, events 3 and 4 have dominance of .15, and event 5 has a dominance of .083. Since these numbers sum to 1.0, it is a reasonable conjecture that the value of each event is equal to this same quantity. This turns out to be the case, as solution of the equilibrium equation, eqn. 4.9 shows:

$$v_i = \sum_j \sum_k v_k c_{kj} x_{ji} \tag{4.9}$$

where $\sum_k v_k c_{kj} = r_j$, the power of individual j. Since $c_{kj} = \frac{1}{6}$ for all events k and actors j, then

$$r_j = \frac{1}{6} \sum_k v_k = \frac{1}{6}.$$

This simplifies eqn. 4.9 to

$$v_i = \sum_j r_j x_{ji} = \frac{1}{6} \sum_j x_{ji},$$

so that the value of event i is merely $\frac{1}{6}$ times the sum of the interests of all actors in that event.

The output of a computer program which solves the equilibrium equations and calculates the measures discussed in the preceding section is shown in the appendix to this chapter. In addition to the value of events and power of actors, this output shows first, the distribution of final control, showing actor 2, for example, with the greatest amount of control over the event with highest value, event 1. Next it shows the probability of a positive outcome for each event, showing that events 1 and 2 have a probability greater than 0.5 of passing, events 3 and 5 have a probability equal to 0.5, and event 4 has a probability less than 0.5. It shows the effect of each actor's actions on each other actor's expected realization of interests, that is, the externalities of each actor's action for each other actor. In this case it shows that because of equally distributed control, the externality from actor A to B is equal to that from B to A. The sum of these increments and decrements, added to 0.5, gives the next output, which is the expected value of the collectivity to each actor, the proportion of his interests that he can expect to be realized. The expected value is 0.5 if the collectivity is neutral toward his interests, realizing exactly half of them. In this case, the collectivity has an expected value greater than 0.5 for all actors except actor 1, whose interests were opposed to the majority on the two most important events, 1 and 2.

The expected realization of interests, weighted by each actor's power (identical in this case) shows the degree to which there is consensus of important people on important events. Again, the base value of this is 0.5, when there is no consensus, and all interests are precisely balanced. The next result, the 'directed power' of the collectivity on each event, incorporates both the value of the event and the coincidence or opposition of direction of interests on it. It shows that on events 2 and 5, opposing interests completely cancel each other (which in this case of equal power of actors, could be seen in the original interest matrix), and that the greatest unopposed power exists for event 1.

Finally, the total external power of the collectivity shows just how much unopposed power, aggregated over all events, there is in this collectivity. If it were 1, the collectivity would be totally united; if 0, it would be totally divided. In this case, the value, .267, shows that the collectivity is more divided than united, but not totally divided.

One of the results of this example, the increment in expected realization of interests of an actor from his own actions (the main diagonal of the matrix shown in the computer output), suggests that the actor's concentration of interests on one or a few events leads him to be able to realize a greater fraction of his interests through the vote market than a dispersed set of interests does, as indicated in the discussion of eqn. 4.4. Actor 2, whose interests are totally concentrated on event 1, realizes .2 of his interests through his actions, while the others range from .09 to .13—not, however, perfectly correlated to the degree of concentration of interests.

Inspection of eqn. 4.4 shows that this increment to his interest-realization from his actions is proportional to the sum of squares of his interests in each event, divided by the value of that event. In effect, this means that his realization of interests through his actions will be greatest when his interests are highly concentrated on unimportant events. In this case, the effect of this can be seen in comparing the interest realization, through their own actions, of different actors. Actors 1 and 6 have exactly the same distribution of interests, except that actor 1 has a greater concentration on event 2, with a value of .2, and actor 6 has a greater concentration on event 4, with a value of .15. The result is slightly higher realization of interests through his own action by actor 6 than by 1 (.101 to .090). Actor 4 has less concentration of interests than actor 3, but concentration on less important events, and consequently has a greater realization of interests through his actions than does actor 3 (.131 to .110).

In the next example, the variation of interest-realization through his actions with concentration of interests will be examined more systematically.

Example 2: Realization of interests as a function of their concentration

A more systematic examination of interest-realization through concentration of interests is suggested by the preceding example. The functional dependence of a_{jj} on the interest concentration, independent of r_j and the values of events, v_i, is not easily determined, because r_j and v_i are themselves a function of interest. However, some simplifications are possible. In a perfect market, the prices of particular goods are independent of the actions of any one actor. Thus in a system of the sort under consideration with many actors, the values v would be independent of his distribution of interests, and in particular, independent of their concentration, as measured by their sum of squares. For this reason, his power, r_j, is independent of his distribution of interests, since his power depends only on his control of events and the values of those events. In such a situation, it is possible to examine the dependence of a_{jj} on $\sum_i x_{ji}^2/v_i$, by taking the partial derivative of a_{jj} with respect to this sum. (It is not possible to examine, in a simple fashion, the effect of concentration apart from the values of those events in which the interests are concentrated.) This shows that the rate of change in a_{jj} with respect to this sum is simply equal to $0.5\, r_j$; i.e. half the actor's power.

Through examples, the effect of interest-concentration on interest-realization can be illustrated. In Table 4.2 are shown three matrices of interest distributions for collectivities of size 5, 4, and 3, with 4, 3, and

Table 4.2
Distributions of actors' interests in three collectivities

	Events 1	2	3	4	$\sum_i x_{ji}^2$
1	.3	.3	.3	.1	
2	.3	.3	.1	.3	
3	.3	.1	.3	.3	
4	.1	.3	.3	.3	
5	1	0	0	0	1.00
5	.8	.2	0	0	.68
5	.5	.5	0	0	.50
5	.6	.3732	.0268	0	.50
5	.4	.4	.2	0	.34
5	.25	.25	.25	.25	.25

	Events 1	2	3	$\sum_i x_{ji}^2$
1	.4	.4	.2	
2	.4	.2	.4	
3	.2	.4	.4	
4	1	0	0	1.00
4	.9	.1	0	.82
4	.8	.2	0	.68
4	.5	.5	0	.50
4	.33	.33	.33	.33

	Events 1	2	$\sum_i x_{ji}^2$
1	.6	.4	
2	.4	.6	
3	1	0	1.00
3	.9	.1	.82
3	.8	.2	.68
3	.7	.3	.58
3	.5	.5	.50

2 events respectively. In each, the interests of all actors but the last have the same distribution, with only a permutation of the events. The last actor will successively have the interest distributions shown in the lower half of the table. Beside these interest distributions is shown the sum of squares of interests. In each of these collectivities, control is assumed to be equally distributed over all actors for all events. This means that power is the same for all actors, 0.2 in the first case, 0.25 in the second, and 0.333 in the third.

Because of the asymmetric distribution of interests of the last actor in each case, the values are not identical for all issues. If they were, the values of all events in the first case would be 0.25, in the second 0.33, and in the third 0.50. If that were the case, then the realization of interests from own action, a_{jj}, could be written as a function of $\sum x_{ji}^2$:

$$a_{jj} = 0.5 \times \frac{.2}{.25} \sum x_{ji}^2 \quad \text{(five actors, four events)}$$

$$= 0.5 \times \frac{.25}{.33} \sum x_{ji}^2 \quad \text{(four actors, three events)}$$

$$= 0.5 \times \frac{.33}{.50} \sum x_{ji}^2 \quad \text{(three actors, two events)}$$

However, the concentration of interests of the last actor increases (in all cases except the final row in each table) the values of those events which his interests are concentrated on. Consequently, the actual values of a_{jj} for the last actor in these examples will be below these, except for the final row of the table. Table 4.3 shows the values

Table 4.3
Increments to expected realization of interests as a function of concentration of interests, in three collectivities

Concentration of interests, $\sum_i x_{ji}^2$	Five actors, four events	Four actors, three events	Three actors, two events
1.00	.250	.250	.250
.82		.218	.218
.68	.194	.194	.194
.58			.179
.50 (.5, .5, 0, 0)	.167	.167	.167
.50 (.6, .3732, .0268, 0)	.164		
.34	.131		
.33		.125	
.25	.100		

of a_{jj} for each value of $\sum x_{ji}^2$ in the above examples, and Figure 4.2 shows these graphically. The three straight lines show the values of a_{jj} as a function of $\sum x_{ji}^2$ when values of all events are equal, for the five actor four event case, the four actor three event case, and the three actor two event case. In the actual examples shown in Table 4.3, values of a_{jj} fall on the same line for the three different collectivities, though this is a consequence of the particular distribution of values that results in these cases.

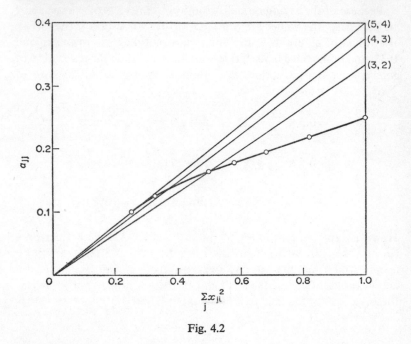

Fig. 4.2

In each of the three collectivities, the final value of a_{jj} results from a flat distribution of interests for the last actor, making values of all events the same. As a result, in Figure 4.2, the point falls on the equal-value line.

In one case, in the five actor four event collectivity, two distributions of interests, both giving a sum of squares of 0.50, are shown. The second produces values that are slightly more skewed in the direction of the concentration of interests of that actor, and thus allows him to realize slightly less of his interests (.164 to .167).

This general effect of concentration of interests on realization of interests shows that beyond an actor's power in a collectivity, his ability to satisfy his interests in it depends on the narrowness of focus of those interests. This becomes even clearer in the interpretation of the model discussed in the preceding chapter, where the value x_{ji} was interpreted as the proportion of persons with control pattern of type j who had sole interests in event i. In this interpretation, then the concentration of interests on event i represents a parallelism of different persons' maximization behaviour. Since the actions of each person in the system impose positive or negative externalities on others, this means (in this interpretation) that all persons represented by control pattern j are creating positive externalities for each other, i.e. reinforcing each others' actions.

Example 3: Paying the cost of a public facility

One of the classical problems of public finance, and of public goods generally, is the 'problem of paying the cost of a public good', or the 'free-rider problem'. The examination of this problem by use of the present model will show its application to cases in which the actions are not 'collective' at all, but under the control of a single actor.

The free-rider problem can be stated as follows: suppose there is a facility or a service which, if supplied by one individual, is available to all, such as a park or playground. Then unless the enjoyment one individual can receive from this facility or service is sufficient to outweigh the costs of supplying it, no one will supply it, even though it would be to everyone's benefit to do so, if costs could be appropriately shared. In sharing the costs, however, each person is motivated to be a 'free rider', to enjoy the benefits without paying his share of the costs.

Consider a simple example of four actors, identical in resources and tastes, who propose to construct a park which costs £24. Each of them would contribute £6. Each estimates to himself that it is worth £8 to him to have the park. Each could construct a park $\frac{1}{4}$ as large for his own use, but each estimates that the value of a park $\frac{1}{4}$ as large would only be $\frac{1}{4}$ as great. That is, the marginal utility of an added unit for the park is constant. Thus if he were able only to construct a park for his own use, it would cost him £6, but only be worth £2 to him. Or if one person constructed a full-sized park, it would cost him £24, and he would experience benefits worth only £8 to him. On the other hand, with a park for all four, the cost to him remains £6, and the value to him is $4 \times £2$, or £8.

If there is nothing to induce each to pay his share of the costs, he sees that the others can construct a park which costs them each £6 and gives each benefits worth £6, or a park which costs each £8 and gives each benefits worth £8. Since the costs exactly equal the benefits, they may or may not build the park. He might try to contribute just enough to make them see a benefit to building the park, so he could receive its benefits at a very small cost. If, however, there are only two actions available to each actor, to contribute £6 or nothing, then the matrices of interest and control are as in Table 4.4 below.

Table 4.4

Interests in and control over actions in supplying a public facility worth £2 per unit to each, and costing £6 per unit

	Events					Actors			
	1	2	3	4		1	2	3	4
Actors 1	−.4	.2	.2	.2	Events 1	1	0	0	0
2	.2	−.4	.2	.2	2	0	1	0	0
3	.2	.2	−.4	.2	3	0	0	1	0
4	.2	.2	.2	−.4	4	0	0	0	1
	Interests					*Control*			

Each has full control over his own action. Each sees £2 benefit to him for each quarter of the park that is built, and a cost of £6 to him for building his quarter. This means that his quarter gives him a net loss of £4, and the others a gain of £2. His total interests are £10 (the sum of absolute values of −4, 2, 2, 2), representing a range from a loss of £4, if he builds and no one else does, to a gain of £6, if they build and he does not. Normalizing to give relative interests gives −.4, .2, .2, .2.

As the matrices show, each actor finds it not to his interest to carry out the one action he has full control over. If the system stands as it is, then the park will not be built.

However, if there are negotiations, each actor finds it to his interest to carry out his action if he can make his contingent on others doing so as well. In a system where this can be achieved, the exchange will be carried out so that the park will be built.

Olson (1965), in an examination of the problem of paying the cost of a public facility, points out that empirically, there is a difference between large and small groups in the degree to which public goods are provided. He points out that in small groups, social psychological pressure can operate to induce individuals to pay their share, while in large groups, such informal pressure cannot be used as effectively. In effect, in terms of the present model, this means that the 'large group' is one so large that a market for exchange of control over actions does not operate, or operates very poorly, while a 'small group' is one in which such a market does operate. This is, of course, related to the fact of enforcement: one or two persons, in a small group, can induce another to live up to his part of the bargain by threatening to withhold their own contributions, simply because their contributions are important if he is to receive his benefits. In the present example, if one other member, say number 2, withholds his contribution, the value of the joint enterprise for number 1 falls to zero.

The solution given by the model to this case, given in appendix p. 172, shows each actor exchanging .6 of the control over his action, in return for .2 of control over the action of each other actor. The control matrix with 1's in the main diagonal means that $r_j = \sum_i v_i c_{ij}$ reduces to $r_j = v_j$. By symmetry, all v_i are equal, so $r_j = v_j = .25$ for all j. Thus $c_{ij}^* = x_{ji}(r_j/v_i) = x_{ji}$. Thus the matrix of final control is identical to the interest matrix. This means that each action will be carried out with probability .6. The reasoning above, however, indicated that if there is to be a social optimum, each action would be carried out with probability 1.0. In that reasoning, an implicit social organization beyond the market was assumed: an implicit pact to make one's action contingent on that of all the others, as described earlier, requires a higher level of social organization than pairwise exchange. It should be noted that the simple principle of individual maximization (rather than proportional allocation) applied here would not lead to a social optimum. Each individual would maintain control over his own action, which compared to any two-party transactions he could make, maximizes his interest realization.[1]

Olson argues that when one party in a public-good or free-rider problem is much larger than the others, it is more likely to be to his benefit to carry out the action. Heuristically, this results from the fact that if one party is larger, equivalent in costs and benefits to two of the others, the external economies that occur in public goods problems are internalized. In the present case, this may be seen by assuming that the first and second actors merge, forming one who is twice as large as before. The cost to the new actor would be £12 instead of £6 and the benefits of his own action would be £8 instead of £2 (£2 for each £6 cost to each of the two previous actors, or £2 × 2 × 2 = £8).

[1] The fact that neither of the individualist actions, maximization or proportional allocation of resources, gives the social optimum indicates what a difficult problem of social organization these public goods situations pose. It is in the nature of the problem that only when the possible externalities are taken into consideration can the social optimum be achieved.

His benefits are, for each of the others' actions, £4. Consequently, his interests are equally divided among the three actions, and the others' interests reflect the combination of these two actors. In effect, rows and columns of the interest and control matrices are collapsed. Below is shown the collapsed interest matrix.

$$
\begin{array}{ccc}
-.333 & .333 & .333 \\
.4 & -.4 & .2 \\
.4 & .2 & -.4
\end{array}
$$

The model shows (see Example 3.2 in the appendix, pp. 173–174) that the probability that action 1 will be taken is higher than the probability that actions 2 or 3 will be taken (.667 to .60). It shows also that the expected value of the collectivity is greater for actors 2 and 3 than for actor 1 (.547 to .511)—he contributes more to them than they do to him. This is true even though the power of 1 is greater than 2 or 3 (but only slightly: .37 to .31). This greater likelihood of the large actor carrying out the action than the smaller ones, and the greater gain they receive from the collectivity, is what Olson describes as the 'exploitation of the large by the small'. Everyone gains more from the actions of the large actor. His gain makes him likely to act. The gain to the small actors makes them willing to let him do it, and leads them to push him to do so. For example, they find it to their interest to gain more control over his action than the action of another small actor. (In this case, each small actor gains one-third control of the large actor's action, but only .2 control of the other small actor's action.)

If we carry this size disparity one step further, collapsing the large actor, 1, with a small actor, then the large actor has costs of $3 \times £6$, and benefits of £2 to each of the three sub-actors for each of the three actions; or costs of $3 \times £6 = £18$, and benefits of $£2 \times 3 \times 3 = £18$. His costs and benefits from his own action are identical, making him indifferent between constructing his three-quarters of the park alone, and not doing so. All his gains or losses arise from the actions of actor 2. The interest matrix becomes:

$$
\begin{array}{cc}
0 & 1 \\
.6 & -.4
\end{array}
$$

The solution of the model indicates that the small actor in effect controls the situation. His power is almost twice as great as that of the large actor (.625 to .375), because the large actor is totally interested in his action, being indifferent to his own. The large actor's action will be carried out with probability 1, and the small actor's only with probability 0.6. The expected value of the collectivity is only .6 to the large, and .76 to the small.[2]

Another kind of question can be asked about this public goods example. The common solution to the free rider problem is to appoint a tax collector, or otherwise to create an organization which will enforce the contributions of each. One way in which this is frequently carried out in society is to impose fines that are slightly greater than the contribution, so that it is to each actor's interest to pay the contribution or the tax, rather than to pay the fine. The tax collector has an interest in collecting the tax, and the others have an interest in not paying the tax, but also in avoiding the fine.

In the present example, this enforcement mechanism may be introduced by adding a fifth actor to the original four. The fifth actor's interests are equally divided among the four events 1–4, the contributions of actors 1–4. His interests are in their payment of taxes. There are four new events, 6, 7, 8, 9, representing the imposition of £6 fines on each actor for failing to contribute. (The £6 fine represents a loss of £2 of benefits compared to making the contribution through action 1, since the £6 contribution there brought him a £2 benefit.) For each of the original four actors, the interests become: −£4 for carrying out

[2] This example might appear to suggest the use of a modified model in which x_{ji} was not relative interest of event i for actor j, but was 'absolute interest', in the sense of some kind of transferable utility. That is, a benefit of £6 to a large actor is represented by a relative interest of 1.0, while a benefit of £6 to an actor only one-third as large is represented by a relative interest of only 0.6. However, the appropriate modification is not to attempt to put these interests on the same scale of transferable utility, but to embed these actions in the context of the larger set of actions in which the actor is engaged. If this were done, then x_{12} would be scaled down to its value relative to the total resources of actor 1, and x_{21} would be scaled to its value relative to the total resources of actor 2. It is not clear, however, how this may be done compactly. Perhaps it could be done through adding a third and fourth actions, over which 1 and 2 had total control respectively, and in which only 1 and 2 had interests respectively, representing the other actions in which 1 and 2 were engaged. The interest matrix might be, if the total resources of actor 1 were £60, and those of actor 2 were £20:

$$\begin{matrix} 0 & .1 & .9 & 0 \\ .3 & -.2 & 0 & .5 \end{matrix}$$

Solution of this system shows that the actor (number 1) who is three times as large as the other (number 2) has a power of .75, compared to .25 for the other, and has three times the control over 2 that 2 has over him (.3 to .1). However, it is still the case that the large actor's contribution will be made with certainty, and the small actor's only with probability .6. Also, if we subtract from each actor's power the value associated with his private goods (event 3 over which actor 1 has total control and in which he has sole interest, and event 4 which is analogous for actor 2), then the remaining power associated with the two contributions to the public good is only .075 for the large actor, and .125 for the small. Thus this formulation gives essentially the same result as the original one.

his own contribution, +£2 for each of the others, and −£6 for imposition of the fine for non-payment of taxes. The matrices of control and interest can be constructed from this description.

Solution of the model shows, in Table 4.5, that each of the first four actors has exchanged three-eighths of his control over his contribution to the fifth actor in return for full control over the fine. The result is that the fines have zero probability of being levied, and the contributions have increased probability (.75) of being made.

Table 4.5
Example 3: Final directed control by actor i of event j

−.25	.125	.125	.125	−1	0	0	0
.125	−.25	.125	.125	0	−1	0	0
.125	.125	−.25	.125	0	0	−1	0
.125	.125	.125	−.25	0	0	0	−1
.375	.375	.375	.375	0	0	0	0

It may be, however, that the formulation of this model to reflect the introduction of an enforcement mechanism is not an appropriate one. It does not link the two events, non-payment of contributions and fines (e.g. events 1 and 5) directly together, but only through the structure of interest and control. Thus there is not direct conditionality of the outcome of event 5 upon the outcome of event 1. There is no way in the model of introducing such full or partial conditionality except through combining the events into one. If that is done in the present case, the event representing payment of the contribution would have a positive benefit of £2, instead of the cost of £4, with a new implicit baseline, which is £6 below his starting point, rather than at his starting point. In this formulation, if non-payment and fine were inextricably bound, all contributions would be made with certainty, since there are no interests opposed to their being made.

Example 4: Formation of a constitution
In the present theory, the two elements that are assumed to be given are the structure of 'constitutional control' over events, and the structure of interests. Sometimes constitutional control is determined by the physical structure of the situation; sometimes by a set of informal norms or customs, and sometimes by a formalized constitution, which defines the structure of decision-making for the collectivity. However, it is useful, also, to ask just what distribution of power in a collectivity will best realize the interests of the members. It need not be, as might be assumed at the outset, one vote for each person. To use

an example: in the decision-making of an academic department in a university, it is sometimes argued by students who favour 'participatory democracy' that there should be equal voting rights of students and faculty. Often, however, the greater numbers of students than of faculty make this seem 'unreasonable', and the argument is made instead that the students should have a number of votes equal to those of the faculty. This explicitly weights each student's vote as n_1/n_2 of that of a faculty member, where there are n_1 faculty members and n_2 students, thus imposing an inequality in which each faculty member's vote has the weight of n_2/n_1 student votes. There is, however, little theoretical justification for this degree of inequality rather than some other, or rather than full equality.

In such a collectivity, the principal power that each individual has *de facto* is that of continuing as a member of the collectivity, or leaving it. If there are m potential or existing members of the potential or existing collectivity, then there are m events, with the ith actor having full control over the ith event, in which a positive outcome is his becoming or continuing as a member of the collectivity, and the negative outcome is his leaving it.

Each actor has a particular degree of interest in each other actor's being a member of the collectivity. For example, it is likely that a student will have a greater interest in a given faculty member's remaining as a collectivity member than in a given student's remaining. His interest, then, in any collective decision, is not merely to realize his desired outcome on that decision, but to realize an outcome that will satisfy those other actors whose continuance in the collectivity is of most importance to him.

Two voting situations for the collective decisions in question must be distinguished. One is a situation in which there is full discussion and full interchange of views, so that each actor knows the position of each other actor, and the importance of the outcome to each other actor. The second is a situation in which there is no prior discussion, and each actor knows only his own position. In both cases, votes would be taken by secret ballot. Actual decisions in collectivities are not at either of these extremes; the smaller the collectivity, the more likely it is to be closer to the full interchange extreme. In both voting situations, each actor will be voting for that outcome which better realizes his interests. In the second, these interests are only the interests directly affected by the decision at hand. In the first, however, these interests include his interests in the satisfaction of other actors whose continuation in the collectivity is important to him. Thus in the first, he may not vote for the outcome he desires, if he sees that the opposing outcome is desired by, and important to, other actors whose continued presence is important to him, making that outcome more in his long-term interests. Something like this may often be observed in small, closely knit groups, in which persons often appear to strongly take into account in their voting the interests of others that are important to them. Even in groups that are less closely knit, such as an academic department in which students vote on an issue, the outcome of the students' vote sometimes seems to reflect the interests of faculty members, or some faculty members, more than their own directly desired outcome.

If voting situations involve no interchange, the only way an actor can ensure that his long-term interests are satisfied is to create a constitution in which the interests of others that he would take into account after full interchange (in pursuit of his own long-term interests) are taken into account through differential amounts of control of the collective decision, such as different numbers of votes. Heuristically, he wants those members whose membership in the collectivity is important to him to have more votes in a decision than those whose membership is less important to him.

Such a constitution could be formed through this procedure: each individual allocates his interest by indicating that fraction of it which is associated with each other member's continuance in the collectivity. He cannot allocate any of his interest to himself; he is in effect indicating the relative importance to him of each other member's continuation in the collectivity. An interest matrix is formed in which the actors are the potential members of the collectivity, and the events are the membership of each actor in the collectivity. The interests as indicated by each individual are the entries in the interest matrix. A control matrix is formed, with each actor having complete control of the event representing his remaining in (or joining) the collectivity, i.e. a matrix with 1's in the main diagonal. In effect, each actor is deciding, through his allocation of interests, how he allocates his autonomy to the collectivity, by allocating it to the different individuals who make it up, according to their importance to him. His importance to the other members of the collectivity will determine the absolute amount of power that he is thereby distributing. An interest matrix in a collectivity of six members might look like that in Table 4.6.

Table 4.6

Interests of each actor in a six-member collectivity in the membership of each other member in the collectivity

		Events					
		1	2	3	4	5	6
	1	0	.4	.3	.2	0	.1
	2	.7	0	.3	0	0	0
Actors	3	.6	.2	0	0	.1	.1
	4	.5	.1	0	0	.1	.3
	5	.7	0	.2	.1	0	0
	6	.6	0	0	.2	.2	0

In this collectivity, actors 2–6 are most interested in the continuance of actor 1 as a member of the collectivity, with different ones among them having most interest in different others. Actors 2 and 3 are most interested in each other's presence, and actors 4 and 6 are associated also.

The solution of this system shows that the proportion of control that each actor should have is .38, .20, .18, .10, .05, .09, rounded to nearest hundredth. Actor 1 should have, in order to satisfy the interests of all members of the collectivity, about eight times the number of votes that actor 5 has.[3] Consequently, a constitution in a collectivity which does not have discussion and interchange of views prior to voting should formally incorporate this inequity if the interests of all members are to be realized. If the collectivity does have full discussion and interchange, then the constitution should give each member a single vote—a distribution which should lead to the same result.

The matrix of final directed control shown in Table 4.7 is useful to examine in this case. It shows the degree to which each actor exercises control, in the mutual compact to form or continue the collectivity, over the others' decisions to join (disregarding for the moment negative signs). Actor 1, who is most powerful, exercises the major control of the decisions to join of actors 2, 3, and 4, and a large fraction of that over 6, through his decision to join. He has no interest in, and thus does not exercise any control over, actor 5's decision. In turn, actors 2 and

[3] The term 'satisfy the interests' rather than 'maximize the interests' is used here because of the ambiguity surrounding the proportional allocation of resources, as discussed in the preceding chapter. Short of the resolution of that ambiguity, these systems cannot be regarded as maximizing interests. If, however, the proportional allocation of interests is regarded, as suggested in one interpretation in Chapter 3, as the proportion of time that the actor regards a given event as most important, then the present model does maximize interests.

3 exercise most control over actor 1's joining, since they are powerful and interested in his joining. Actors 2 and 3, who have relatively strong interests in one another, exercise strong control over each other's joining, as is also true for actors 4 and 6. Actor 3, although he has only half as much interest in 6's joining as in 2's joining, exercises even more control over 6's joining than over 2's, because there is so little interest of anyone else in 6's joining. (This of course depends on the assumptions, shown in Table 4.6, that each actor has no interest in his own membership. See footnote 4 below for a relaxation of that assumption.)

A variant in this 'constitution-constructing' procedure can be achieved by allowing each individual to write down not just his relative interest in having each other individual as a member of the collectivity, but also his interest in having any individuals out of the group. Here

Table 4.7
Example 4: Final directed control by actor *i* of event *j*

0	.767	.625	.779	0	.444
.365	0	.326	0	0	0
.288	.184	0	0	−.404	.213
.128	.049	0	0	−.216	.342
.083	0	.049	.046	0	0
.135	0	0	.175	−.379	0

he writes, not merely the fraction of interest that he has in each other actor, but includes also a negative sign if he has a quantity of interest in another actor's not being a member of the group.

In the example for which results are shown in Table 4.7, negative signs were included. In particular, all actors who had an interest in actor 5's joining the group were opposed to it. In the final control over events, these actors, 3, 4, and 6, have full control of 5's membership (actors 1 and 2 being uninterested), and unanimously oppose it. In effect, actor 5 has given over his control of the decision to stay or leave to actors 3, 4, and 6 in order to ensure that actor 1, and to a slight extent, actors 3 and 4, join. But he is rejected by 3, 4, and 6, and thus the group, with probability 1.0.

In such a case, after elimination of such potential but unsuccessful actors, a new solution should be obtained, in order to determine the appropriate constitutional power. For if the eliminated actor had strong interests in favour of one member, then this would result in that member having too much power, relative to the interests of those actors who in fact would comprise the system.

Example 5: Patterns of influence in informal groups

When a group's decision process includes a full discussion and interchange of views, so that each person in the group knows the position and importance of the event to each other person, then each can modify his own vote so that the interests of the other actors enter. In such a collectivity, we must take the constitution, which establishes the number of votes held by each member, as given. Then, given this, for example one vote per person, it is possible to examine the outcome of a decision and the degree of informal influence that each member will have over each other member. One interesting result of this examination is that the distribution of formal voting power has less effect on the outcome in a case like this than in one where there is not full informal discussion and interchange of views.

The problem can be formulated by adding to the previous interest matrix in Example 4 another column and to the control matrix another row, representing the collective action. The row in the control matrix consists of control of one sixth by each actor; and the column in the interest matrix shows the relative interest that each has in this decision, compared to his interest in each other actor's remaining in the collectivity. (Interests directed toward actor 5 have been changed in this matrix to positive, to allow him to remain a member of the group.) In this case, I will assume that the interest in the collective action (event 7) is .2, −.2, −.2, .2, .2, −.2, for actors 1 to 6 respectively. This means that for each of the actors, the collective action is only one-quarter as important as the total importance of the group membership of the five actors other than himself. Results are shown in the appendix, page 175.

The probability of positive outcome in this case is not .5, as would be expected from the equal votes and equally divided group, but .54, because of the informal influence exerted by actor 1, whose presence is very important to all other members of the group. The outcome would be even more unbalanced except that actors 2 and 3, who together have power about equal to 1, oppose it. The outcome of the vote derives wholly from the relative power of the different members who favour it and oppose it, and that power derives from the interests that others have in their remaining in the group. Actor 1's power in determining the outcome is .35, rather than one-sixth, very nearly what it was in the preceding example of constitution-formation. It is reduced slightly from .38 toward one-sixth, because in this case .2 of the total interest of each group member was in the particular action to be taken, while in the preceding case, all of it was directed toward the other members' presence.[4] The net result of transactions can be seen from the matrix of final directed control of events. For example, actors 4 and 6, on opposing sides, have exchanged about equal amounts of influence (.208 and .228), but both have given up control to actor 1 (obtaining .140 and .153 of the control of his presence) to ensure his satisfaction (and thus continued membership). Thus the influence of members who are 'important' to the group by being important to the members makes its effect felt in the group decision. In a collectivity with full discussion and interchange, but with institutional inequalities in votes, this would presumably be manifested by a non-zero probability that group members would vote the way they knew particular other group members were voting. For example, actor 6, whose control over the decision is shown by the model to be reduced from $(-).16667$ to $(-).10259$, would be expected to have a probability of $(.16667 - .10259)/.16667$, or .384, of voting the way actors 1, 4, and 5 vote, which is positive, since he is influenced by those three.

The effect of changing the formal distribution of voting power in such informal groups with full interchange can be seen by giving different members different numbers of votes. For example, suppose actors 2, 4, and 6 are given two votes, and actors 1, 3, 5 are given one, making nine votes in all. By a counting of formal vote power, this means that the negative side has five votes of the nine, or .55 of the total formal power. However, because of the informal system of influence, the probability of a positive outcome is reduced only from .540 to .533, in the solution given by the theory. When the voting power is switched the other way, so that actors 1, 3, and 5 each have two of the nine votes, this increases the probability of a positive outcome only to .546.

Thus because of the importance of the other actions in the system over which actors have individual control, their actions of remaining

---

[4] This suggests that a modification of the constitution-formation procedure could be carried out, in which each member allocates a certain fraction of his interest to himself, representing the proportion of his interest that would normally be associated with the outcome of a given decision, independent of the continued membership of any of the other actors in the system. This would appear to invite strategy, with each individual reserving to himself all his interest; but as discussed earlier, it is not in his interest to do so, if he is to induce the actors he wants in the group to join it or remain in it.

in or leaving the collectivity, the formal distribution of power in the collective decision is far less important in determining the outcome than the informal structure of interests that leads to a structure of influence.

Example 6: The exchange between representative and constituents
One of the essential processes in a representative democracy is the exchange between a legislator and his constituents. The structure of representative democracy is designed so that the legislator has control over those actions which interest the constituents, through his seat in the legislature, while the constituents have control over the action which interests the legislator, his election to office. Actual representative systems have design defects, as I will illustrate later; but at this point, we may focus attention on the ideal representative system.

To consider only one constituency in that system, we may conceive of the actors as types of voters having particular patterns of interest. In the example to be used in illustration, there are six types of voters, distinguished according to their interests. Types 1 and 2 each constitute one-sixth of the constituency, types 3 and 4 each constitute one-quarter of the constituency, and types 5 and 6 each constitute one-twelfth of the constituency. These fractions represent the fraction of control over the election (event 1 in the example) that each group in the electorate has. This event is the one event that interests the representative.

There are five events of interest to the constituents, and the representative has full control of those. (If the matrices of control and interests covered the full system, the representative would have only $1/n$th of the control of those events, where n is the size of the legislature. Nothing is lost, however, by reducing the system to the one constituency, for there can be no transactions across constituencies, since electors in constituency A have no control over the event that interests the representative in constituency B.) The matrices of interest and control in this example are as shown in Table 4.8.

In each pair of constituent types with equal constituency power, one has highly concentrated interests, and the other highly dispersed interests. Results from the solution for this example are shown in Table 4.9. The matrix of final control shows that the representative has gained full control over the election, and in return various constituent types have gained control of the decisions in the legislature. The group represented by actor 2, with one-sixth of the electorate,

Table 4.8

Interest and control of representative (actor I) and groups of constituents (actors 2–7) over election of representative (event I) and actions of legislature (events 2–6)

			Events								Actors					
		1	2	3	4	5	6			1	2	3	4	5	6	7
	1	1	0	0	0	0	0		1	0	$\frac{1}{6}$	$\frac{1}{6}$	$\frac{1}{4}$	$\frac{1}{4}$	$\frac{1}{12}$	$\frac{1}{12}$
	2	0	−.8	−.1	0	.1	0		2	1	0	0	0	0	0	0
	3	0	.2	−.2	.2	.2	.2	Events	3	1	0	0	0	0	0	0
Actors	4	0	0	.1	0	−.1	.8		4	1	0	0	0	0	0	0
	5	0	.2	.2	.2	−.2	.2		5	1	0	0	0	0	0	0
	6	0	0	.1	.8	.1	0		6	1	0	0	0	0	0	0
	7	0	.2	−.2	.2	.2	.2									

Interest	Control

has gained over half the control of event 2; and the group represented by actor 4, with one-quarter of the electorate, has gained over half the control of event 6. Those constituency groups with dispersed interests have gained smaller proportions of control over a wider range of issues. The amount of final control over an event in this case depends on the constituency's size, on its degree of interest in the event, and on the amount of competition for control of the event, which determines that event's value or price.

Table 4.9
Results for Example 6

Value of each event

.5	.117	.075	.083	.075	.150

Power of each actor

.5	.083	.083	.125	.125	.042	.042

Final directed control by actor I of event J

I	0	0	0	0	0
0	−.571	−.111	0	.111	0
0	.143	−.222	.200	.222	.111
0	0	.167	0	−.167	.667
0	.214	.333	.300	−.333	.167
0	0	.056	.400	.056	0
0	.071	−.111	.100	.111	.056

Probability of positive outcome of event J

I	.429	.556	I	.500	I

Expected value of collectivity to actor J

I	.552	.675	.906	.697	.906	.675

Directed power of collectivity on event J

.5	−.017	.008	.083	0	.15

The direction of interests of each constituent type in each event is included in this example. In one event, 5, constituency types represented by actors 4 and 5 are opposed to a positive outcome, and cancel out completely the positive interests of actors 2, 3, 6, 7. The probability of a positive outcome, which in this case may be interpreted as the proportion of the constituent pressure on a legislator toward a positive outcome, is in this case .5. Also the directed power of the collectivity on this event is zero, showing the balance. In two other events, event 2 and event 3, there is a near cancellation of interests, making the directed power of the collectivity very small, much smaller than the value of these events. For events 4 and 6, there is consensus of direction of interests in the constituency, so that the power the constituency is able to exercise on these issues is equal to the value of those events to the constituency. In effect, this means that the resulting interests of the representative, which he must pursue in the legislature, are primarily on events 4 and 6. Although his constituents have strong interests in other events as well, these interests largely cancel each other out.

The vector of directed power of the collectivity gives (excluding event 1, the election) the relative sizes of interests for the representative to pursue in the legislature. This vector, scaled up so that the absolute values scale to 1.0, would constitute the vector of interests of the representative in the legislature, in so far as his votes are totally dependent on constituents' interests. In this example, we have assumed that they are, assuming that his total interests were in election, and he saw his constituents having complete control over that event.

An additional result shown by this example is the effect of concentration of interests on an actor's ability to realize his interests through his efforts. In two of the three pairs of constituency groups with equal power (2 and 3, 4 and 5, 6 and 7), the actor with concentrated interests (4, 6) is able to increment his expected realization of interests more than the actor with dispersed interests. In the other pair, 2 and 3, 3 is able to increment his expected realization of interests more because his interests (in events 4 and 6) are allied with those of others.

Example 7: A parliamentary system

In a parliamentary system with single-member constituencies, in which the winning party controls the parliament and organizes the government, the party exercises a larger portion of control over the representatives' election. (In the above example, there was assumed zero party control.) The party is able to determine who will be its candidate in the election. Thus a potential candidate is in a different position, with the party exercising a large fraction of control over his election. Since the election consists of two events, the party's nomination of him and the constituency's electing him, and since both must have a positive outcome for him to be a representative, we can say that he has equal interest in the two events. The party, in turn, is interested in the outcome of the election, for this affects its chances of governing. It is also interested in committing him to vote in the directions it dictates, because it cannot continue to govern without a parliamentary majority on important bills. (The majority voting rule distorts matters here again, by making the party's interest in the outcome high only when the election over all constituencies will be close, and by making the party's pursuit of this interest high only when the election in that constituency is expected to be close. I will neglect these distortions here.) This introduces another actor, the party, into the situation, and the control matrix is changed (see Table 4.10) by adding a row for the event representing the party's nomination of the candidate (event 7), and a column, actor (actor 8) representing the party. The candidate's interests are now equally divided between events 8 and 1 (the nomination and the election), and the party's interests are divided between his election and certain legislative issues. It is not clear *a priori* just how this interest will be divided; but since his utility to the party in any bill depends on the conjunction of two events, his election and his vote on that bill, it is reasonable to suppose that the party's interest is half on the election and half divided among the bills of interest to it. Matrices of interest and control would be like those in Table 4.10. In this case, the party has interest only in events 2 and 5. The other events may be bills principally of interest to persons in this constituency, such as pork barrel legislation. The result of this situation as predicted by the theory is given in Table 4.11. The party and the candidate jointly gain control of the election, and the party gains a large portion of control of events 2 and 5, the two legislative issues it is interested in. The introduction of the party changes greatly the probability of a positive outcome on events 2 and 5, increasing 2 from .43 to .69, and 5 from .5 to .74. The directed power of the collectivity, in effect, the interests to be pursued by the legislator in parliament, changes greatly, with a larger fraction of the power on events 2–7 now going to events 2 and 5. In effect, this legislator has relatively strong interests to pursue on bills 2, 4, 5, and 6, two as commitments to his party, and two as commitments to his constituency. This representative, however, is in an especially fortunate situation, for there is little conflict between the commitments his party demands of him and those his constituents want from him. For all constituency types except the one represented by actor 2, the expected value of these transactions is greater than .5 (the baseline). A different

Table 4.10

Interest and control of candidate for representative (actor 1), party (actor 8) and groups of constituents (actors 2–7) over nomination (event 7) and election (event 1) of candidate, and actions of legislature (events 2–6) in a parliamentary system

		Events									Actors							
		1	2	3	4	5	6	7			1	2	3	4	5	6	7	8
	1	.5	0	0	0	0	0	.5		1	0	$\frac{1}{6}$	$\frac{1}{6}$	$\frac{1}{4}$	$\frac{1}{4}$	$\frac{1}{12}$	$\frac{1}{12}$	0
	2	0	−.8	−.1	0	0	.1	0		2	1	0	0	0	0	0	0	0
	3	0	.2	−.2	.2	.2	.2	0		3	1	0	0	0	0	0	0	0
Actors	4	0	0	.1	0	−.1	.8	0	Events	4	1	0	0	0	0	0	0	0
	5	0	.2	.2	.2	−.2	.2	0		5	1	0	0	0	0	0	0	0
	6	0	0	.1	.8	.1	0	0		6	1	0	0	0	0	0	0	0
	7	0	.2	−.2	.2	.2	.2	0		7	0	0	0	0	0	0	0	1
	8	.5	.3	0	0	.2	0	0										

Interest	Control

Table 4.11
Results for Example

Value of each event
.333	.144	.050	.056	.094	.100	.222

Power of each actor
.444	.056	.056	.083	.083	.028	.028	.222

Final directed control by actor I of event J
.667	0	0	0	0	0	1
0	−.308	−.111	0	.059	0	0
0	.078	−.222	.200	.118	.111	0
0	0	.167	0	−.088	.667	0
0	.115	.333	.300	−.176	.167	0
0	0	.056	.400	.029	0	0
0	.038	−.111	.100	.059	.056	0
.333	.462	0	0	.471	0	0

Probability of positive outcome of event J
1	.692	.556	1	.735	1	1

Expected value of collectivity to actor J
1	.364	.774	.882	.703	.929	.774	.855

Directed power of collectivity on event J
.333	.056	.006	.056	.044	.100	.222

5

structure of interests among constituents would create much greater conflict for him, and lead him not to be able to realize, for party and constituents alike, expected values as high as these.

Example 8: Money as power on legislative issues

In Example 5, it was assumed that candidates for representative were interested only in election to office. However, this is never wholly true, and sometimes far from true. For example, state legislatures in the United States provide very little pay and are not full-time. Lawyers are often motivated to run for office because of the benefits this would bring to their law practices, and other private pecuniary gains it would bring. In many legislatures, the legislators leave office with considerably greater private wealth than they had upon entering office, gained through practices which range from fully legal to fully illegal, but always involving an exchange of some control over political issues for control of some wealth.

This structure of interest and control can be described by the present theory, by adding another event to Example 6. This 'event' is private monetary wealth, which can be described both by the distribution of interests in it, and the distribution of control over it. The simplest assumption to make about the interests are that each actor, including the candidate, has the same fraction of his interests in monetary wealth, assumed here to be .2. The distribution, of control of wealth, however, is skewed, and I will assume it is generally distributed roughly in inverse proportion to the size of the constituency type. The legislator initially has .1 of the total, actor 7 has .45, actor 6 has .225, actor 5 has .1125, actor 4, .05625, and actors 2 and 3, .028125.

It is important to recognize what is assumed in the present application. It is assumed that there is no insulation between political resources and monetary ones—that exchange of one for the other takes place freely, at exchange rates determined by the relative interest of various parties in control over collective actions and in control over private goods. In real systems, there are constraints on this exchange, attempts through legal prohibitions to insulate each from the other, though these constraints are never completely effective.

The solution shows in Table 4.12 the sharp effect of private wealth with free exchange on the power of each actor, giving, for example, .12 of the control to constituency type represented by actor 7, although it is one of the two smallest size constituency types. There is a redistribution of wealth, principally from the constituency types with much wealth and little political power to the representative; but also to a lesser extent to those constituency types with little wealth but a high amount of political power. In fact, all constituency types except those represented by actors 6 and 7, the two wealthiest, have increased their wealth by giving up power over the issues they were interested in, to actors 6 and 7. The wealth of the representative has increased most, even though he had no greater interest in wealth than any other actor, for it is his power in which those with wealth (e.g. actors 6, 7) are primarily interested.

Table 4.12
Results from Example 8

Value of each event

.364	.091	.068	.096	.062	.120	.200

Power of each actor

.456	.066	.066	.102	.113	.075	.120

Final directed control by actor I of event J

1	0	0	0	0	0	.456
0	−.469	−.079	0	.086	0	.066
0	.117	−.157	.110	.173	.089	.066
0	0	.121	0	−.133	.548	.102
0	.201	.269	.188	−.295	.152	.113
0	0	.089	.501	0	.050	.075
0	.213	−.285	.200	.313	.161	.120

Probability of positive outcome of event J

1	.531	.479	1		.572	1

Expected value of collectivity to actor J

1	.588	.780	.913	.750	.958	.780

Expected wtd. realization of interests for all actors = .891
Directed power of collectivity on event J

.364	.006	−.003	.096	.009	.120	.2

Total external power of collectivity = .798

Examining the effect on outcomes of the introduction of wealth with no constraints against exchange, the probability of a positive outcome on event 2 changes (compared to example 6) from .43 to .53; that for event 3 changes from .56 to .48, and that for event 5 changes from .50 to .57. The directed power (i.e. the representative's interests in pursuit of legislation) has changed somewhat, though much of the power is still counterbalanced by opposition within the collectivity. The principal effect has been to strengthen the (positively directed) power on event 4 from .083 to .096. (For direct comparison, these numbers should be renormalized without event 1, in Example 6, or events 1 and 7 in the present example, since they are outside the legislature.)

Example 9: Committee structure in a legislature

Committees in a legislature constitute a way of organizing the affairs of the legislature, so that some members, those on the committee, can give sufficient attention to bills in a given area, and can carry out the preliminary work of the legislature on those bills. At the same time, the existence of committees changes the decision process significantly. It means that each bill must go through two decisions, rather than one: first past the committee, and then the legislature as a whole. It also gives very great power to men who sit on important committees, because of their control of legislation in that area.

If committees were wholly insulated from the rest of the legislature, then the present theory could be applied to two-stage decision processes by in fact applying it independently in two stages. The outcome of the decision would be positive if it were positive in both the first and second stage. However, in actual committees in a legislature, there is a great volume of transactions between committee members and those in the legislature outside the committee, and one of the commodities in these transactions is the legislation that is the province of the committee. The market is not completely open, for committee boundaries constitute some insulation. However, a defect of the present theory is that it must assume either a completely free market or one without exchange, and cannot mirror systems with partially constrained exchange (or exchange with extra costs attached, which would probably be the most appropriate way of conceptualizing constrained exchanges). Consequently, in this example, I will illustrate a collectivity in which decisions are made in two stages, with a completely open market. There are, in this example of a five-actor collectivity, three collective actions to be decided. On the first two, actors 1 and 2 constitute a 2-man committee, with equal power on the committee. On the third, actors 3 and 4 constitute a 2-man committee, with equal power. The decision procedure is that first the bill must pass the committee, and then it must pass the legislature as a whole.

In the case of a perfect market between decision stages, so that the interests of the members of the total collectivity can affect the outcome of the committee decision, it should be possible to elaborate the present theory into a two-stage theory, obtaining a solution for the committee decision within the solution of the larger collectivity decision. I will discuss the way this might be approached as part of the further developments discussed in Chapter 5. However, as a first approach to treating a collectivity with uninsulated committees as a first decision stage, we may incorporate the committee members' control of the committee decisions into the larger collectivity's action. Each bill involves in fact two events: action in the committee, and action in the collectivity as a whole. Each of these actions has .5 of the control of the final outcome, because the final outcome depends equally upon the committee action and the total collectivity's action.

Consequently, when these events are collapsed into one, as they will be in this example, the committee member's control of the action consists of his control of the final action, multiplied by .5, plus his control of the committee's action, multiplied by .5. Thus if actors 1 and 2 each have equal control of the committee action, this constitutes for each $.5 \times .5 = .25$ control of the overall action. In addition, each has one vote of five in the final action, so that his control in the final action is $.2 \times .5 = .1$. Each committee member, then, has $.25 + .1 = .35$ control of each event representing bills which his committee must pass. More generally, his control, if he has equal control in committee i of n_i members, and equal control in the final decision involving all n members, his overall control is $.5(1/n_i) + .5(1/n)$, or $.5(n_i + n)/(n_i n)$. The control matrix in this example of a five-member collectivity with two committees of two members each is given in Table 4.13, together with an arbitrary interest matrix.

Table 4.13

Interest and control for five actors and three issues, in a 2-stage decision process collapsed into one

		Events					Actors				
		1	2	3			1	2	3	4	5
committee 1	1	−.6	.2	−.2		1	.35	.35	.1	.1	.1
Actors	2	.2	−.4	−.4	Events 2	.35	.35	.1	.1	.1
committee 2	3	0	.2	.8		3	.1	.1	.35	.35	.1
	4	.2	−.6	.2							
	5	.2	−.2	.6							

| | Interest | | Control |

The power and value vectors for this example, given in Table 4.14, show that the power of the first two actors is highest, at .25, the power of actors 3 and 4 is next at .20, and the power of actor 5 is least, at .1.

The disparity in power between actors 1 and 2, whose committee has control of two events, and that of actors 3 and 4, whose committee has control of only one, is small in this example because of the large amount of interests in event 3, making it the most important event in the system. (Values of events are .258, .331, and .411 for events 1, 2, and 3 respectively.) Because the two members of committee 1 are opposed on both issues covered by their committee, they act to reduce for one another the expected value of the collective actions: despite their power, the expected value of the collectivity to them is lower than to any of the other three actors. Actor 1, in fact, experiences negative externalities (decrements in expected realization of interests) from each of the other members of the collectivity, because his positions are generally opposed to theirs. Nevertheless, his power, together with concentration of negatively directed interests on event 1, are sufficient to reduce the probability of a positive outcome of that event below .5.

Table 4.14
Example 9: Value of events and power of actors

Value:	.258	.331	.411		
Power:	.247	.247	.203	.203	.10

Example 10: A simple bureaucratic structure

One structure that can be examined with the present theory is that of an ideal-type bureaucracy, in which each actor is interested only in his job, but his job is under the complete control of his direct superior. In one form of such ideal-type bureaucracy, the actor at the very top of the pyramid, with no superior, has an interest wholly in the output of those at the lowest level in the bureaucracy. In such a system, with three levels, a span of control of two at each level, and the output of each lowest-level employee of equal importance to the actor at the top, the interest and control matrices would be as shown in Table 4.15. (Actors are labelled 1–7 from top to bottom, and the event i in which actor j has complete interest (his job) is given a corresponding label, so that actor j has an interest of 1.0 in event i.) The organizational chart looks like this:

Table 4.15
Interest and control matrices in an ideal type bureaucracy

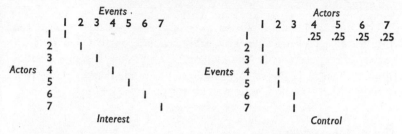

	Events								Actors						
	1	2	3	4	5	6	7		1	2	3	4	5	6	7
1	1							1				.25	.25	.25	.25
2		1						2	1						
3			1					3	1						
Actors 4			1					Events 4		1					
5				1				5		1					
6					1			6			1				
7						1		7			1				
	Interest								Control						

Rational behaviour on the part of each actor in gaining control of events, as described in the theory, would lead each actor to exchange control of those events he controls for the one in which he has interest. The matrix of final control is identical to the interest matrix. It is important to note, however, that such transactions cannot be pairwise, for the event in which actors 2–7 have interest is controlled from above, while the resources each of them has is of interest only to those below. It is at least in part for this reason that a bureaucracy does not spontaneously emerge from social interaction, but requires conscious organization, with 'the organization' acting as the central agency which facilitates and balances these asymmetric transactions. Or, to describe the problem differently, if a computer simulation of an exchange system were constructed, with each individual attempting to make an exchange with others, no exchanges would be carried out in a structure like that of Table 4.15, while such a simulation would lead to exchanges in many of the previous examples.

Results of the theory for this simple bureaucracy are:

(1) The value of control over each event is inversely proportional to the number of actors at that level. Event 1 has a value of $\frac{4}{12}$, events 2 and 3 values of $\frac{2}{12}$ each, and events 4, 5, 6, 7 values of $\frac{1}{12}$ each.

(2) The power of each actor is inversely proportional to the number of actors at that level. Actor 1 has a power of $\frac{4}{12}$, actors 2 and 3 power of $\frac{2}{12}$ each, and actors 4, 5, 6, 7 power of $\frac{1}{12}$ each.

(3) Each actor carries out exchanges so that he achieves full control over the event that interests him, his job, through giving up complete control of the event he initially controls, performance of his task. This means concretely that those at the lowest level and the intermediate level allow their immediate superiors to dictate their activities, in return for being able to dictate their own continued employment, and

the actor at the top allows his supervision activities to be dictated by the aggregate output of those at the lowest level.

This simple ideal-type bureaucracy of course contains none of the 'interesting' structural aspects of real bureaucracies, in which there is a variety of events controlled by each actor, and more than one event of interest to each. It shows, nevertheless, the fundamental transaction around which hierarchical organizations are constructed.

The problem of data

The above examples have shown a variety of applications of the theory of collective decisions. These applications are all based on hypothetical data, and are intended to show some of the possible areas of application of the theory. It is useful, however, to raise the question of how the theory would be used with actual data.

It should be quite clear from some of the examples above that the theory does make predictions, and thus is not empty. If the interest and control matrices are known for a set of collective actions (possibly including those actions controlled by a single individual, but of interest to others in the group), the theory predicts the degree to which each will exercise control over each collective action, as well as the probability of a positive outcome for the collective action. For those collective actions governed by a formal decision rule involving voting, the theory cannot be regarded as wholly appropriate, because of its assumption of a probabilistic decision rule, as discussed in the preceding chapter.

The theory in addition predicts the expected value of the collectivity for each actor, as well as the positive and negative externalities that he experiences as a result of the actions of each other actor. If the theory were amplified to include a process through which satisfaction or dissatisfaction with the collectivity developed as a consequence of the returns it brought each actor, this would give an additional prediction from the theory. Even as it stands, one can hypothesize that satisfaction will be monotonically related to the expected value the actor receives from the collectivity. Similarly, it can be hypothesized that positive and negative sentiments will develop as a consequence of positive and negative externalities experienced at the hand of other actors, quite without an explicit theory about the process through which these sentiments develop. With this hypothesis, the model predicts qualitatively the development of positive and negative sentiments among group members.

In applying the model to real situations, two kinds of data are necessary. One is data on the structure of control over events in the collectivity. Such data are easily obtained in collectivities with formally defined decision rules; but those decision rules ordinarily violate the assumptions of the theory about a probabilistic decision rule. In informally organized collectivities, it is ordinarily possible to isolate those activities over which specific individuals have full control, and beginning from those (as in Example 5) observed in qualitative observation, a matrix of control over events can be written.

The matrix of interests in events is ordinarily not so easily obtained as the matrix of control. In some situations, it is possible, after laying out those events in which it appears that persons other than those with control over them have interest, to ask members of the collectivity to indicate the proportion of their interests associated with each event.

If, however, interests were to be measured following the canons of measurement theory, it would be necessary to infer their values from the transactions that individuals were willing to make, and those they were unwilling to make. Here, the measurement procedures are precisely those used in obtaining interval measurement of utility under risk. Such interval measurement of utilities gives measurement of utility differences (i.e. interests, cf. Chapter 3) that are unique up to a scale transformation, which is all that is necessary for the present theory. (All interests are scaled so that the absolute sum of interests is 1.0 for each individual.)

Thus the present theory may be used with data either in a very precise fashion, in which case the measures are difficult to construct, or more loosely, by accepting individuals' reports of the distribution of their interests among events circumscribed by the collectivity. It should be pointed out, however, that such application with quantitative data has not been carried out.[5] As with classical economic theory or the theory of games, the present theory is a set of logically interrelated concepts which describe behaviour that rational individuals will carry out (subject to caveats discussed in Chapter 3), and as in those theories, should be normatively useful apart from its ability to mirror descriptively the behaviour of actual groups.

[5] An application with some sense of quantitative data has been carried out by Gudmund Hernes (1971) for decision-making in the Norwegian parliament. Another, with somewhat less quantitative data, has been carried out by Sherif El Hakim (1972) for the functioning of a Sub-Saharan village.

Appendix: Chapter 4

Notes on Trad II: Computer program to solve for equilibrium

This computer program calculates the equilibrium power of actors and value of events, and other results described in this chapter. The program is written in Extended Basic, a language used with time-shared computers.[1] The program uses the equilibrium relation from eqn. 4.9,

$$V = VCX$$

where $V = \{v_i\}$, $X = \{x_{ji}\}$, $C = \{c_{ij}\}$, and CX is a stochastic matrix (since C is row stochastic, and X is row stochastic). This can be rewritten as $0 = V(CX - I)$, and then the first $m - 1$ equations rewritten as $0 = V^*(CX - I)^* + Y$, where V^* contains the first $m - 1$ entries of V, each divided by v_m, and $(CX - I)^*$ contains the first $m - 1$ columns and rows of $(CX - I)$, and Y is the last row of $(CX - I)$ (multiplied by 1, which is the last element of V after dividing through by v_m). Thus

$$-Y(CX - I)^{*-1} = V^*$$

thus giving a solution for V^* in terms of the initially given matrices C and X. Then since

$$v_i^* = v_i/v_m, \quad \text{and} \quad \sum_{i=1}^{m-1} v_i^* + 1 = \sum_{i=1}^{m-1} (v_i/v_m) + 1 = 1/v_m$$

the vector V may be found by dividing each element of V^* by

$$\sum_{i=1}^{m-1} v_i^* + 1$$

---

[1] In the form of Basic used for this program, the term 'LET' may be omitted from instructions. For the use of the program with some other systems it will be necessary to reinstate 'LET'.

Solution of these equations for V then allows calculation of the other results described in this chapter. These results are described below in the description of program output.

Input parameters
Read statements   *Data statements*

40 READ N1	805 DATA 2
50 READ N,M,Cl	810 DATA 8,7,0
130 MAT READ C(N,M)	815 DATA (see program listing)
170 MAT READ X(M,N)	820 DATA (see program listing)
	825 ——— (repeat of 810–820 for new problem)

N1 = number of separate problems to be analysed in current run
M = number of actors
N = number of events
Cl: If Cl $\neq$ 1, control matrix is read via statement 50 and correspond-ing data statements. If Cl = 1, control is assumed to be identical for all actors, for all events, and is calculated in program (in statements 770, 775).
C(N,M): matrix of constitutional control, read in as C(1,1), C(1,2) …, C(1,m), …, C(n,m).
X(M,N): matrix of *signed* interests, read in as $X(1,1)$, $X(1,2)$, …, $X(1,n)$, …, $X(m,n)$. (These are labelled y_{ji} in Chapter 3, with $X_{ji} = |y_{ji}|$.)
Statements 95–245 in appended program are for the purpose of setting defining matrices, reading in data, testing that row totals of C and X matrices equal 1.0, and printing out C* and X.

Outputs of program
(Refer to Example 1 for example of output.)
Constitutional control by actor i of event j (statements 220–230). This is matrix C', i.e. C transformed so that actors are represented by rows. It is directly printed out from input.
Directed interest of actor i in event j (statements 240–245). This is matrix of directed interests including both sign of interest, sgn(y_{ji}), and absolute value x_{ji} directly printed out from input.
Control of actor i by actor j (statements 285–295). This is matrix XC (see Table 3.1).

Control of event i by event j (statements 300–315). This is matrix CX (see Table 3.1).

Value of each event (statements 320–470). This is the vector of values V obtained as indicated above.

Power of each actor (statements 475–485). This is power, r_j, calculated as $r_j = \sum_{i=1}^{m} v_i c_{ij}$.

Final directed control by actor i of event j (statements 490–550). This is calculated as $c_{ij}^* = (x_{ji}/v_i) r_j$, and then directed control is $c_{ij}^* \operatorname{sgn}(y_{ji})$.

Probability of positive outcome of event j (statements 530–560). This is calculated as $0.5 + 0.5 \sum_{j=1}^{n} c_{ij}^* \operatorname{sgn}(y_{ji})$.

Increment in expected realization of interests of actor i from j (statements 590–645). This is calculated as

$$a_{ij} = 0.5 \sum_{k=1}^{m} x_{ik} \operatorname{sgn}(y_{ik}) c_{kj}^* \operatorname{sgn}(y_{kj})$$

Expected value of collectivity to actor j (statements 650–690). This is calculated from above step, as

$$a_j = 0.5 + \sum_{k=1}^{n} a_{jk}.$$

Expected wtd. realization of interests for all actors (statements 695–710). This is calculated from above step, as

$$\sum_{j=1}^{n} a_j r_j.$$

Directed power of collectivity on event J (statements 720–730). This is calculated as

$$b_i = \sum_{j=1}^{n} r_j x_{ji} \operatorname{sgn}(y_{ji}).$$

Total external power of collectivity (statements 735–755). This is calculated from above step, as

$$b = \sum_{i=1}^{m} |b_i|.$$

See page 167 for computer program and output Examples 1, 3(1), 3(2), and 5.

5 The Dynamic System, and Other Elaborations

The model of collective actions as developed in Chapters 3 and 4 constitutes a first step toward a well-developed theory of collective actions. In this chapter, modifications and extensions of the basic theory will be discussed, indicating some of the directions in which future work can go.

Dynamics and the movement to equilibrium

In the preceding chapter, the solutions obtained in the various examples are equilibrium solutions, obtained by solving the system of equilibrium equations. However, it is useful to return to the dynamic model, in which supply of and demand for control of an event are not necessarily in equilibrium, but move toward one another through adjustments of the price or value of control over events. The dynamic equation is presented as eqn. 3.7. This equation, reproduced as eqn. 5.1 here, shows the modification of the value of an event as demand for control of each event and supply of control are brought into equilibrium by the modification of value.

$$\frac{dv_i}{dt} = k(D_i - S_i), \text{ for all events } i = 1, \ldots, n \qquad (5.1)$$

where k is a constant expressing the rate at which demand and supply come into equilibrium, and D_i and S_i are expressed in terms of value. Supply of control over i, S_i, is always equal to v_i, since the total control over i is 1.0. For the basic model in which actors express demand proportional to their interest in the event, demand D_l, takes a particular form, and eqn. 5.1 becomes

$$\frac{dv_i}{dt} = k\left(\sum\sum v_h c_{hj} x_{jl} - v_i\right) \qquad i = 1, \ldots, n \qquad (5.2)$$

The solution of this set of equations for $V(t)$ as a function of C, X, and $V(0)$ may be obtained by defining a new matrix, G, which is the product matrix, CX, minus the identity matrix I, multiplied by the scalar quantity k. That is, $G = k \cdot (CX - I)$, where the dot represents multiplication of each term of the matrix by the scalar k. Then from eqn. 5.2,

$$\dot{V}(t) = V(t)G \qquad (5.3)$$

(where $\dot{V}(t)$ is the time derivative of $V(t)$). The solution of this equation is:

$$V(t) = V(0)e^{Gt}, \qquad (5.4)$$

where e^{Gt} is defined as the matrix which is the sum of the infinite series,

$$I + Gt + \frac{G^2 t^2}{2!} + \frac{G^3 t^3}{3!} + \ldots,$$

a series which converges when CX is a stochastic matrix, as it is in this case. Given the matrix G, one can calculate the values or prices v_i at any point in time after the negotiation process has begun, if the initial set of values, $V(0)$, is known. Equation 5.4 appears not to be of much interest, because the matrix of interests is ordinarily not well enough known in empirical cases to allow actual fitting of data, and if such fitting were done, it would of necessity be within the context of the somewhat artificial structure embodied in the assumptions of the model: the set of events is fixed in advance; the decision rule is probabilistic; and the exchange is carried out through a central medium which automatically adjusts prices as offers and demands are made.

There is, however, one use that may be made of this equation, if the artificial structure is in fact imposed. It offers a means of estimating the interest matrix X, which can ordinarily not be estimated with any confidence from direct observation or report. If appropriate experiments beginning with different values of $V(0)$ (in particular, n experiments, in which $v_i = 1$ and all other $v_{j \neq i}$ are zero, for each i), and observing the system a sufficient time later for some price changes to have occurred, but not for long enough for the system to be close to equilibrium, then the matrix G may be estimated. From this, if the control matrix C is known, and has a rank of $n - 1$, the matrix X can be estimated so long as the number of actors does not exceed the number of events. This, in fact, is the appropriate way to estimate the interests X: from the very transactions that people are willing to carry out, rather than from verbal reports from the actors themselves.

Beyond this capability of describing the time path of the system, the dynamic formulation has other important values. By providing an algorithm by which demand and supply come into equilibrium, it allows the possibility of modifying the assumptions on which the quantity of demand is based. This is particularly important because of the two difficulties with the basic model discussed in Chapter 3: (1) demand does not arise through maximization of expected utility, as rational behaviour dictates (except under a special interpretation, in which each actor j represents many individuals, and x_{ji} is the proportion of individuals of type j who have sole interest in event i, or the interpretation in which each actor j is only one individual, but x_{ji} represents the fraction of his time that he has sole interest in event i), but through allocation of resources proportional to the fraction of interest in each event; and (2) demand is assumed independent of the alignment of interests pro and con, an assumption that is valid only for the probabilistic decision rule. The use of the dynamic equation makes possible introducing different assumptions about demand to treat these two problems. It is to the first of these that I now turn.

Maximization versus proportional allocation of interests

In Chapter 3, the possibility of introducing a demand function in which each actor was maximizing his expected utility in the market was discussed. If y_{ji} is a measure of the utility difference he will experience as a consequence of a positive outcome for event i rather than a negative one, he will seek at each point in time to exchange a unit of his resources for control over that event which, at current prices, gives him maximum increment in expected utility. If, for a given amount of resources he places on the market, he can get a unit of control c_{ij}, then he will buy control over that event $i*$ which maximizes the product of the increment in control times his expected utility, that is he will maximize $\Delta c_{ij}x_{ji}$ over events i. However, the amount of control Δc_{ij} he can buy with a given unit of resources is inversely proportional to the price of that control. Consequently, he will buy control over that event in which the ratio, x_{ji}/v_i is maximized. Furthermore, since the marginal expected utility of a unit of control is constant under a probabilistic voting rule, he will seek to buy as much control as his resources make possible over that event which maximizes x_{ji}/v_i. If his resources are more than sufficient to buy complete control over event i, he will use the remaining resources to buy control over the event which maximizes x_{ji}/v_i from the set of remaining events other than $i*$. Assuming for the moment that the number of actors is sufficiently large, and the constitutional control held by any one is sufficiently small that such total control over an event by a single actor does not occur, then the demand for control over event i is

$$D_i = \sum_{j \in B_i} \sum_h v_h c_{hj} \qquad (5.5)$$

where the set B_i is the set of all actors for which i maximizes x_{ji}/v_i, and $\sum_h v_h c_{hj}$ is the value of the constitutional control held by j. When this demand function is employed in the price adjustment equation, eqn. 5.1, it becomes

$$\frac{dv_i}{dt} = k \left(\sum_{j \in B_i} \sum_h v_h c_{hj} - v_i \right) \qquad (5.6)$$

Since a given actor is in only one set B_i $(i = 1, \ldots, n)$ and since the sum of $\sum v_h c_{hj}$ over all j is equal to $\sum_i v_i(=1)$, then the overall value demanded equals the value supplied.

Equation 5.6, consequently, expresses the dynamics for the change in value of each event i when actors are engaged in maximization as defined above. This equation, however, presents more difficulties than eqn. 5.2 for the basic model with allocation of resources proportional to interests. Two difficulties are most apparent. First, when an actor has sufficient resources to gain full control over an event, that is, when for some actor j in set B_i, $\sum_h v_h c_{hj} > v_i$, then he must turn to his second-best event, as described above. The conceptual and operational difficulties this creates can be exemplified by considering the case in which the set B_i contains only this actor j. According to the assumption expressed earlier, this actor will express a demand for event i not equal to $\sum v_h c_{hj}$, but only a portion of this equal to v_i. If this is so, however, then since he is the only actor in set B_i, demand equals supply for this event, and there is no mechanism to increase the price v_i. What this corresponds to empirically is a special case of the situation in which actor j is a monopsonist for event i at this price. Thus not only can he limit his demand to v_i, he can reduce it below v_i until the price decreases to just above the point at which i maximizes x_{ji}/v_i for another actor.

To be sure, it is possible to establish rules of the game in which actor j must place *all* his resources on the market for that event i which maximizes x_{ji}/v_i, and thus eliminate this difficulty. (In the basic theory, the assumption that each will place on the market exactly that value of control over i beyond the amount equal to $r_j x_{ji}$ is in a sense such an arbitrary rule.) It is questionable, however, whether such rules correspond to any situation in actual political processes. Since this modification of the basic model is designed explicitly to bring it into closer correspondence with actual political processes, this is a serious defect. It is a defect which arises when the number of actors is small relative to the number of events, or when the number of actors is large, but the resources held by one or more actors is large relative to the prices of control over some events. This again suggests that the model, in this modification at least, breaks down when the number of actors and events, and the structure of control and interest, is such as to make possible a monopsonist, or something close to it. This, of course, is to be expected, since when numbers of actors are small, and rules do not prevent it, strategic considerations enter, and the individual actor is no longer facing an impersonal market in which he cannot affect prices, but is instead in a strategic game in which prices are partially controlled by his behaviour.

This example of monopsonist strategy directs attention to the complementary situation, in which there is one or more actors with monopoly of control over a single event. It is clear that in this case as well, unless there are specific rules to the contrary, the monopolist can withhold his control from the market to extract the highest price he can obtain for it. In the basic model, this was explicitly prevented by the rules, which dictated that all actors tentatively place all control on the market at the given price. In the absence of such rules that make strategy to affect prices impossible, strategy will arise, invalidating the models described here, for they invalidate the simplifications permitted by the concept of an actor facing a risky environment, not an actor facing a purposive strategic environment. One may take either of two approaches to the problems created by strategic considerations. One is to formulate in game-theoretic terms the strategic situation confronted by each actor, and examine the 'solution' of the game according to the various solution concepts that have been developed for non-zero sum games. The other, which I will take here, is to assume either a set of rules which makes strategic actions impossible, or a set of actors large enough that strategic actions are no longer profitable. While this second approach in effect assumes away some of the problems that arise in real situations of social organization, and can only be taken in cognizance of such unsolved problems, it allows investigation of organizational structures of greater complexity.

In the appendix to this chapter, a computer program is listed which gives the dynamic behaviour of the system, following eqn. 5.1 (or rather its discrete approximation). This program incorporates as one option the maximization principle described above. In this program, there are two rules that govern action and prevent strategic behaviour: each actor must place all his resources on the market at the given price, thus not withholding resources to increase their price, and each actor j must offer all his resources as demand for the event which maximizes x_{ji}/v_i, even when these resources are greater than v_i.

The second difficulty with the maximization modification of the model is the fact that it need not give a unique equilibrium. Heuristically, the source of the difficulty may be seen by considering what happens to eqn. 5.6 when there is a disequilibrium of demand and supply. If demand is greater than supply, the price v_i slowly rises, then it reaches a point at which for one actor j, i no longer maximizes x_{ji}/v_i. Actor j leaves the set B_i, and the demand drops discontinuously, to the level of demand created by the remaining actors in B_i. But when that price drops, actor j again enters B_i, and the demand discontinuously increases, to bring about another slow rise in price again to the point of where actor j leaves B_i.

This instability (and the instability caused in the opposite direction by a slow decline in the price of event i until a new actor j enters the set B_i) will not always arise, but I have not found the conditions for stability.

Example of maximization

The computer program listed in the appendix to this chapter finds the price equilibrium through an iterative process, using the dynamic equation (5.1) to trace a path for the values v_i. For proportional allocation, demand is calculated as indicated in eqn. 5.2; for maximization, it is calculated as indicated in eqn. 5.6. An example in which maximization does give a stable equilibrium point is shown by the control and interest matrices of Table 5.1. At the same time, this example illustrates the limitations of the model, as I will indicate below.

For these data, use of the basic model, with proportional allocation, results in values $v_1 = .545$, $v_2 = .455$ for the two events. The first four actors each have power equal to .114, and the last has power equal to .545. Actors 1–4 each have control of .125 over the first event, and .1 control over the second, while actor 5 has control of .5 of the first event, and .6 of the second. His greater power, exhibited both in his overall power of .545 and in his large amount of control over both events, is due to the fact that he has full control over the first event, in which most of the interest of the system lies. The probability of a positive outcome is .75 for the first event, .2 for the second.

Table 5.1
Control and interest matrices, five actors and two events

		Actors							Events	
		1	2	3	4	5			1	2
Events	1	0	0	0	0	1		1	−.6	.4
	2	.25	.25	.25	.25	0		2	.6	−.4
			Control				Actors	3	−.6	.4
								4	.6	−.4
								5	.5	−.5
									Interest	

Allocation of resources by maximization gives very different results. The program output is shown in the appendix to this chapter. The events are now of equal value, and the power of each of the first four actors has increased to .125, reducing the power of the fifth actor to .5. The source of the change is evident in examining the distribution of final control. The first four actors, who have .4 of their interest in event 2, exercise no final control over it. The fifth actor, with .5 of his interest in each event, exercises no control over the first event, and total control over the second. For him, the interest-to-price ratio is identical for the two events, so it is arbitrary that he makes his total demand for the second event. This indicates one defect of the maximization principle: if two events will bring identical expected return or very nearly identical expected return, the actor will arbitrarily choose a single event.

A second weakness of the model is its failure to give a stable equilibrium set of values in nearly all cases. In none of the examples of Chapter 4, for example, does the program give a stable equilibrium.

A third defect is evident in comparing the values of the two events. In this model it is assumed that with no strategic considerations each actor places his resources on the market. In fact, we would expect actor 5, with complete control over event 1, to withhold his resources, and through bargaining obtain a price for his control such that x_{11}/v_1 was only slightly higher than x_{12}/v_2, that is, a price of slightly less than .6 for event 1. By doing this, he would be able to retain some control over event 1 while gaining full control over event 2. Each of the first four actors would have only one-sixth of the control of event 1, and he would retain one third control.

Because of this absence of strategic considerations in the model of the sort that exists in small groups, the model (both in proportional allocation form and in maximization form) is only appropriate for larger groups with control so distributed that no monopoly or near-monopoly conditions exist.

Before turning to the second difficulty discussed in Chapter 3, related to decision rules other than probabilistic ones, it is useful to reconsider briefly the interpretation of proportional allocation of resources as a special kind of maximization involving time. Suppose we consider maximizing behaviour slightly differently from that ordinarily assumed. We assume that a given individual j will vary over time in the event in which he has maximum interests. We assume that this variation is random over the time period in which political transactions take place, and that at a given point in time he has interest only in a single event. Further, in any finite segment of time during this period, he has interest in event i for a given proportion of that time, θ_{ji}. We assume also that he commits his resources at a constant rate over the period during which transactions take place. Given these assumptions, the demand he makes for event i will always be a constant proportion, θ_{ji}, of his total demand. If the price is high, he will obtain less control over the event; but the proportion of his resources of value that he commits remains the same. In a private market, this is equivalent to the condition in which the price elasticity of demand is -1, a condition which is sometimes assumed in the absence of specific data.

In such a situation, if the quantities θ_{ji} take the place of the quantities x_{ji} in the present theory, the resulting behaviour is that of the basic theory: allocation of resources proportional to θ_{ji} (or in the basic theory, x_{ji}). Thus the behaviour specified in the basic theory is compatible with a principle of maximization, when that principle is defined as described above. If the basic theory were reformulated in these terms, it would be necessary to define operationally the x_{ji}'s not in terms of utility differences in a theory of rationality under risk, but in terms of the assumptions used to define the quantities θ_{ji} above, that is, sequential maximization. Whether such quantities are compatible with behaviour (in the sense that at any instant of time, an individual has total interest in only one event, and will commit resources to control of that event, whatever the price) is an open question. If so, it is likely that the operational definition will not correspond in practice to the operational definition of x_{ji} based on utility under risk. There will likely be some events whose outcomes have a non-zero utility difference which would never 'come to his attention', that is, never enter in the sequence of events in which he had instantaneous sole interest. The values of θ_{ji} would as a consequence likely be more skewed toward high values than the utility differences.

There is a final point of interest concerning this reinterpretation of proportional allocation as utility-maximization over time. In a two-person bargaining situation, i.e. a bilateral monopoly of the sort considered in the example of Chapter 3, classical economic analysis results in a contract curve rather than a unique equilibrium point. The classical analysis begins with utility curves in an Edgeworth box representing the current level of utility of the individual deriving from the resources he currently holds. The Edgeworth box, together with the contract curve, representing the points of tangency of the two persons' utility curves, is shown in Figure 5.1, assuming that actor 1 begins with full control over good (or event) 1, and actor 2 begins with full control over good (or event) 2. If these are interpreted as goods, they are scaled so that the total quantity of each in the system equals 1.0.

Solution of the set of equations of the theory using the proportional allocation of resources, given the interests shown in the example of Chapter 3 ($x_{11} = .4$, $x_{12} = .6$, $x_{21} = .8$, $x_{22} = .2$), gives a unique equilibrium point. If the x_{ji}'s represent not utility differences as described earlier, but proportions of time that actor j has sole interest in event (or good) i, then the x_{ji}'s constitute rates at which each actor makes demands, i.e. offers, for goods of the other actor. Consequently, a unique path to a unique equilibrium point on the contract curve is predicted by the theory, shown as e on the contract curve in Figure 5.1. In this case, actor 1 had .4 of his interests realized before the transactions (complete control of event 1, in which he has .4 of his interests), and .64 after the transactions $[(.4)(.4) + (.8)(.6) = .64]$. His gain in interests through the transactions is $.64 - .4 = .24$ of his total possible interest realization. Actor 2 had only .2 of his interests realized by his initial holdings, and .52 afterwards $[(.6)(.8) + (.2)(.2) = .52]$. His gain

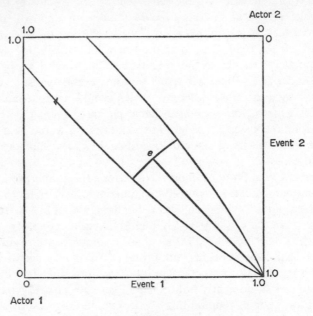

Fig. 5.1

in interests is $.52 - .2 = .32$. Thus actor 2 gained a larger portion of his total interest in this negotiation than did actor 1, although actor 1 has more power, and a higher absolute level of interest-realization at the end than does actor 2.

This interpretation of proportional allocation as a time-mixture of sequential maximization that determines the rate at which resources are offered up as demand provides a possible solution of the indeterminacy of transaction systems which involve small numbers of participants, bringing together normative theory of what the 'rational, utility-maximizing' individual will do, and descriptive theory which seeks to predict unique outcomes in behaviour systems. What remains open, however, is the question of whether people can be validly characterized according to such sequentially variable maximization.[1]

This reinterpretation of proportional allocation as a special kind of utility maximization provides another rationale for use of the behaviour principle of proportional allocation, rather than the behaviour principle described by eqn. 5.5. It remains, of course, for empirical investigation to assess which behaviour principle better describes reality; but it is clear from this discussion that the proportional allocation need not be regarded *a priori* as behaviour other than rational.

Relaxing the probabilistic decision rule

The difficulty of the basic theory discussed in the preceding section is a difficulty related to the actors' behaviour principle. The probabilistic decision rule, however, is of a different order. It is a difficulty related to the structural rules under which collectivities act. Collectivities could act through use of a probabilistic decision rule; and if they did, the existence of a probabilistic decision rule in the theory would not be a difficulty, but wholly a reflection of social reality. There are, in fact, definite virtues of the probabilistic decision rule, principally in their ability to reflect appropriately the interests of a minority, no matter how small its size, a virtue held by no empirically used decision rule except a unanimity rule, which has other defects.[2] There is, however, one serious disadvantage to the probabilistic decision rule: if the introduction of issues for consideration is itself determined from

[1] The fact that individuals can attend to only one thing at a time has always constituted a problem in normative theories of social action, which have assumed an infinite capacity for simultaneous attention to different activities. Some theories of management in organizations have repaired this deficiency by assuming that managers sequentially attend to problems as those problems rise to a point where they demand attention, rather than assuming that managers engage in simultaneous adjustment of all activities to maximize some criterion quantity (see March and Cyert, 1963).

[2] Knut Wicksell (1958) argued, in tax bills, for unanimity decision rules, together with the possibility for continuous adjustment of the bill until unanimity was achieved. Wicksell's general argument was that by such adjustment, the benefits could be made to outweigh the costs for each voter, and that only in a bill on which unanimity was reached could this excess of benefits over costs for each voter be assured. His procedure was designed for the protection of minorities from majority interests. For bills in which no such continuous adjustment is possible, a probabilistic decision rule has many of the characteristics that a unanimity decision rule has for continuous-adjustment bills.

within the system (as it is in most of those under consideration here), an issue can be reintroduced by those dissatisfied with the outcome. If such a decision rule were to be used, its use would necessarily be accompanied by a limitation on the introduction of new issues. In some collectivities, this could be carried out, for example, by explicit constitutional distribution of the power to initiate action, just as there is explicit constitutional distribution of power to determine the outcome of issues.

With a probabilistic decision rule, the division of interests between those in favour of, and those opposing, the action has no effect on the price of control over an event, only on the outcome. For, as described in Chapter 3, even if all interests are favourable to a positive outcome, an actor holding more control over a given issue than he desires can merely threaten to cast it in the direction against his interests, and it becomes to the interest of others to buy that control. Because of the constant marginal utility of a fraction of control, independent of the amount held by others, that last fraction of control has a given value to them, independent of the distribution of remaining control between those favouring and those opposing.

When the voting rule is a majority rule, or any rule other than the probabilistic rule, the balance of positive and negative interests is important not merely in determining the outcome, as it should be, but also in determining the value or price of control over an event. If the interests are unbalanced in one direction or the other, then control over the event is of lesser value, because there is little competition for votes on that event between the two sides, than if the interests are closely balanced.[3]

In order to modify the theory for a non-probabilistic decision rule, but with vote exchange, it is necessary to think what a set of rational actors would do. Two different sets of assumptions will be outlined below.

Separation of resource-allocation from interests

If tentative values for the set of events were established (say by a central bank which set values and acted as a market place), and it occurred that on the basis of these values, those favouring one event had strong enough interests and strong enough power to obtain more than half the control over the events, then neither those favouring it

---

[3] I have shown how this occurs in another paper (Coleman, 1968) in which I examine the 'marginal utility' of a vote commitment in a collectivity with a majority rule.

nor those opposing it would strongly compete for control over the event. Its value would drop. The question is, just how far would it drop? Clearly it would not drop to near zero, because at that value, those who oppose the issue could buy over half the control over it, and win. The drop in its value is clearly limited by the potential threat posed by the weaker side (weaker in the sum of their products of power and interest) to control the event. Thus the value must be maintained above the point at which the power of the weaker side on this issue would be sufficient to buy half the control over the issue.

If y_{ji} is the signed interest of member j in issue i (where the sign is positive if he favours the issue, and negative if he opposes it and $x_{ji} = |y_{ji}|$), then for a given value of each event, we can calculate the total strength of those favouring the event and the total strength of those opposing it, in eqns. 5.7 and 5.8, labelling v_i^+ the total power directed in favour of the event, and v_i^- the total power directed against it.

$$v_i^+ = \sum r_j y_{ji} \text{ (summed over all } j \text{ such that } y > 0) \qquad (5.7)$$

$$v_i^- = -\sum r_j y_{ji} \text{ (summed over all } j \text{ such that } y < 0) \qquad (5.8)$$

Then if $v_i^+ = v_i^-$, the power on the issue is balanced, and neither those who favour the event nor those who oppose it can afford to reduce their investment in this issue. However, if $v_i^+ > v_i^-$, then the power is unbalanced, with those favouring the event mobilizing more strength in favour of it than those against it can mobilize on the other side.

Under such circumstances, it would be rational for those favouring the event to devote some of their power elsewhere, since they can afford to reduce their power devoted to this event down to the point that in sum is equal to (or slightly greater than) v_i^-.

The rational strategy, then, for each of those favouring the issue, acting independently, is to redeploy some of their power on other issues in which they are currently in a weak position, to attempt to gain control of those issues for the side they favour.

What is rational for those who oppose the issue in this case, or more generally, those who are in the weaker position on an event? Is it to their interest to continue to deploy their power on this issue, or to shift it elsewhere, by trading off their control over this event? If all actors on this side trade off their control of the event since they cannot win it at current price levels of the various events, then the price will drop to zero, and the event will be valueless, since those on the other side are not interested in further purchases of this event and the market would not be cleared of this issue: 50 per cent of it (or slightly less) would remain unsold. But if this occurred on event i, it would occur on all events, since each event will have one side with greater power.

This would lead to further instability, with a new set of exchanges being made, since an actor j who was on the winning side on event i, but the losing side on event k, but who felt more strongly about k than i, could make an exchange of his partial control over i for partial control over k with someone in a mirror-image position to his own. Then he could pick up all the free votes on issue k (slightly less than 50 per cent) and his trading partner could pick up all the free votes on issue i, and they could each thereby reverse the collective decision on each of these two issues.

This fundamental instability has recently been noted (Park, 1967, Coleman, 1967, Wilson, 1969); it does not, however, make impossible vote exchanges, but merely complicates the process through which they take place.

It is not clear what is the optimum strategy in this situation, because of the great number of complexities facing the actor: uncertainty about the ultimate disposition of a vote he trades; external economies and diseconomies he will experience at the hand of the other; and the obvious importance of time with a majority rule because votes committed after 50 per cent are committed on one side are worthless. What is possible, however; is to proceed one step toward more complex strategy by assuming limited increases in information. Two such extensions have been made, and these will be described below.

Reduction of resource allocation to threat level of losing side on each event

In the first case, we assume that the intermediary who sets prices makes available at each point in time information about the amount of control held by those who favour the action, and the amount held by those who oppose it.

With this information, we assume that, under a majority rule, the more powerful side will reduce their control to a point just above that of the weaker side. The amount controlled by the weaker side is its 'threat level': it is control that would be worthless if sold on the market, but is valuable in forcing those who can buy majority control to pay for that control. The algorithm which is used for this modification is:

(1) A tentative price is established.

(2) For each issue, the demand from actors who favour a positive outcome is calculated, and the demand from actors who favour a negative outcome is calculated. The excess demand for or against is determined and saved.[4]

(3) For each actor j, each event is examined to determine whether he is on the side with excess demand. If so, he takes a fraction $2/n$ of the total excess, and stores that up as his excess demand to be used on other issues (labelled u_j).[5]

(4) After each actor's total excess demand is calculated, that demand is allocated among those events in which he was on the losing side, proportional to the existing size of his interest in those events. This is accomplished through separating conceptually his distribution of *current efforts* from his distribution of *basic interests*. Initially, his basic interests determine his distribution of current efforts (or current resource allocation). In the proportional allocation model, resources are allocated in proportion to basic interests; in the maximization model, resources are allocated to the one event which maximizes x_{ji}/v_i. However, subsequently, his distribution of current efforts is distinct from his distribution of basic interests; and the quantities that represent his 'current efforts', a_{ji}, play the same role in resource-allocation that interests, x_{ji}, play in the basic theory. The quantities a_{ji} begin equal to x_{ji}, and are modified on each iteration, according to eqns. 5.9 and 5.10:

$$a_{ji,\,t+1} = a_{ji,\,t} + \frac{a_{ji,\,t}}{\sum a_{ji,\,t}}\,u_j \qquad (5.9)$$

(for all i in which demand on his side was deficient)

$$a_{ji,\,t+1} = a_{ji,\,t} - \frac{a_{ji,\,t}}{\sum a_{ji,\,t}}\,u_j \qquad (5.10)$$

---

[4] When the voting rule is a majority rule, a unit of control held by those favouring a positive outcome counts equally to a unit of control held by those favouring a negative outcome. For a $\frac{2}{3}$ rule, however, two positive votes are necessary to offset one negative vote. Thus in calculating the balance of demand, when the voting rule states a proportion p necessary for passage, the positive demand is weighted by $1 - p$ and the negative demand by p. This makes possible a generalization to a voting rule with any proportion p necessary for passage. In the computer program in the appendix to this chapter, a parameter K4 is used to specify the voting rule.

[5] The fraction $2/n$ is used as a fraction of the total excess demand merely as a convenient fraction of that demand. The sum of these fractions will not in general equal the total, but since the process is iterative, that will not affect its convergence.

(for all i in which demand on his side was in excess) where the summations in eqns. 5.9 and 5.10 are taken only over the sets of events governed by eqns. 5.9 and 5.10 respectively.

(5) Steps 2–4 are repeated, until convergence to a set of values of a_{ji} that are consistent with the existing price levels, or until a fixed number of cycles is carried out, indicating non-convergence of a_{ji}.

(6) If convergence is reached in the cycle 2–5, then using the new values a_{ji} in place of the interests x_{ji}, a new price equilibrium is established for those values of a_{ji}, and there is return to step 1 for iteration. If the new prices v_i are less than a given small amount different from preceding prices, overall equilibrium is reached.

In this procedure, it may well be the case that no general equilibrium occurs. The conditions for no equilibrium can be intuitively seen in terms of the political process: if one actor is in the majority on all events, after there has been whatever adjustment possible of resource allocation (a_{ji}) and of prices or values v_i, then he has excess resources for which there is no use. He has unused power in the system, and the market will not be cleared of all resources. This, of course, happens in practice in collective decisions; it means in effect that the set of events on which collective decisions are made does not exhaust the power of all actors in the system. However, a direct means of mirroring this through modifications of this theory has not yet been developed.

Another means of modification of resource allocation, more fundamental than the one described above, has been developed by Robert Harris (1972). Harris has made resource allocation by actor j dependent on the perceived marginal utility of the increment of control over event i.

In the probabilistic voting rule, the marginal utility to actor j of an increment of control over an event is constant, $\Delta c_{ij} x_{ji}$. However, for any other voting rule, the marginal utility of an increment of control, as perceived by actor j, depends on his assumption about the way that each other actor in the system will vote. With such assumptions, it is possible to calculate the marginal utility of a vote commitment to actor j, and it is this marginal utility that should govern his resource allocation. A model for calculating such marginal utility has been presented elsewhere (Coleman, 1968). Extending and developing further this calculation, Harris has devised a procedure embodied in a computer program for resource allocation based on marginal utility. This procedure has been presented in a publication by Harris (1972).

Example of modified resource allocation by reducing demand to threat level of losing side

A problem showing the use of a non-probabilistic decision rule leading to modified deployment of resources among events, using in this case a majority rule, is given in the appendix on page 182 as Example 2a. The control and interest matrices are shown as the first output of the program. Except for the last event, in which two actors have one-third control, two have one-sixth, and two have zero, each actor has one-sixth control of each event.

For comparison purposes, the same problem with a probabilistic voting rule (described on p. 69) is analysed in Example 2b. The effect of the modification of resource allocation can be seen in Example 2a by comparing the initial matrix of interests (neglecting signs) with the output labelled 'Pursuits of Interests by Actor I on Event J'. This is the transposed matrix $\{a_{ji}\}$, using the notation of the present section. Examining the first event shows that those opposed have increased their efforts on this event, and those in favour have reduced theirs to the threat level posed by the opposition. The issue passes with a bare majority.[6] (With the probabilistic decision rule of Example 2b, the probability of passage is .664.) For event 2, the opponents had an excess of interest, so that each actor opposed to the event reduced his allocation of resources, and each actor favourable to it increased his. The event fails to pass, showing a proportion of favourable votes slightly less than .5. (In the probabilistic decision rule case, probability of passage is .164.) The third event is similar to the second: all those opposed, with an excess of power, decreased their allocation to this event, and all those favourable increased their allocation. Again, the event fails to pass. With the probabilistic decision rule, the probability of passage is .287. For the fourth event, a slightly different pattern arises. Actors 1, 3, and 4, who are opposed, reduce their resource allocation below their interests. Actor 6, who is favourable, increases his. But actor 5, who is opposed to the event, increases his resource allocation to the event. The way this occurs can be seen by noting that the equilibrium value for this event is .213, compared to .154 with the probabilistic

---

[6] Passage of the event is shown by a proportion of votes very slightly above the voting rule. Because equilibrium is achieved only subject to a given level of accuracy, the reduction of resources of the more powerful side is not quite to the level of the weaker side, resulting in a very slight excess for the stronger side.

decision rule. There is high competition for control of this event, due to a relative balance of interests. Thus, although those opposed show a slight excess of power on it in the first round, actor 6, who is favourable, is able to put a large amount of resources in the event, because of his excess on events 1, 2, and 3. This leads to an increase in the resources allocated by the opponents, and then further adjustments by both sides, with the final result that actor 5 remains with a higher allocation of resources to event 4 than he began with, even though at the end of the competition for control, his side wins.

Event 5 shows still a different pattern. From the outset, there is very high competition, with the opponents only slightly ahead of the proponents. Their minority position leads the proponents (actors 5 and 6) to allocate their excess resources to the event, thus overcoming the resources of the opponents, and putting them in a majority position. Both actors 5 and 6 are in a relatively advantageous position, because of being on the winning side in the relatively one-sided events 1, 2, and 3. This increases the competition, as in event 4, with the final result that both of the opponents, as well as both of the proponents, have increased their resource allocations to this event. Its final value is .112 compared to .083 in the probabilistic decision rule where directionality of interests is ignored. The final outcome shows the opponents to have won, but in this case, it is only after they have had to throw extra resources into the battle to win. The probability of passage with the probabilistic decision rule shows the degree of competition, for it is .488, close to .5.

Thus in this model, there is a continual reallocation of resources by each actor, throwing excess resources into those events in which he is currently losing, with the result of changing back and forth the balance of power on each event, until there is a bare majority on each event. The dynamics of this process could be examined by printing out resource allocations (matrix A in the program) at each stage.

This process appears to mirror much more closely the actual processes by which issues are decided in legislatures, because it takes into account the direction of interests, and leads the actors to allocate their resources toward events in which there is relatively equal power on both sides. There are several aspects of empirical power allocation that are not mirrored by this process, however. First, on a one-sided issue, rational behaviour of those in the minority is not simply to allocate some of their excess resources from other issues in the hope of winning; it is to estimate the expected probability of winning, reducing their resource-allocation if that expected probability will give them a low expected return compared to their estimates on other issues. The program described in Harris (1972) does this.

Short of such calculations of expected returns, if there is any uncertainty about the locus of control (as there will be in empirical cases), those with majority control should allocate somewhat more resources than the bare minimum necessary to win. The current program (TRAD I2 listed in appendix to this chapter) could be modified to include such an insurance by addition or modification of a few statements in the program. The modification introduced by changes indicated below uses the following criterion: let e_i be the net demand directed against passage of event i, a_8 be the total demand on both sides, and a_3 the proportion of votes necessary for passage. Then if $|e_i/a_8 - a_3| \leqslant k_5$, there is no excess demand on event i, where k_5 is an input parameter. When $k_5 = 0$, the program functions as at present, with $B1 = 2$; when $k_5 = 1.0$, there is never reallocation of resources, and the program operates as with $B1 = 1$. If the decision rule is such that a proportion a_3 is necessary for passage, then there is excess demand only if the net demand for i divided by the total demand for i is outside the range $a_3 \pm k_5$. The necessary program modifications to introduce such insurance are given below.

```
  80   READ M, N, K1, K2, K3, K4, K5
  85   A3 = K4
 586   A8 = 0
 594   A2 = Z(I,J)*(K4 − Q(J,I))
 595   E(I,1) = E(I,1) + A2
 596   A8 = A8 + ABS(A2)
 602   IF ABS(E(I,1)/A8 − A3) > K5 THEN 605
 603   E(I,1) = 0
1200   DATA 5, 2, .3, .001, 0, .5, .1
```

Another defect of this model is that even though actors take into account directionality of interests in deciding how to allocate their resources, they do not do so in determining with whom to trade. Rational actors would take into account the direction of trading partners' interests, in estimating the expected loss they will experience from giving up a given unit of control, an estimate which depends on the other's direction of interests in the event. The current program, however, does not make such an estimate, and each actor examines only the overall prices of events when allocating his resources.

Should a rational actor discriminate in vote purchases and sales?

I have assumed in all the foregoing that there is an intermediary in the market who sets tentative prices, and then receives bids to buy and sell at that price. Such an intermediary removes any identity of buyer and seller from the transaction, and thus makes impossible any price discrimination. If, however, such an intermediary does not exist, so that buyers can identify sellers, and sellers can identify buyers, does it become to a seller's interest to have different prices for different buyers, or to a buyer's interest to make different price offers to different sellers?

It is clear that the rational buyer or seller will answer this question by examining the effect of different sales on his expected utility. Heuristically, if a seller sells to another person whose interest in the issue is in the same direction as his own (but, perhaps, stronger), then he will not suffer an expected loss of utility from giving up this control, as he would if he were selling to the other side. On the other hand, it may not be to that buyer's interest to buy control from this seller, since he may be gaining nothing by doing so. What each actor needs to know, in deciding at what price he will buy control from, or sell control to, another actor, is just what will be the expected ultimate disposition of that control which lies in, or falls into, the other's hands.

The theory of Chapters 3 and 4, using an intermediary, is equivalent to assuming that he treats all other actors alike. There can be several ways of complicating this assumption, depending on what kind of information is available to each actor about the others and about the system. The information that is of use to both buyer and seller is the other's directed interest, both to know the direction it will be voted if that actor keeps it, and the probability that he will keep it. The information problem becomes enormous, and there appears to be no simple addition to the theory that will allow use of different price transactions.[7]

Altogether, then, the answer is that the rational voter should

---

[7] One might characterize transactions according to their probability of producing a vote reversal. From this could be calculated an expected utility gain or loss to both parties. The demand for control of events could be made a function of the probability that the transaction would create a vote reversal, and the supply would also be made a function of the probability. Thus rather than a single level of demand and supply and a single price for each event, there is a continuum of prices, one for each probability that the transaction will bring a vote reversal, say $v_i(p)$, where p is the probability that the transaction will bring a vote reversal, and p is a function of the interests of both parties.

discriminate in buying and selling control; but that his ability to do so depends on the information available to him. The most promising direction of work appears to be to let price be a function of the probability that the transaction will result in a vote reversal, giving a continuum of price for each event.

Sequential introduction of events

To this point, it has been assumed that the set of actors is confronted with a fixed set of events at one time, and negotiations are carried out for this fixed set of events. However, in two important ways, this simplifies reality. First, the introduction of events is itself in part endogenous to the system in many empirical situations. Since the action on each event involves utilization of power that may be employed on other events, the introduction of events (or bills, or issues) is itself a source of power. In legislatures, there are mechanisms to govern the distribution of this power, ordinarily in the form of filtering committees which determine what bills will be considered in the total body.

The sequential introduction of events has a second kind of effect as well. Even if the events are introduced exogenously, by external circumstances beyond the control of the collectivity, the time order affects the market in votes. There is ordinarily not a set of events for which a market can be developed through their simultaneous consideration. It appears that sometimes the activities of legislatures are designed to create such simultaneous consideration: many bills will be introduced in early days of a legislative session, but very few will be passed or even voted on. In the final days of the session, many bills are voted. While this is in part due to the time required for formal legislative procedures to take place, it appears in part to be due to the necessity for the extended negotiations which involve consideration of a number of bills rather than only the single bill. Thus it appears that legislatures, and perhaps other bodies as well, proceed so as to ensure that a number of collective actions are simultaneously under discussion, to create a market in which vote trading can occur.

At the same time, it appears empirically that there is extensive use of political credit, due to the sequential character of much collective action. Rather than explicit trade of votes, a member gives up his vote on an issue in which he has little interest in return for implicit

6

credit from the member or group of members to whom he gave the vote. This credit is then called when an issue arises in which he has a strong interest. When such an issue is already on the horizon, it may be that a discounting process occurs, so that the promised future vote is discounted back to a present value.

This introduction of time indicates some ways in which the theory might be elaborated to take into account more aspects of reality. These developments, however, lie in the future.

Multi-stage decision processes

Closer to incorporation into the present theory are multi-stage decision processes. In many collectivities, there are committees, and the committee decision is not insulated from the larger collectivity. A first attempt at incorporating such uninsulated two-stage decisions into this theory was carried out in Example 9 of Chapter 4. (Fully insulated two-stage decisions, in which no transactions occur between decisions at one stage and decisions at another, may be treated as two decisions, the first independent of the second, and the second contingent upon the outcome of the first.) However, a more fundamental approach appears possible within the framework presented in previous chapters. In that example, the two stages were merely collapsed into one, by giving each committee member control over the first event, plus his control over the final event, each weighted by .5.

If there are two stages preceding a final outcome, then it is possible to specify each actor's constitutional control of the event constituting each stage. In Example 9 of Chapter 4, there were three final actions of the collectivity, and an interest matrix was specified for those three final actions and the five actors. However, rather than a direct collapsing of the first and second stages of the decision, as was done in constructing the control matrix, another matrix can be introduced, showing the control of the first stage and the second stage of the final action. We now use three indices: i representing the final composite event, k representing the primary events over which actors have direct constitutional control, and j representing actors. In this representation, $k = 1, 2,$ and 3 are the three committee actions, $k = 4, 5, 6$ are the actions of the total collectivity, after the committee actions. In this representation, they are distinguished from the final event viewed as a composite of this action and the committee action. Table 5.2 shows the matrix of actors' control over primary events, and primary events' control over composite events.

Multiplication of these matrices will give the overall control of each actor over each final event, which is the matrix shown in Example 9 of Chapter 4. Formally, if the matrix of final events controlled by primary events is D, with elements d_{ik} and the matrix of constitutional control of primary events by actors is labelled C_1, with elements c_{1kj} then the matrix C of control of composite events, used in the analysis with the interest matrix is $C = DC_1$.

Table 5.2
Control of actors over primary events, and control of primary events over composite events in a two stage decision process
(Example 9 of Chapter 4)

		Primary events								Actors				
		1	2	3	4	5	6			1	2	3	4	5
Composite events	1	.5	0	0	.5	0	0		1	.5	.5	0	0	0
	2	0	.5	0	0	.5	0		2	.5	.5	0	0	0
	3	0	0	.5	0	0	.5	Primary events	3	0	0	.5	.5	0
									4	.2	.2	.2	.2	.2
									5	.2	.2	.2	.2	.2
									6	.2	.2	.2	.2	.2

The value of expanding the representation to represent explicitly control over primary events lies in the fact that the process can be repeated for multi-stage discussions. In doing so, if there were another stage subsequent to the stage represented in this example, the matrix C would replace the matrix C_1 as the matrix of primary events, and the second composite control would be calculated by use of another matrix D_1 representing the control of these events over the final events. Thus the final control matrix becomes $C = D_1 DC_1$. Such elaboration can be carried out for any number of stages, allowing representation of very complex decision procedures by specification of the actors' control over primary events, and the way these events control other events.

Appendix: Chapter 5

Notes on Trad 12: Computer program for systems of vote exchange

This program, written in Extended Basic (an extended Basic programming language used for time-shared consoles), is designed to simulate systems of vote exchange. The model is one in which there is a system of m actors and n events, with an interest matrix X (x_{ji} is relative interest of individual j in event i, and $\sum_i x_{ji} = 0$) and a control matrix C (c_{ij} is control of individual j over event i, $\sum_j c_{ij} = 0$). The interest matrix guides the way individuals make exchanges, in one of several ways, depending on options in the program. There are two binary options, which allow for four kinds of exchange systems.

Options with parameter A1

(1) *Resources allocated proportional to interests: $A1 = 0$.* The basic model outlined in Chapters 3 and 4 is one which assumes that individual actors exercise demand for control over events by allocating their resources (actor j's resources are r_j) according to the proportional interests x_{ji}. In the option with $A1 = 0$, this assumption is made. The basic model is a system of linear differential equations:

$$\frac{dv_i}{dt} = k \text{ (demand for } i - \text{supply of } i)$$

where both demand for i and supply of i are expressed in terms of value. Demand for i is the value of all resources offered on the market for i, and v_i is the total supply of value of event i.

$$\frac{dv_i}{dt} = k \left(\sum_j x_{ji} \sum_k v_k c_{kj} - v_i \right)$$

The program adjusts values according to this differential equation until the demand and supply on each issue are effectively the same (i.e. less than a criterion value).

(2) *Resources allocated only to that event for which x_{ji}/v_i is maximum: $A1 = 1$.* This behavioural assumption is one of maximization of the sum of products $\sum_i c_{ij}^* x_{ji}$, where c_{ij}^* is the control after exchange (subject to the constraint that $\sum_j c_{ij}^* = 1$). This is a maximization of the 'controlled interests' of j.

The model is:

$$\frac{dv_i}{dt} = k \, (\text{demand for } i - \text{supply of } i)$$

$$= k \left(\sum_{j \in B_i} \sum_k v_k c_{kj} - v_i \right)$$

where the set B_i is the set of actors j for whom x_{ji}/v_i is maximum over all events.

Note: It may be the case that under $A1 = 1$ there is no equilibrium set of values. In this case, the program will give oscillation of values rather than an equilibrium.

Option with parameter B1

(1) *Probabilistic decision rule or private goods exchange: $B1 = 1$.* This model is one in which individuals are motivated to gain control over an event independently of the distribution of others' interests in the event. Each individual assumes in effect that he can realize his interests only in proportion to his control of the event, apart from where the remaining control resides. Consequently his efforts (i.e. his demands) are always exercised precisely as dictated by his interests x_{ji}, either proportionally ($A1 = 0$) or by maximization ($A1 = 1$).

(2) *Signed interests: $B1 = 2$.* In this option, individual actors examine the level of others' demand for and against the issue, and modify their own demand down to that just sufficient for passage. The voting rule is as follows: Let $K4$ be a non-negative number less than or equal to 1. Then if the proportion of control held after exchange by those whose interests are in favour of passage is greater than $K4$, the issue passes. If less, it fails, and if exactly equal to $K4$, it passes with probability equal to $K4$. ($K4$ is a parameter which is specified by the user. Under probabilistic decision rule ($B1 = 1$), $K4 = 0.5$ arbitrarily. For a majority rule, $K4 = 0.5$. For a two-thirds rule, $K4 = .66667$.)

In this situation, it is necessary to make an assumption about the way individuals react to control that is (tentatively) held by those on their side and those on the opposing side. The assumption made here is as follows: Beginning with the interest as given, and some initial values, a tentative assessment of the demand by those in favour of the issue and those against it is made. If the demand by those in favour exceeds that of those against, each of those in favour can afford to reduce his demand, employing his resources elsewhere, so that the level of demand by those in favour can drop to a point just greater than that of those against. The size of the potential threat by those against the issue is expressed by their level of demand, and those in favour reduce their demand to just above that level (in this program, they reduce it exactly to that level).

This implies a redeployment of resources, expressed in the program by the matrix A. The matrix A begins (for a particular set of values v_i) as identical to the interest matrix X. It is then modified by redeployment as indicated above. The final matrix A represents the allocation of effort or resources, or at least is the key to such allocation. In this, it plays the role that the matrix X played for $B = 1$.

Note: As for $A1 = 1$, it may be for $B2 = 2$ that no stable equilibrium exists.

Use of the program

Data are read from the data statements into the executed program as follows: when the computer encounters a READ statement, it reads the first data statement that has not already been read. In this program, data statements are massed at the end of the program, beginning with 1195. The read statements and corresponding data statements are:

READ A1, B1	DATA 1, 1
READ M, N, K1, K2, K3	DATA 2, 2, .3, .001, 0
READ K4, K5	DATA .5
MAT READ C(N, M)	DATA 0, 1, 1, 0, .8, .2, .4, .6
MAT READ X(M, N)	

Meaning of input data

$A1$, $B1$: Parameters specifying which of four kinds of exchange systems is to be used:
0, 1: proportional allocation, probabilistic decision rule or private goods exchange

1, 1: maximization, probabilistic decision rule or private goods exchange

0, 2: proportional allocation, deterministic decision rules, demand contingent on others' demand

1, 2: Maximization, deterministic decision rules, demand contingent on others' demand

M number of actors

N number of events

$K1$ rate of movement toward equilibrium in value (k in eqn. 5.2 or 5.6)

$K2$ criterion test for equilibrium against sum of absolute values of difference between values on successive iterations

$K3$ 1 for printing path to equilibrium, 0 for no print

$K4$ decision rule: proportion of positive votes required for passage (probabilistic rule is arbitrarily .5)

C matrix with elements c_{ij} of constitutional control

X matrix with elements x_{ji} of interest

Outputs are listed in the Chapter 4 appendix. Their calculation is like that for Trad 11, discussed in Chapter 4 and the appendix to Chapter 4.

To run a new problem with new X and C matrices, it is necessary to change values for M and N and values for X and C. For matrix X, the order of reading data is events 1, 2, ..., n, for individual 1, events 1, 2, ..., n for individual 2, and so on. For matrix C, the order is individuals 1, 2, ..., m, for event 1, individuals 1, 2, ..., m for event 2, and so on.

Maximum numbers of actors and events may be increased by running the program on a computer with a capacity greater than that of the GE 235, used in constructing this program. The maximum product of actors and events is now such that $(m + 1)(n + 1) \leqslant 81$.

Additional comments

It is quite possible that no equilibrium will be reached in all combinations of $A1$, $B1$ except $A1 = 0$, $B1 = 1$, which is the classical model. If convergence does not occur, one may try to bring about equilibrium by reducing $K1$. For diagnostic or other purposes $K3$ may be set equal to 1. PRINT statements can be introduced wherever desired.

General guide to the program

Statements 50–145: Dimensioning of vectors and matrices, reading in parameters, and initializing matrices.

158 THE MATHEMATICS OF COLLECTIVE ACTION

Statements 150–245: Reading in the C and X matrices and testing to insure that $\sum_j c_{ij} = 1$ and $\sum_i x_{ji} = 1$ for all i and j respectively.

Statements 250–325: Initial settings for various variables, and testing values of parameters $A1$ and $B1$.

Statements 330–370: This is the basic iterative loop for the program. For the simple case of $A1 = 0$, $B1 = 1$, this set of statements contains all the work of creating Δv_i, then adding Δv_i to v_i, and recycling. In this case, the only exit to a subroutine (GOSUB 780) is to test whether the sum of $|\Delta v_i|$ is below the exit criterion.

Statements 420–435: These are entered from the read statements for C and X, and provide a stop if the input data of X and C don't satisfy constraints.

Statements 440–520: This is the basic subroutine for calculating demand when the maximization option is used ($A1 = 1$). The added complexity of maximization is illustrated by the fact that this long subroutine performs for maximization the same function that statement 118 performs for the proportional allocation of resources. The loop from 450 to 515 is a loop for each individual, processed sequentially in calculating individual demands. Within this, statements 460–495 search through the issues I to find that issue (labelled K at the end of the search) for which a_{ji}/v_i is maximum. (For present purposes, consider a_{ji} the same as x_{ji}, representing his effective interest in obtaining control over issue i.) The statements 465–470 and 505 treat the special case when $a_{ji} > 0$ and $v_i = 0$, and in this case set $K = I$. The I-loop finds the I for which a_{ji}/v_i is maximum, and labels it K. Then statement 271 fills a cell of a Z matrix with the amount of demand he exercises for issue K.

Statements 525–765: This subroutine is only used under the option $B1 = 2$, when interests are directed (by the Q matrix) for or against passage. This is the most complex subroutine of the program. Overall, it first sets a variable matrix A equal to the interest matrix X, and progressively modifies A so as to take account of the directed demand. In effect, for each individual, it examines the demand on both sides of the issue, and stores in vector E the excess demand *against* the issue. The entry in E is positive if there is more demand against the issue than for it, negative if there is more for it than against.

It is useful to note that if a two-thirds majority is required to pass, each vote against balances two votes in favour. Thus the calculation of demand, in 595, gives the appropriate weight to votes for and against, through use of parameter $K4$.

After the E vector is calculated, then for each individual, J, a cycling through all issues is carried out in 635–665. (Statements 620–630 are necessary housekeeping.) In this, a quantity D $(1,I)$ is calculated for each issue i, which is a fraction of ($K6$ is the fraction, which is $2/N$) the excess of demand on his side. If this is positive, this fraction of excess demand is stored up for him in U $(1,J)$, and his total interest on issues where there is this excess demand is summed in S $(J,1)$. If it is negative, then there is simply a cycle to the next issue.

After all issues have been processed, we have for him a supply (U) of excess demand (which is, in fact, merely a fraction, $K6$, of the total excess demand on his sides), then in 680–710, he increases a_{ji} for all events i in which he was on the losing side, by a fraction of the excess demand, U, which he is working with. (In this case, $D(1,I)$ in 695 and 705 is always a negative number, so in 705, a_{ji} is increased.) Then in 720–735, the other a_{ji}'s where he was on the winning side are decreased appropriately to maintain the sum of a_{ji} over $i = 1$.

This is done for all individuals, looping through 615–740. Then there is a recycling to modify the A matrix again, until some equilibrium is reached through elimination of excess demand (in 745, the exit criterion is that the sum of excess demand is less than .015), or until 100 cycles have occurred, in which case there is a 'no equilibrium' exit, in 770 and 775.

Statements 780–833: This subroutine is one used in all versions of the program. It merely tests whether the sum of the absolute values of Δv_i are greater than some exit criterion ($K2$), and if not, returns to recycle. There are really two tests. For the option in which $B1 = 1$ (no directionality of interests), there is a simple test. In the case where $B1 = 2$ (directional interests), the aim is to find a local equilibrium under a given matrix A, then (by setting $A4 = 1$) to go back into the 525 subroutine (from 290) to get a new equilibrium A matrix. At the same time, one wants an overall test to determine whether these local equilibria have converged to a general equilibrium of A and V. This is done through the variable $A3$. The program is now set so that a maximum of eleven of these grand cycles takes place (statement 845), though this can be increased by changing 845.

Statements 860–1185: This section is a general routine for calculating final results after equilibrium has been reached or cycle limits have been exceeded. In 880 and 890, the individual power and issue value are printed out. Then the final control matrix is calculated, using the final demand of actor j divided by v_i to determine his control. This is either calculated by subroutine 440 and statements 920–940, when the maximization option is used, or statement 960 if the proportional allocation of resources is used. In addition, in statement 975, the realization of interests of each actor $(= \sum_i x_{ji} c_{ij}^*$, where c_{ij}^* is the final control, expressed here by the matrix $Z)$ is calculated for each actor. At the same time, a directed interest matrix is calculated, in statement 980, for calculating in statement 1140 the external power that the group can exercise on each event, and in 1160–1170, the total external power the group can exert. In addition, the total realization of interests, which merely sums up individual realization, is calculated in 1135. These various items are printed out, and the program has a normal stop at 1190.

See page 177 for computer program and output of examples 1, 2a, and 2b.

References

ANDERSON, T. W. 'Probability Models for Analyzing Time Changes in Attitudes', in P. F. Lazarsfeld, ed., *Mathematical Thinking in the Social Sciences* (New York: Free Press, 1954).

BAILEY, N. T. J. *The Mathematical Theory of Epidemics* (London: Griffin, 1957).

BARTHOLEMEW, D. J. *Stochastic Models for Social Processes* (New York: Wiley, 1967).

BAUER, R. A., I. de SOLA POOL, and L. A. DEXTER. *American Business and Public Policy: The Politics of Foreign Trade* (New York: Atherton, 1963).

BEAUCHAMP, MURRAY A. *Elements of Mathematical Sociology* (New York: Random, 1970).

BECKER, GARY S. 'Irrational Behavior and Economic Theory', *Journal of Political Economy*, 1962, vol. LXX, (February), 1.

BLAU, PETER. *Exchange and Power in Social Life* (New York: Wiley, 1964).

BLUMEN, I., M. KOGAN, and P. J. McCARTHY. *The Industrial Mobility of Labor as a Probability Process*, Cornell Studies of Industrial and Labor Relations, vol. 6 (Ithaca: Cornell University Press, 1955).

BOUDON, RAYMOND. *L'Analyse Mathematique des faits Sociaux* (Paris: Plon, 1967).

COLEMAN, JAMES S. *Introduction to Mathematical Sociology* (New York: Free Press, 1964a).

COLEMAN, JAMES S. *Models of Change and Response Uncertainty* (Englewood Cliffs, New Jersey: Prentice-Hall, 1964b).

COLEMAN, JAMES S. 'Collective Decisions', *Sociological Inquiry*, 1964c, Spring: pp. 166–81.

COLEMAN, JAMES S. 'The Possibility of a Social Welfare Function', *American Economic Review*, 1966, vol. 61, 5 (December), pp. 1105–22.

COLEMAN, JAMES S. 'The Possibility of a Social Welfare Function: Reply', *American Economic Review*, 1967, vol. 58, 5 (December): pp. 1311–17.

COLEMAN, JAMES S. 'The Mathematical Study of Change', pp. 428–478 in Hubert M. and Ann B. Blalock (eds.), *Methodology in Social Research* (New York: McGraw-Hill, 1968a).

COLEMAN, JAMES S. 'The Marginal Utility of a Vote Commitment', *Public Choice*, Fall 1968b, vol. V.

COLEMAN, JAMES S. 'Multivariate Analysis for Attribute Data', in E. F. Borgatta and G. W. Bohrnstedt (eds.), *Sociological Methodology* (San Francisco: Jossey-Bass, 1970).

COLEMAN, JAMES S. 'Control of Collectivities and the Power of a Collectivity to Act', in B. Lieberman (ed.), *Social Choice* (Gordon, 1971).

COLEMAN, JAMES S. 'Systems of Social Exchange', *Journal of Mathematical Sociology* (Fall), 1972, 2 (December).

COLEMAN, JAMES S. 'Loss of Power', *American Sociological Review*, February 1973a.

COLEMAN, JAMES S. 'A model for the Mutual Effects of Attributes', in P. Suppes, L. Henkin, A. Jogi, G. C. Moisil (eds.), *Logic, Methodology and Philosophy of Science IV* (Amsterdam: North Holland, 1973b).

COX, D. R., and H. D. MILLER. *The Theory of Stochastic Processes* (London: Methuen, 1965).

CROZIER, MICHEL. *The Bureaucratic Phenomenon* (Chicago: University of Chicago Press, 1964).

FARRELL, M. J. 'The Demand for Motorcars in the U.S.', *Journal of the Royal Statistical Society*, 1954, Series B, vol. 16, pp. 171–201.

FINNEY, D. J. *Statistical Method in Biological Assay*, 2nd edition (London: Griffin, 1964).

FRANK, R. E. 'Brand Choice as a Probability Process', *Journal of Business*, 1962, vol. 35, pp. 43–56.

GINSBERG, RALPH B. 'Critique of Probabilistic Models: Application of the semi-Markov model to migration,' *Journal of Mathematical Sociology*, 1972, vol. 2.

GOODMAN, LEO. 'On Some Statistical Tests for M-th Order Markov Chains', *Annals of Mathematical Statistics*, 1959, vol. 30, pp. 154–64.

GOODMAN, LEO. 'Statistical Methods for the "Mover-Stayer" Model', *Journal of the American Statistical Association*, 1961, vol. 56, pp. 841–68.

GOODMAN, LEO, 'Partitioning of chi-square, analysis of marginal contingency tables, and estimation of expected frequencies in multidimensional contingency tables,' *J. of Amer. Statistical Assoc. 66*: 339–344, 1971.

el HAKIM, SHERIF M. 'Collective Decisions in a South Saharan Village', unpublished Ph.D. dissertation, Baltimore: Johns Hopkins University, 1972.

HARRIS, T. ROBERT. 'Public and Private Goods Markets: Optimality and Alternative Methods of Logrolling', Carnegie-Mellon University, Pittsburgh, 1972, mimeographed.

HARSANYI, JOHN C. 'A General Theory of Rational Behavior in Game Situations', *Econometrica*, 1966, vol. 34, p. 3.

HARSANYI, JOHN C. 'Games with Incomplete Information Played by "Bayesian" Players, Part I: The Basic Model', *Management Science*, 1967, vol. 14, 3 (November), pp. 159–82.

HARSANYI, JOHN C. 'Games with Incomplete Information Played by "Bayesian" Players, Part III: The Basic Probability Distribution of the Game', *Management Science*, 1968, vol. 14, 7 (March), pp. 486–502.

HERNES, GUDMUND. 'Interest, Influence, and Cooperation: A Study of the Norwegian Parliament', Johns Hopkins University, 1971, unpublished Ph.D. Dissertation.

HERNES, GUDMUND. 'The Process of Entry into First Marriage', *American Sociological Review*, 1972, vol. 37, pp. 173–82.

HODGE, R. W. 'Occupational Mobility as a Probability Process', *Demography*, 1966, vol. 3, pp. 19–34.

HOMANS, GEORGE. *Social Behavior: Its Elementary Forms* (New York: Harcourt, Brace, 1961).

ISAACS, RUFUS. *Differential Games* (New York: Wiley, 1965).

KEMENY, J. G., and J. L. SNELL. *Finite Markov Chains* (Princeton: Van Nostrand, 1960).

KOTARBINSKI, TADEUSZ. *Praxiology: An Introduction to the Sciences of Efficient Action* (Oxford, New York: Pergamon Press, 1965).

KUEHN, A. A. 'An Analysis of the Dynamics of Consumer Behavior and its Implications for Marketing Management', Carnegie-Mellon University, 1958, unpublished Ph.D. Dissertation.

KUHN, H. W., and G. P. SZEGO. *Differential Games and Related Topics* (Anasterdaro-North Holland, 1971).

LASKER, EMMANUEL. *Struggle* (New York: Lasker's Publishing Co., 1907).

LAZARSFELD, PAUL F. (ed.). *Mathematical Thinking in the Social Sciences* (New York: Free Press, 1954).

LAZARSFELD, PAUL F. 'Latent Structure Analysis', pp. 476–543 in Sigmund Koch (ed.), *Psychology: A study of a science* (New York: McGraw-Hill, 1959).

LUCE, R. D., and H. RAIFFA. *Games and Decisions* (New York: Wiley, 1957).

MAPES, ROY. 'The Pattern of Insured Absence', *Journal of Management Studies*, 1967, vol. 4, 1 (February), pp. 89–94.

MAPES, ROY. *Mathematics and Sociology* (London: Batsford, 1971).

MARCH, JAMES G., and RICHARD M. CYERT. *A Behavioral Theory of the Firm* (Englewood Cliffs, New Jersey: Prentice-Hall, 1963).

MASSY, WILLIAM F., DAVID B. MONTGOMERY, and DONALD G. MORRISON. *Stochastic Models of Buying Behavior* (Cambridge, Mass.: M.I.T. Press, 1970).

MATRAS, JUDAH. 'Comparison of Intergenerational Occupational Mobility Patterns: An application of the formal theory of social mobility', *Population Studies*, 1960, vol. 14, pp. 163–9.

McDILL, EDWARD L., and JAMES S. COLEMAN. 'High School Social Status, College Plans, and Interest in Academic Achievement: A panel analysis', *American Sociological Review*, 1963, vol. 28, 6 (December), pp. 905–18.

McFARLAND, DAVID D. 'Intra-Generational Society Mobility as a Markov Process: Including a time-stationary Markovian model that explains observed declines in mobility rates over time', *American Sociological Review*, 1970, vol. 35, pp. 463–76.

McGINNIS, ROBERT. 'A Stochastic Model of Social Mobility', *American Sociological Review*, 1968, vol. 33, pp. 712–22.

MORRISON, PETER A. 'Duration of Residence and Prospective Migration: Evaluation of a stochastic model', *Demography*, 1967, vol. 4, pp. 553–61.

OLSON, MANCUR. *The Logic of Collective Action* (Cambridge, Mass.: Harvard University Press, 1965).

PARK, R. E. 'The Possibility of a Social Welfare Function: Comment', *American Economic Review*, 1967, vol. 58, 5 (December), pp. 1301–4.

PARSONS, TALCOTT. *The Structure of Social Action* (New York: McGraw-Hill, 1937).

PEABODY, ROBERT L., and NELSON W. POLSBY. *New Perspectives on the House of Representatives* (Chicago: Rand McNally, 1963).

RAE, DOUGLAS, 'Decision-rules and individual values in constitutional change,' *American Political Science Review, 63*, 1969, 40–86.

RAPOPORT, ANATOL. *Two-Person Game Theory: The essential ideas* (Ann Arbor: University of Michigan Press, 1966).

RAPOPORT, ANATOL. 'Escape from Paradox', *Scientific American*, 1967 (July), 50.

RAPOPORT, ANATOL, and ALBERT M. CHAMMAH. *Prisoner's Dilemma: A study in conflict and cooperation* (Ann Arbor: University of Michigan Press, 1965).

RUBIN, RICHARD. 'A Comparison of Models for the Analysis of Dichotomous Attribute Data', mimeographed, Johns Hopkins University, 1972.

SAVAGE, L. J. *The Foundations of Statistics* (New York: Wiley, 1954).

SCHELLING, THOMAS C. *The Strategy of Conflict* (Cambridge, Mass.: Harvard University Press, 1960).

SHAPLEY, LLOYD S. 'A Value for n-Person Games', in H. W. Kuhn and A. W. Tucker (eds.), 'Contribution to the Theory of Games II', *Annals of Mathematical Studies*, vol. 28 (Princeton: Princeton University Press, 1953).

SHAPLEY, LLOYD S. 'Utility Comparison and the Theory of Games', Paper No. 3582, Santa Monica, Calif.: The Rand Corporation, April 1967.

SHAPLEY, LLOYD S., and MARTIN SHUBIK. 'A Method for Evaluating the Distribution of Power in a Committee System', *American Political Science Review*, 1954, vol. 48, pp. 787–92.

SHUBIK, MARTIN. *Game Theory and Related Approaches to Social Behavior: Selections* (New York: Wiley, 1964).

SPILERMAN, SEYMOUR. 'The Causes of Racial Disturbances: Test of an explanation', *American Sociological Review*, 1971, vol. 36, pp. 427–42.

SØRENSEN, AAGE B. 'The Occupational Mobility Process: An analysis of occupational careers', Johns Hopkins University, 1972, Ph.D. dissertation.

STARR, A. W., and Y. C. HO. 'Further Properties of Nonzero-sum Differential Games', *Journal of Optimization Theory and Applications*, 1969, vol. 3, 4 (April), pp. 207–19.

STARR, A. W., and Y. C. HO. 'Nonzero-sum Differential Games', *Journal of Optimization Theory and Applications*, 1969, vol. 3, 3 (March), pp. 184–206.

SVALASTOGA, K. *Prestige, Class, and Mobility* (London: Heinemann, 1959).

THIBAUT, J. W., and H. H. KELLEY. *The Social Psychology of Groups* (New York: Wiley, 1959).

THIEL, H. 'A Multinomial Extension of the Linear Logit Model', *International Economic Review*, 1969, vol. 10, pp. 251–65.

TOBIN, J. 'The Application of Multivariate Probit Analysis to Economic Survey Data', Cowles Foundation Discussion Paper No. 1, Yale University, 1955.

TVERSKY, AMOS. 'Elimination by Aspects: A Theory of Choice', *Psychological Review*, 1972, vol. 79, 4, 281–99.

UZAWA, H. 'Preference and Rational Choice in the Theory of Consumption', in K. J. Arrow, S. Karlin, and P. Suppes (eds.), *Mathematical Methods in the Social Sciences* (Stanford: Stanford University Press, 1959).

VON MISES, LUDWIG. *Human Action: A treatise on Economics* (New Haven: Yale University Press, 1949).

VON NEUMANN, J., AND OSKAR MORGENSTERN. *Theory of Games and Economic Behavior*, 2nd edition (Princeton: Princeton University Press, 1947).

WHITE, HARRISON. *Chains of Opportunity* (Cambridge, Mass.: Harvard University Press, 1970).

WICKSELL, KNUT. 'A New Principle of Just Taxation', in Richard A. Musgrave and Alan T. Peacock (eds.), *Classics in the Theory of Public Finance* (London: Macmillan, 1958).

WILSON, ROBERT. 'An Axiomatic Model of Logrolling', *American Economic Review*, 1969, vol. 59, 3 (June), pp. 331–41.

Computer program and output, Chapter 4

```
20  DIM W(14,11),Q(14,11)
25  DIM E(11,1),Z(11,14)
30  DIM P(1,14),V(1,11),C(11,14),X(14,11)
35  DIM D(1,11),S(14,1),T(1,1),Y(1,14)
40   READ N1
45   FOR I3=1 TO N1
50   READ M,N,C1
55   PRINT
60   PRINT "PROBLEM";I3
65   PRINT
70   PRINT
75  PRINT "***********************************************************"
80  PRINT "*********"M" ACTORS******"N" EVENTS*****"C1
85   PRINT
90   PRINT
95   MAT Z=ZER[M,N]
100   MAT D=ZER[1,N]
105   MAT E=ZER[N,1]
110   MAT Q=ZER[M,N]
115   MAT S=CON[M,1]
120   MAT Y=ZER[1,N-1]
125   IF C1=1 THEN 770
130   MAT  READ C[N,M]
135   MAT P=ZER[1,M]
140   MAT E=C*S
145   MAT D=TRN(E)
150   FOR I=1 TO N
155   IF D[1,I]>1.001 THEN 785
160   IF D[1,I]<.999 THEN 785
165   NEXT I
170   MAT  READ X[M,N]
175   GOTO 220
180   MAT E=CON[N,1]
185   MAT S=X*E
190   MAT P=TRN(S)
195   FOR J=1 TO M
200   IF P[1,J]>1.001 THEN 795
205   IF P[1,J]<.999 THEN 795
210   NEXT J
215   GOTO 285
220   PRINT "CONSTITUTIONAL CONTROL BY ACTOR I OF EVENT J"
225   MAT Z=TRN(C)
230   MAT  PRINT Z;
235   MAT Z=ZER[M,N]
240   PRINT "DIRECTED INTEREST OF ACTOR I IN EVENT J"
245   MAT  PRINT X;
250   FOR I=1 TO M
255   FOR J=1 TO N
260   LET Q[I,J]=SGN(X[I,J])
265   LET X[I,J]=ABS(X[I,J])
270   NEXT J
275   NEXT I
280   GOTO 180
285   MAT Z=X*C
290   PRINT "CONTROL OF ACTOR I BY ACTOR J"
```

167

```
295   MAT  PRINT Z;
300   MAT Z=ZER[N,N]
305   MAT Z=C*X
310   PRINT "CONTROL OF EVENT I BY EVENT J"
315   MAT  PRINT Z;
320   MAT W=ZER[N-1,N-1]
325   'OR I=1 TO N-1
330   LET Y[1,I]=0
335   FOR K=1 TO N-1
340   LET W[I,K]=0
345   'OR J=1 TO M
350   LET W[I,K]=W[I,K]+C[I,J]*X[J,K]
355   NEXT J
360   NEXT K
365   FOR J=1 TO M
370   LET Y[1,I]=Y[1,I]+C[N,J]*X[J,I]
375   NEXT J
380   NEXT I
385   MAT E=CON[N-1,1]
390   MAT V=ZER[1,N-1]
395   MAT T=ZER[1,1]
400   MAT Z=IDN[N-1,N-1]
405   MAT W=W-Z
410   MAT Z=INV(W)
415   MAT Y=(-1)*Y
420   MAT V=Y*Z
425   MAT T=V*E
430   MAT D=ZER[1,N]
435   LET D[1,N]=1/(T[1,1]+1)
440   FOR I=1 TO N-1
445   LET D[1,I]=D[1,N]*V[1,I]
450   NEXT I
455   MAT V=ZER[1,N]
460   MAT V=(1)*D
465   PRINT "VALUE OF EACH EVENT ="
470   MAT  PRINT V;
475   MAT P=V*C
480   PRINT "POWER OF EACH ACTOR ="
485   MAT  PRINT P;
490   MAT Z=ZER[M,N]
495   FOR I=1 TO M
500   FOR J=1 TO N
505   LET Z[I,J]=P[1,I]*X[I,J]/V[1,J]
510   NEXT J
515   NEXT I
520   FOR I=1 TO M
525   FOR J=1 TO N
530   LET Z[I,J]=Z[I,J]*Q[I,J]
535   NEXT J
540   NEXT I
545   PRINT "FINAL DIRECTED CONTROL BY ACTOR I OF EVENT J"
550   MAT  PRINT Z;
555   MAT S=CON[1,M]
560   MAT D=S*Z
565   MAT V=CON[1,N]
570   MAT D=V+D
575   MAT D=(.5)*D
580   PRINT "PROBABILITY OF POSITIVE OUTCOME OF EVENT J"
585   MAT  PRINT D;
590   MAT W=ZER[N,M]
595   MAT W=TRN(Z)
600   FOR I=1 TO M
605   FOR J=1 TO N
610   LET Z[I,J]=X[I,J]*Q[I,J]
```

168

```
615    NEXT J
620    NEXT I
625    MAT Q=ZER[M,M]
630    MAT Q=Z*W
635    MAT Q=(.5)*Q
640    PRINT "INCREMENT IN EXP REALIZATION OF INTERESTS OF ACTOR I FROM J"
645    MAT  PRINT Q;
650    MAT S=CON[M,1]
655    MAT E=ZER[M,1]
660    MAT E=Q*S
665    MAT S=(.5)*S
670    MAT E=S+E
675    PRINT "EXPECTED VALUE OF COLLECTIVITY TO ACTOR J"
680    MAT /=ZER[1,M]
685    MAT V=TRN(E)
690    MAT  PRINT V;
695    MAT E=(2)*E
700    MAT E=E-S
705    MAT T=P*E
710    PRINT "EXPECTED WTD. REALIZATION OF INTERESTS FOR ALL ACTORS="T[1,1
715    PRINT
720    MAT D=P*Z
725    PRINT "DIRECTED POWER OF COLLECTIVITY ON EVENT J"
730    MAT  PRINT D;
735    LET B9=0
740    FOR I=1 TO N
745    LET B9=B9+ABS(D[1,I])
750    NEXT I
755    PRINT "TOTAL EXTERNAL POWER OF COLLECTIVITY ="B9
760    NEXT I3
765    STOP
770    MAT C=CON[N,M]
775    MAT C=(1/M)*C
780    GOTO 135
785    PRINT "FOR I="I;" SUM OF CONTROL ="D[1,I]
790    STOP
795    PRINT "FOR J="J;" SUM OF INTERESTS ="P[1,J]
800    STOP
805    DATA 4
810    DATA 6,5,1
815    DATA -.4,-.3,-.15,-.1,-.05, 1,0,0,0,0, -.4,.4,-.1,.1,0
820    DATA .1,.2,.3,-.2,-.2, .2,.2,-.2,-.2,.2, .4,.1,.15,.3,.05
825    DATA 4,4,0
830    DATA 1,0,0,0, 0,1,0,0, 0,0,1,0, 0,0,0,1
835    DATA -.4,.2,.2,.2, .2,-.4,.2,.2, .2,.2,-.4,.2, .2,.2,.2,-.4
840    DATA 3,3,0
845    DATA 1,0,0, 0,1,0, 0,0,1
850    DATA -.3333,.3333,.3333, .4,-.4,.2, .4,.2,-.4
855    DATA 6,7,0
860    DATA 1,0,0,0,0,0, 0,1,0,0,0,0, 0,0,1,0,0,0, 0,0,0,1,0,0, 0,0,0,0,1,0
865    DATA 0,0,0,0,0,1, .16667,.16667,.16667,.16667,.16667,.16667
870    DATA 0,.32,.24,.16,0,.08,.2, .56,0,.24,0,0,0,-.2
875    DATA .48,.16,0,0,.08,.08,-.2, .4,.08,0,0,.08,.24,.2
880    DATA .56,0,.16,.08,0,0,.2, .48,0,0,.16,.16,0,-.2


SAVE

READY.

BYE

*** OFF AT 16:22   FRI.   10-13-72.
```

Example I

PROBLEM 1

```
************************************************************
********* 6   ACTORS****** 5   EVENTS***** 1
```

CONSTITUTIONAL CONTROL BY ACTOR I OF EVENT J
```
.166667   .166667   .166667   .166667   .166667

.166667   .166667   .166667   .166667   .166667

.166667   .166667   .166667   .166667   .166667

.166667   .166667   .166667   .166667  · .166667

.166667   .166667   .166667   .166667   .166667

.166667   .166667   .166667   .166667   .166667
```

DIRECTED INTEREST OF ACTOR I IN EVENT J
```
-.4    -.3    -.15    -.1    -.05

 1    0    0    0    0

-.4     .4    -.1     .1     0

 .1     .2     .3    -.2    -.2

 .2     .2    -.2    -.2     .2

 .4     .1     .15    .3     .05
```

CONTROL OF ACTOR I BY ACTOR J
```
.166667   .166667   .166667   .166667   .166667   .166667

.166667   .166667   .166667   .166667   .166667   .166667

.166667   .166667   .166667   .166667   .166667   .166667

.166667   .166667   .166667   .166667  · .166667   .166667

.166667   .166667   .166667   .166667   .166667   .166667

.166667   .166667   .166667   .166667   .166667   .166667
```

CONTROL OF EVENT I BY EVENT J
```
.416667   .2     .15    .15    8.33333E-02

.416667   .2     .15    .15    8.33333E-02

.416667   .2     .15    .15    8.33333E-02

.416667   .2     .15    .15    8.33333E-02

.416667   .2     .15    .15    8.33333E-02
```

170

VALUE OF EACH EVENT =
 .416667   .2   .15   .15   8.33333E-02

POWER OF EACH ACTOR =
 .166667   .166667   .166667   .166667   .166667   .166667

FINAL DIRECTED CONTROL BY ACTOR I OF EVENT J
-.16   -.25   -.166667 -.111111 -.1

 .4   0   0   0   0

-.16   .333333 -.111111   .111111   0

 .04   .166667   .333333 -.222222 -.4

 .08   .166667 - 222222 -.222222   .4

 .16   8.33333E-02   .166667   .333333   .1

PROBABILITY OF POSITIVE OUTCOME OF EVENT J
 .68   .75   .5   .444444   .5

INCREMENT IN EXP REALIZATION OF INTERESTS OF ACTOR I FROM J
 9.00556E-02   -.08   -1.52222E-02   -3.68889E-02   -2.32222E-02
-7.61667E-02

- 08   .2   -.08   .02   .04   .08

-1.52222E-02   -.08   .109778 -2.44444E-03   1.73333E-02   -.007

-3.68889E-02   .02   -2.44444E-03   .130889 -3 04444E-02   -.002

-2 32222E-02   .04   1.73333E-02   -3.04444E-02   .109111 -1.56667E-02

-7.61667E-02   .08   -.007 -.002 -1.56667E-02   .101167

EXPECTED VALUE OF COLLECTIVITY TO ACTOR J
 .358556   .68   .522444   .579111   .597111   .580333

EXPECTED WTD. REALIZATION OF INTERESTS FOR ALL ACTORS= .605852

DIRECTED POWER OF COLLECTIVITY ON EVENT J
 .15   .1   -8.73115E-11   -1.66667E-02   -7.27596E-11

TOTAL EXTERNAL POWER OF COLLECTIVITY = .266667

Example 3(1)

```
***********************************************************
********* 4  ACTORS****** 4   EVENTS***** 0
```

CONSTITUTIONAL CONTROL BY ACTOR I OF EVENT J
```
 1   0   0   0

 0   1   0   0

 0   0   1   0

 0   0   0   1
```

DIRECTED INTEREST OF ACTOR I IN EVENT J
```
-.4     .2      .2      .2

 .2    -.4      .2      .2

 .2     .2     -.4      .2

 .2     .2      .2     -.4
```

CONTROL OF ACTOR I BY ACTOR J
```
 .4     .2      .2      .2

 .2     .4      .2      .2

 .2     .2      .4      .2

 .2     .2      .2      .4
```

CONTROL OF EVENT I BY EVENT J
```
 .4     .2      .2      .2

 .2     .4      .2      .2

 .2     .2      .4      .2

 .2     .2      .2      .4
```

VALUE OF EACH EVENT =
```
 .25    .25     .25     .25
```

POWER OF EACH ACTOR =
```
 .25    .25     .25     .25
```

FINAL DIRECTED CONTROL BY ACTOR I OF EVENT J
```
-.4     .2      .2      .2

 .2    -.4      .2      .2

 .2     .2     -.4      .2

 .2     .2      .2     -.4
```

172

```
PROBABILITY OF POSITIVE OUTCOME OF EVENT J
 .6    .6    .6    .6


INCREMENT IN EXP REALIZATION OF INTERESTS OF ACTOR I FROM J
 .14  -.04  -.04  -.04

-.04   .14  -.04  -.04

-.04  -.04   .14  -.04

-.04  -.04  -.04   .14


EXPECTED VALUE OF COLLECTIVITY TO ACTOR J
 .52   .52   .52   .52


EXPECTED WTD . REALIZATION OF INTERESTS FOR ALL ACTORS= .54

DIRECTED POWER OF COLLECTIVITY ON EVENT J
 .05   .05   .05   .05


TOTAL EXTERNAL POWER OF COLLECTIVITY = .2
```

Example 3(2)

```
************************************************************
********* 3  ACTORS****** 3  EVENTS***** 0

CONSTITUTIONAL CONTROL BY ACTOR I OF EVENT J
 1   0   0

 0   1   0

 0   0   1


DIRECTED INTEREST OF ACTOR I IN EVENT J
-.3333    .3333    .3333

 .4   -.4    .2

 .4    .2   -.4


CONTROL OF ACTOR I BY ACTOR J
 .3333    .3333    .3333

 .4    .4    .2

- 4    .2    .4
```

CONTROL OF EVENT I BY EVENT J
 .3333   .3333   .3333

 .4   .4   .2

 .4   .2   .4

VALUE OF EACH EVENT =
 .374988   .312482   .312529

POWER OF EACH ACTOR =
 .374988   .312482   .312529

FINAL DIRECTED CONTROL BY ACTOR I OF EVENT J
 -.3333   .39997   .39991

 .333325 -.4   .19997

 .333375 .20003   -.4

PROBABILITY OF POSITIVE OUTCOME OF EVENT J
 .6667   .6   .59994

INCREMENT IN EXP REALIZATION OF INTERESTS OF ACTOR I FROM J
 .188844 -8.88836E-02   -8.88819E-02

 -.106663   .166662 -.013331

 -.106645 - .013329   .166678

EXPECTED VALUE OF COLLECTIVITY TO ACTOR J
 .511079   .546668   .546704

EXPECTED WTD. REALIZATION OF INTERESTS FOR ALL ACTORS= .566668

DIRECTED POWER OF COLLECTIVITY ON EVENT J
 .125021   6.24965E-02   6.24684E-02

TOTAL EXTERNAL POWER OF COLLECTIVITY = .249986

174

Example 5

```
************************************************************
********* 6   ACTORS****** 7   EVENTS***** 0

CONSTITUTIONAL CONTROL BY ACTOR I OF EVENT J
 1   0   0   0   0   0   .16667

 0   1   0   0   0   0   .16667

 0   0   1   0   0   0   .16667

 0   0   0   1   0   0   .16667

 0   0   0   0   1   0   .16667

 0   0   0   0   0   1   .16667


DIRECTED INTEREST OF ACTOR I IN EVENT J
 0   .32   .24   .16    0   .08    .2

 .56   0   .24    0    0    0  -.2

 .48   .16    0    0   .08   .08  - .2

 .4   .08    0    0   .08   .24    .2

 .56    0   .16   .08    0    0    .2

 .48    0    0   .16   .16    0  -.2


CONTROL OF ACTOR I BY ACTOR J
 .033334   .353334   .273334   .193334   .033334   .113334

 .593334   .033334   .273334   .033334   .033334   .033334

 -.513334   .193334   .033334   .033334   .113334   .113334

 .433334   .113334   .033334   .033334   .113334   .273334

 .593334   .033334   .193334   .113334   .033334   .033334

 .513334   .033334   .033334   .193334   .193334   .033334


CONTROL OF EVENT I BY EVENT J
 0   .32   .24   .16    0   .08    .2

 .56    0   .24    0    0    0    .2

 .48   .16    0    0   .08   .08    .2

 .4   .08    0    0   .08   .24    .2

 .56    0   .16   .08    0    0    .2

 .48    0    0   .16   .16    0    .2

 .413342  9.33352E-02   .106669   .066668  5.33344E-02   .066668   .2000
```

175

VALUE OF EACH EVENT =
 .3213   .150331   .140818   7.89687E-02   3.93305E-02   6.92553E-02
 .199997

POWER OF EACH ACTOR =
 .354633   .183665   .174151   .112302   7.26639E-02   .102589

FINAL DIRECTED CONTROL BY ACTOR I OF EVENT J
 0   .754885   .604413   .71853   0   .409654   .354639

 .320112   0   .313025   0   0   0 -.183667

 .26017   .185352   0   0   .354232   .20117   -.174154

 .13981   5.97626E-02   0   0   .228428   .389176   .112304

 .126647   0   8.25622E-02   7.36129E-02   0   0   7.26651E-02

 .153261   0   0   .207857   .417341   0 -.10259

PROBABILITY OF POSITIVE OUTCOME OF EVENT J
 1.   1   1   1   1.   1.   .539598

INCREMENT IN EXP REALIZATION OF INTERESTS OF ACTOR I FROM J
 .302644   1.91963E-02   2.02878E-02   3.63595E-02   .023063
6.36953E-03

 3.70656E-02   .145561   .090263   2.79163E-02   3.81022E-02   .053172

 4.13131E-02   9.51937E-02   .1169   5.18091E-02   2.31289E-02
6.37352E-02

 .114818   4.56558E-02   8.03424E-02   9.74211E-02   .032596
3.70867E-02

 .112558   9.63068E-02   5.54322E-02   5.03771E-02   5.22773E-02
4.09682E-02

 2.20185E-02   9.51937E-02   .108195   4.05982E-02   2.90179E-02
9.70574E-02

EXPECTED VALUE OF COLLECTIVITY TO ACTOR J
 .90792   .89208   .89208   .90792   .90792   .89208

EXPECTED WTD. REALIZATION OF INTERESTS FOR ALL ACTORS= 1.30126

DIRECTED POWER OF COLLECTIVITY ON EVENT J
 .3213   .150331   .140818   7.89687E-02   3.93305E-02   6.92553E-02
 .015839

TOTAL EXTERNAL POWER OF COLLECTIVITY = .815842

TIME: 13 SECS.

176

Computer program and output, Chapter 5

```
J  READ A1,B1
55 PRINT "*PROPORTIONAL ALLOCATION, A1=0;  MAXIMIZATION, A1=1:  A1=";A1
60 PRINT "*PROB. DECISION RULE, B1=1;  DETERMINISTIC, B1=2:  B1=";B1
65 DIM A(8,8),Q(8,8)
70 DIM E(8,1),Z(8,8)
75 DIM P(1,8),V(1,8),C(8,8),X(8,8),D(1,8),S(8,1),T(1,1),U(1,8)
80 READ M,N,K1,K2,K3
85 READ K4
90 K8=2*(1-K4)
95 MAT A=ZER(M,N)
100 MAT Q=CON(M,N)
105 MAT V=CON(1,N)
110 MAT V=(1/N)*V
115 MAT Z=ZER(N,M)
120 MAT D=CON(1,N)
125 MAT E=CON(N,1)
130 MAT U=ZER(1,M)
135 MAT S=CON(M,1)
140 MAT P=ZER(1,M)
145 K4=K4/(1-K4)
150 MAT READ C(N,M)
155 PRINT "*CONSTITUTIONAL CONTROL BY ACTOR I OF EVENT J"
160 MAT A=TRN(C)
165 MAT PRINT A;
170 MAT F=C*S
175 MAT D=TRN(E)
180 FOR I=1 TO N
185 IF D(1,I)>1.001 THEN 420
190 IF D(1,I)<.999 THEN 420
195 NEXT I
200 MAT READ X(M,N)
205 GOTO 375
210 MAT A=(1)*X
215 MAT E=CON(N,1)
220 MAT S=X*F
225 MAT P=TRN(S)
230 FOR J=1 TO M
235 IF P(1,J)>1.001 THEN 430
240 IF P(1,J) <.999 THEN 430
245 NEXT J
250 MAT Q=(K4+1)*Q
255 P(0,0)=1
260 A4=0
265 K6=2/N
270 B2=0
275 MAT P=V*C
```

```
280 IF A4=0 THEN 305
285 IF B1=1 THEN 300
290 GOSUB 525
295 B2=B2+1
300 A3=0
305 IF A1=0 THEN 330
310 GOSUB 440
315 MAT F=Z*S
320 MAT D=TRN(F)
325 GO TO 335
330 MAT D=P*A
335 MAT D=D-V
340 GOSUB 780
345 MAT D=(K1)*D
350 MAT V=V+D
355 IF K3=0 THEN 365
360 MAT PRINT V
365 P(0,0)=P(0,0)+1
370 GO TO 275
375 PRINT"'*DIRECTED INTEREST OF ACTOR I IN EVENT J"
380 MAT PRINT X;
385 FOR I=1 TO M
390 FOR J=1 TO N
395 Q(I,J)=(SGN(X(I,J)) +1)/2
400 X(I,J)=ABS(X(I,J))
405 NEXT J
410 NEXT I
415 GO TO 210
420 PRINT "FOR I= "I;" SUM OF CONTROL ="D(1,I)
425 STOP
430 PRINT "FOR J="J;" SUM OF INTERESTS ="P(1,J)
435 STOP
440 MAT Z=ZER(N,M)
445 MAT S=CON(M,1)
450 FOR J=1 TO M
455 L=0
460 FOR I=1 TO N
465 IF V(1,I)>0 THEN 480
470 IF A(J,I)<=0 THEN 495
475 GO TO 505
480 IF A(J,I)/V(1,I)<=L THEN 495
485 L=A(J,I)/V(1,I)
490 K=I
495 NEXT I
500 GOTO 510
505 K=I
510 Z(K,J)=Z(K,J)+P(1,J)
515 NEXT J
520 RETURN
525 MAT A=(1)*X
530 A4=0
535 A9=0
540 IF A1=0 THEN 555
545 GOSUB 440
550 GO TO 580
555 FOR I=1 TO N
560 FOR J=1 TO M
565 Z(I,J)=P(1,J)*A(J,I)
570 NEXT J
575 NEXT I
580 FOR I=1 TO N
585 F(I,1)=0
590 FOR J=1 TO M
```

178

```
595 E(I,1)=E(I,1)+Z(I,J)*(K4-Q(J,I))
600 NEXT J
605 NEXT I
610 A2=0
615 FOR J=1 TO M
620 U(1,J)=0
625 S(J,1)=0
630 A8=0
635 FOR I=1 TO N
640 D(1,I)=K6*E(I,1)*(1-K8*Q(J,I))
645 IF D (1,I)<=0 THEN 665
650 U(1,J)=U(1,J)+D(1,I)
655 S(J,1)=S(J,1)+X(J,I)
660 A8=A8 + A(J,I)
665 NEXT I
670 IF A8=0 THEN 740
675 A7=0
680 FOR I=1 TO N
685 IF D(1,I)>0 THEN 710
690 IF X(J,I)<.001 THEN 710
695 D(1,I)=-U(1,J)*(1-A(J,I))*X(J,I)/(1-S(J,1))
700 A7=A7+D(1,I)
705 A(J,I)=A(J,I)-D(1,I)
710 NEXT I
715 A2=A2+U(1,J)
720 FOR I=1 TO N
725 IF D(1,I)<=0 THEN 735
730 A(J,I)=A(J,I)+A7*A(J,I)/A8
735 NEXT I
740 NEXT J
745 IF A2<.015 THEN 765
750 IF A9>100 THEN 770
755 A9=A9+1
760 GO TO 555
765 RETURN
770 PRINT "*NO EQUIL. ON EFFORT CHANGES"
775 GO TO 875
780 T(1,1)=0
785 FOR J=1 TO N
790 T(1,1)=T(1,1)+ABS(D(1,J))
795 NEXT J
800 A3=A3+T(1,1)
805 IF A3<K2 THEN 870
810 IF T(1,1)>K2 THEN 820
815 A4=1
820 IF K3=0 THEN 830
825 PRINT "SUM ABS DV="T(1,1)," VALUES ARE:"
830 IF P(0,0)>100 THEN 840
835 RETURN
840 IF B1=1 THEN 860
845 IF B2>10 THEN 860
850 A4=1
855 GO TO 835
860 PRINT "*NO EQUILIBRIUM"
865 GO TO 875
870 PRINT "*EQUILIBRIUM AFTER"P(0,0);"ROUNDS"
875 PRINT "*POWER OF EACH ACTOR ="
880 MAT PRINT P;
885 PRINT "*VALUE OF EACH EVENT ="
890 MAT PRINT V;
895 PRINT "/OTING RULE ="K4/(K4+1);" -1 FOR PROB, 2 FOR DETERM :"B1
900 PRINT "*FINAL DIRECTED CONTROL BY ACTOR I OF EVENT J"
905 MAT C=ZER(M,N)
```

179

```
910 IF A1=0 THEN 945
915 GOSUB 440
920 FOR I=1 TO N
925 FOR J=1 TO M
930 Z(I,J)=Z(I,J)/V(1,I)
935 NEXT J
940 NEXT I
945 FOR J=1 TO M
950 FOR I=1 TO N
955 IF A1=1 THEN 965
960 Z(I,J)=(A(J,I)/V(1,I))*P(1,J)
965 V2=(Q(J,I)/(K4+1))*2 -1
970 C(J,I)=Z(I,J)*V2
975 Z(I,J)=X(J,I)*V2
980 Q(J,I)=X(J,I)*(Q(J,I)-K4)
985 NEXT I
990 NEXT J
995 MAT PRINT C;
1000 MAT S=CON(1,M)
1005 MAT D=S*C
1010 MAT V=CON(1,N)
1015 MAT D=V+D
1020 MAT D=(.5)*D
1025 PRINT "*PROPORTION OF VOTES IN FAVOR OF EVENT I"
1030 MAT PRINT D;
1035 MAT X=ZER(M,M)
1040 MAT X=C*Z
1045 MAT X=(.5)*X
1050 MAT C=ZER(M,M)
1055 MAT C=TRN(X)
1060 PRINT "*INCREMENT IN EXP. REALIZATION OF INTERESTS OF ACTOR I FROMJ
1065 MAT PRINT C;
1070 MAT S=CON(M,1)
1075 MAT E=ZER(M,1)
1080 MAT E=C*S
1085 MAT S=(.5)*S
1090 MAT E=S+E
1095 PRINT "*EXP. VALUE OF COLLECTIVITY TO ACTOR J"
1100 MAT V=ZER(1,M)
1105 MAT V=TRN(E)
1110 MAT PRINT V;
1115 MAT E=(2)*E
1120 MAT E=E-S
1125 PRINT "*PURSUIT OF INTERESTS BY ACTOR I ON EVENT J"
1130 MAT PRINT A;
1135 MAT T=P*E
1140 MAT D=P*Q
1145 PRINT "*POWER OF GROUP ON EVENT I"
1150 MAT PRINT D;
1155 A5=0
1160 FOR I=1 TO N
1165 A5=A5+ABS(D(1,I))
1170 NEXT I
1175 PRINT "*EXTERNAL POWER = "A5;"  INTERNAL CONFLICT ="1-A5
1180 PRINT "*TOTAL REALIZATION OF INTERESTS ="T(1,1)
1185 PRINT "*NO. EFFORT CHANGES ="B2
1190 STOP
1195 DATA 1,1
1200 DATA 5,2,.3,.001,0,.5
1205 DATA 0,0,0,0,1, .25,.25,.25,.25,0
1210 DATA -.6,.4,.6,-.4,-.6,.4,.6,-.4,.5,-.5
```

180

Example I

```
*PROPORTIONAL ALLOCATION, A1=0;  MAXIMIZATION, A1=1:  A1= 1
*PROB. DECISION RULE, B1=1;  DETERMINISTIC, B1=2:  B1= 1
*CONSTITUTIONAL CONTROL BY ACTOR I OF EVENT J
 0  .25

 0  .25

 0  .25

 0  .25

 1  0


*DIRECTED INTEREST OF ACTOR I IN EVENT J
-.6     .4

 .6    -.4

-.6     .4

 .6    -.4

 .5    -.5


*EQUILIBRIUM AFTER 16    ROUNDS
*POWER OF EACH ACTOR =
 .124984  .124984  .124984  .124984  .500063


*VALUE OF EACH EVENT =
 .500063  .499937


VOTING RULE = .5      1 FOR PROB, 2 FOR DETERM : 1
*FINAL DIRECTED CONTROL BY ACTOR I OF EVENT J
-.249937  0

 .249937  0

-.249937  0

 .249937  0

 0 -1.00025


*PROPORTION OF VOTES IN FAVOR OF EVENT I
 .5    -1.25190E-04


*INCREMENT IN EXP. REALIZATION OF INTERESTS OF ACTOR I FROM J
 7.49812E-02   -7.49812E-02    7.49812E-02   -7.49812E-02   -.20005

-7.49812E-02    7.49812E-02   -7.49812E-02    7.49812E-02    .20005

 7.49812E-02   -7.49812E-02    7.49812E-02   -7.49812E-02   -.20005

-7.49812E-02    7.49812E-02   -7.49812E-02    7.49812E-02    .20005

-6.24844E-02    6.24844E-02   -6.24844E-02    6.24844E-02    .250063
```

181

*EXP. VALUE OF COLLECTIVITY TO ACTOR J
 .29995   .70005   .29995   .70005   .750063

*PURSUIT OF,INTERESTS BY ACTOR I ON EVENT J
 .6   .4

 .6   .4

 .6   .4

 .6   .4

 .5   .5

*POWER OF GROUP ON EVENT I
 .250031 -.250031

*EXTERNAL POWER =   .500063   INTERNAL CONFLICT = .499937
*TOTAL REALIZATION OF INTERESTS = .750094
*NO. EFFORT CHANGES = 0

TIME: 11 SECS.

Example 2(a)

*PROPORTIONAL ALLOCATION, A1=0; MAXIMIZATION, A1=1: A1= 0
*PROB. DECISION RULE, B1=1; DETERMINISTIC, B1=2: B1= 2
*CONSTITUTIONAL CONTROL BY ACTOR I OF EVENT J
 .166667   .166667   .166667   .166667   .166667

 .166667   .166667   .166667   .166667   0

 .166667   .166667   .166667   .166667   .333333

 .166667   .166667   .166667   .166667   .166667

 .166667   .166667   .166667   .166667   0

 .166667   .166667   .166667   .166667   .333333

*DIRECTED INTEREST OF ACTOR I IN EVENT J
 -.4   -.3   .15   -.1   -.05

 1 0 0 0 0

 -.4   -.4   .1   -.1   0

 .1   .2   -.3   -.2   -.2

 .2   -.2   -.2   -.2   .2

 .4   -.1   -.15   .3   .05

182

```
*EQUILIBRIUM AFTER 46   ROUNDS
*POWER OF EACH ACTOR =
 .166671  .148148  .185194  .166671  .148148  .185194


*VALUE OF EACH EVENT =
 .401692  .14162  .132356  .213217  .111138


VOTING RULE = .5     1 FOR PROB, 2 FOR DETERM : 2
*FINAL DIRECTED CONTROL BY ACTOR I OF EVENT J
-.230678 -.108443  .276481 -5.63584E-02   -9.03504E-02

 .368809  0  0  0  0

-.26471  -.237323  .222907 -.073865  0

 1.04523E-02     .48639  - .16154  -.124585 -.410707

 3.80226E-02   -.107848 -.164902 -.245568  .390651

 8.70676E-02   -6.17399E-02   -.173209  .499246  .108899


*PROPORTION OF VOTES IN FAVOR OF EVENT I
 .504482  .485519  .499869  .499435  .499246


*INCREMENT IN EXP. REALIZATION OF INTERESTS OF ACTOR I FROM J
 8.82147E-02   -7.37619E-02    .108952 -7.06675E-02   -1.28291E-03
-.048828

-.115339  .184405 -.132355  5.22616E-03   1.90113E-02   4.35338E-02

 .084466 -7.37619E-02    .115245 -.101216  1.79983E-02   -3.86883E-02

-4.91794E-02   1.84405E-02   -6.30173E-02    .126922  1.34332E-03
-3.66538E-02

-4.32708E-02   3.68809E-02   -1.76429E-02   -6.00521E-02    .094699
-6.83305E-03

-.072162  7.37619E-02   -6.88735E-02   -3.90691E-02   -1.70434E-03
 .111101


*EXP. VALUE OF COLLECTIVITY TO ACTOR J
 .502626  .504482  .504043  .497855  .503781  .503053


*PURSUIT OF INTERESTS BY ACTOR I ON EVENT J
 .555954  9.21434E-02    .219558  7.20976E-02   6.02466E-02

 1  0  0  0  0

 .574165  .181484  .159309  8.50422E-02    0

 2.51911E-02    .413285  .128281  .159378  .273864

 .103095  .103095  .147324  .353425  .29306

 .188853  4.72132E-02    .12379   .574791  6.53522E-02
```

*POWER OF GROUP ON EVENT I
 .127776 - .138894 -6.38899E-02   -4.25921E-02   -2.77846E-03

*FXTERNAL POWER = .37593   INTERNAL CONFLICT = .62407
*TOTAL REALIZATION OF INTERESTS = .50525
*NO. EFFORT CHANGES = 3

TIME: 1 MINS. 21 SECS.

Example 2(b)

*PROPORTIONAL ALLOCATION, A1=0; MAXIMIZATION, A1=1: A1= 0
*PROB. DECISION RULE, B1=1; DETERMINISTIC, B1=2: B1= 1
*CONSTITUTIONAL CONTROL BY ACTOR I OF EVENT J
 .166667 .166667 .166667 .166667 .166667

 .166667 .166667 .166667 .166667 0

 .166667 .166667 .166667 .166667 .333333

 .166667 .166667 .166667 .166667 .166667

 .166667 .166667 .166667 .166667 0

 .166667 .166667 .166667 .166667 .333333

*DIRECTED INTEREST OF ACTOR I IN EVENT J
 -.4   -.3   .15 -.1   -.05

 1   0   0   0   0

 -.4   -.4   .1   -.1   0

 .1   .2   -.3   -.2   -.2

 .2   -.2   -.2   -.2   .2

 .4   -.1   -.15 .3   .05

*EQUILIBRIUM AFTER 20   ROUNDS
*POWER OF EACH ACTOR =
 .166669 .1531   .180237 .166669 .1531   .180237

*VALUE OF EACH EVENT =
 .410943 .204113 .150744 .152799 8.14119E-02

184

VOTING RULE = .5   1 FOR PROB, 2 FOR DETERM : 1
*FINAL DIRECTED CONTROL BY ACTOR I OF EVENT J
 -.16223   -.244966   .165847 -.109077 -.102361

  .372558   0   0   0   0

 -.175438 -.353212   .119565 -.117957   0

  4.05576E-02   .163311 -.331693 -.218154 -.409445

  7.45115E-02   -.150015 -.203126 -.200394   .376112

  .175438 -8.83029E-02   -.179348   .353872   .110695

*PROPORTION OF VOTES IN FAVOR OF EVENT I
 .662698   .163407   .285622   .354144   .4875

*INCREMENT IN EXP. REALIZATION OF INTERESTS OF ACTOR I FROM J
 8.96423E-02   -7.45115E-02   .102935 -3.63412E-02   -7.01758E-03
-5.57542E-02

-8.11152E-02   .186279 -8.77188E-02   2.02788E-02   3.72558E-02
 8.77188E-02

 9.51854E-02   -7.45115E-02   .117606 -4.64506E-02   1.49641E-02
-4.40879E-02

-3.63412E-02   1.86279E-02   -5.02321E-02   .130873 1.62121E-03
-1.96128E-02

-7.63952E-03   3.72558E-02   1.76166E-02   1.76489E-03   .100416
 1.99912E-02

-5.15569E-02   7.45115E-02   -4.40879E-02   -1.81363E-02   1.69812E-02
 .108802

*EXP. VALUE OF COLLECTIVITY TO ACTOR J
 .518952   .662698   .562706   .544936   .669405   .586513

*PURSUIT OF INTERESTS BY ACTOR I ON EVENT J
 .4   .3   .15   .1   .05

 1   0   0   0   0

 .4   .4   .1   .1   0

 .1   .2   .3   .2   .2

 .2   ·2   .2   .2   .2

 .4   .1   .15   .3   .05

*POWER OF GROUP ON EVENT I
 .133719 -.137406 -6.46322E-02   -4.45732E-02   -2.03531E-03

*EXTERNAL POWER = .382366   INTERNAL CONFLICT = .617634
*TOTAL REALIZATION OF INTERESTS = .676782
*NO. EFFORT CHANGES = 0

TIME: 13 SECS.
185

Index

190   INDEX

National Science Foundation, viii
negotiations, vii, 104, 140, 151
Nth-order Markov Process, 14, 22

occupational mobility, 11, 23
occupations, 10, 11
Olson, M., 104–6
optimization, 5
outcome of an event, 95

paradigm, 39
parameters, 9, 10, 19, 21–5, 27, 51, 129, 145, 149, 154, 156, 157
Park, R. E., 144
Parson, T., 1, 33, 34
Peabody, R. L., viin, viii
Poisson processes, 5, 6, 7, 8, 14, 18, 19, 20, 25, 29, 32
political credit, viii
Polsby, N. W., viin
Pool, I. de Sola, viin
Power of actor, 95, 130
Praxiology, 35, 42n
Probabilistic decision rule, 88–90, 141, 142, 147, 148, 155–7
probability, 5–7, 9–15, 17–21, 23, 25–7, 30, 39–42, 46n, 48, 49, 51, 52,
    55–7, 61, 65–9, 83n, 88, 90, 91, 93, 98, 105–8, 113, 114, 118, 119, 121, 124,
    130, 137, 147–9, 150
probit analysis, 17, 18
psychological theory, 1
purchase, 10–14, 18, 144
purposive action, viii, 3–5, 29, 32–3, 39, 48, 49

Rae, D., 88n
Raiffa, H., 39n, 41n, 42n
Rand Corporation, viii
Rapoport, A., 42n, 57n, 59n
rationality, 1, 31, 30, 31–8, 39–54, 57, 59, 60, 66, 73, 83, 87, 139–43, 148–50
regression analysis, 17, 18
relative utility differences, 71, 72, 95
republican, 10
response, 1, 15
response probabilities, 16, 18
response unreliability, 13, 14
Rubin, R., 24, 25

Savage, L. J., 41n
Schelling, T., 52
separable events, 64
sequential dependence, 10